A HEALTHY
STATE OF
PANIC

ALSO BY FARNOOSH TORABI

You're So Money

Psych Yourself Rich

When She Makes More

A HEALTHY STATE OF PANIC

Follow Your Fears to Build Wealth, Crush Your Career, and Win at Life

FARNOOSH TORABI

ATRIA BOOKS
New York • London • Toronto • Sydney • New Delhi

An Imprint of Simon & Schuster, Inc.
1230 Avenue of the Americas
New York, NY 10020

Names and identifying characteristics of some individuals have been changed.

This publication contains the opinions and ideas of its author. It is sold with the understanding that neither the author nor the publisher is engaged in rendering financial or other professional advice or services. If readers require such advice or services, certified professionals should be consulted.

First Atria Books hardcover edition October 2023

ATRIA BOOKS and colophon are trademarks of Simon & Schuster, Inc.

For information about special discounts for bulk purchases, please contact Simon & Schuster Special Sales at 1-866-506-1949 or business@simonandschuster.com.

The Simon & Schuster Speakers Bureau can bring authors to your live event. For more information or to book an event, contact the Simon & Schuster Speakers Bureau at 1-866-248-3049 or visit our website at www.simonspeakers.com.

Interior design by Dana Sloan

Manufactured in the United States of America

1 3 5 7 9 10 8 6 4 2

Library of Congress Cataloging-in-Publication Data
Names: Torabi, Farnoosh, author.
Title: A healthy state of panic : follow your fears to build wealth, crush your career, and win at life / Farnoosh Torabi.
Description: First Atria Books hardcover edition. | New York, NY : Atria Books, an imprint of Simon & Schuster, Inc., 2023. | Includes bibliographical references and index.
Identifiers: LCCN 2023009256 (print) | LCCN 2023009257 (ebook) | ISBN 9781982199197 (hardcover) | ISBN 9781982199203 (trade paperback) | ISBN 9781982199210 (ebook)
Subjects: LCSH: Fear. | Success. | Wealth. | Self-realization.
Classification: LCC BF575.F2 T67 2023 (print) | LCC BF575.F2 (ebook) | DDC 152.4/6--dc23/eng/20230602
LC record available at https://lccn.loc.gov/2023009256
LC ebook record available at https://lccn.loc.gov/2023009257

ISBN 978-1-9821-9919-7
ISBN 978-1-9821-9921-0 (ebook)

For my tooties, Evan and Colette

CONTENTS

PROLOGUE

—————

TARSOO

N OT TO BRAG, BUT I've known the world's a scary place since growing up in Worcester, a rough and tough central Massachusetts city
where crime and violence happened on the reg. That's according to my
immigrant parents, who watched a lot of 5 p.m. news. And the *New York
Times*, which once described our city as nobody's "first choice."[1]

My earliest traumatic flashback stems from the summer of 1984,
that time I threw myself onto a running vehicle at four years old. The
car was in park, but still.

"*Boro-keh-NAWR!*" My mom's friend Soraya ordered me to get the
hell off. She sat seething behind the steering wheel, questioning her
life's decisions.

But her rage only intensified my commitment. "Please take me!" My
voice cracked pitifully as I clung to her Oldsmobile's side mirror. The
soles of my Disney-themed Velcro sneakers hovered several inches off
the pavement. Soraya was free to speed away, but I was intent on joining her, even if it meant getting dragged through the mud.

Soraya was someone I had believed I could trust. A fellow Persian, neighbor, and close friend of my mother, she'd happily agreed to look after me while Mom attended an English language class at the local college. I'd arrived in the morning and joined Sanaz, her six-year-old daughter, in staring at cartoon reruns in their living room. During the commercial breaks, Sanaz regaled me with details of her mom's new curling iron and how she couldn't wait to twist my thick brown hair around the scorching rod. "You're going to look great," she said, without smiling.

An hour into the visit, Soraya began shuffling around the front entrance. She was adjusting the strap on her crossbody bag and reaching for keys, burgundy lipstick freshly applied.

It was then that I realized we had a *situation*.

As she reached for the metal knob, Soraya announced she was going to Duffy's Discount, one of the city's many bargain basements, and that she'd be back in an hour. "Stay in the house and leave the door locked," she instructed. As Sanaz went to the kitchen to pour herself a bowl of Apple Jacks, I sensed this was business as usual in their home. But to me, as the constantly on-edge kid, this act of abandonment almost guaranteed a tragic ending. I envisioned one of us choking. Robbers breaking in. Death by hot iron.

This is when my pleading began. "Leave Sanaz here, but please take me!"

"*Stop it or I'm going to tell your mom!*" Soraya shot back.

I yanked on the ends of her sweater and attempted to block the front door. But like a true Irooni, Soraya was determined to get what she wanted, especially if it was on sale. I made sure my loud, intense begging carried from her ground-level apartment to the outdoor parking lot, hoping a sympathetic onlooker would step in and save me. But when no one rushed to my rescue, it quickly became clear: surviving was single-handedly my job.

What happened next—throwing myself against her sedan, in

a last-ditch effort to knock sense into Soraya, and her dragging me back by my arm and rage-pacing the house until my mother arrived— would go down as a classic tale of young Farnoosh, retold many times at family gatherings as something of a joke.

"Oh my god, Farnoosh, you were so *tarsoo*," Soraya laughs, as she and my mom sit together decades later exchanging memories over chai.

In Farsi, calling someone *tarsoo* is equivalent to *scaredy cat*. The word is a derivative of *tars*, meaning "fear." Said mockingly, *tarsoo* implies that your fears are unjustified. *Get a hold of yourself, kid.*

As Soraya recounts the day, I manage a smile, regretting nothing.

INTRODUCTION

YOU'RE NOT A PSYCHOPATH . . . ARE YOU?

For generations, fear has been the victim of some unfortunate PR. At least as far back as President Franklin D. Roosevelt's famous inauguration speech during the Great Depression, where he told financially desperate Americans that "the only thing we have to fear is fear itself,"[1] our culture has ventured an aggressive campaign to belittle and undermine our fears. We're told it's a barrier to living our best life. If you let fear drive your decisions, brace yourself. You're headed for dead ends, collisions, and hellish embarrassments.

Search for a book with the word "fearless" in the title and tens of thousands of results will pop up, featuring war heroes, millionaire entrepreneurs with six-pack abs, and persistent romantics. All this seems to be saying, *Fight your fears and you, too, can get rich, achieve your career dreams, live healthy, free, and happy.*

Scientists have even invested time and dollars in seeking a "cure" or "conversion" for what they believe is a treacherous emotion. A study out of the University of South Australia concluded that smiling more can actually trick the brain into reducing fear.[2] I tried this, forcing a wide grin during a recent mammogram to see if it would calm my jitters while in the waiting room. It didn't. Because the threat of cancer is beyond terrifying. My elated face only made the patients around me wonder, *What's her deal?*

Here it is: Being a feverishly scared young girl and, today, a continuously frightened woman, I've arrived at a far different understanding of fear and how it works: It's not out to get you. It wants a healthy relationship with you so you can reach your greatest potential with a net at your back.

I'm not saying to let fear boss you around. Fear can absolutely make us feel stuck and insecure. Unchecked, it can trigger irrational and impulsive moves that backfire. But this book is about what it's like to turn and stare fear in the face, then ask it some questions, and most of all, trust it's here to help. When you do this, something miraculous happens: your world opens up.

American primatologist Dian Fossey, known for her groundbreaking research on apes, moved around with herds of chimpanzees for years, noting how fear and anxiety were integral to their protection and survival. In each tribe, she inevitably discovered a small subset of more concerned chimps that tended to stay on the outskirts of the settlement. They insisted on lying awake to survey the land for predators. As an experiment, Fossey removed the anxious chimps from their tribe. Several months later, their community was obliterated. What had seemed at first like an excess of fear was actually an essential shield that kept the settlement safe and thriving.

Modern science reinforces the merits of siding with fear. A 2023 study led by academics in the fields of brain science and psychology found that those who viewed emotions like fear, anger, and sadness as *bad* or *wrong* were unhappier than people with a positive or even just neutral relationship to these "negative" feelings.[3]

So what would happen if we, too, chose to view fear as a friend and leveraged it with purpose and precision to triumph and get good at life? Thanks to living in our complex and divisive world, we've certainly got the talent. If we were to go by Malcolm Gladwell's ten-thousand-hour rule, which says that dedicating that much time to a field equates to mastery, we are all bona fide fear *experts*.[4] (Go ahead—add it to your LinkedIn profile.)

From the shock waves of recessions, gun violence, pandemics, and climate disasters to everyday aggressions like getting dumped or discriminated against, we cannot avoid the adrenaline. The twenty-four-hour news cycle profits from fear-driven headlines, while corporations benefit from alarming marketing that lures us to buy their crap. And social media does little to help. A whole system is stirring up the scaries.

Dr. Ellen Vora, a psychologist and author of *The Anatomy of Anxiety*, who first taught me about Dian Fossey and those protective apes, puts it bluntly when she describes us as "a generation afraid." Anxiety, she writes, "is the tone of modern western culture."[5]

But rather than deny anxiety, or its very close relative fear, why not choose to work with it? I'm here to (finally!) validate your fears, instead of urging you to combat them. When fear arrives, it's exciting. It has key insights to share about you, your goals, and what you hold dear. In these pages you will find out how when you process and learn from fear, it can bring you safety, satisfaction, and all kinds of success. *This is an opportunity you can't afford to miss.*

As Dr. Vora continues in her book, "Sometimes anxiety is your body's way of telling you, '*Please look at this . . .*' When you listen closely, this anxiety can point you in the direction of actions you need to take as well as the unique contributions you are here to make."[6]

I admire how Olympic extreme skier Eileen Gu calls herself a "hopeless romantic" when it comes to fear. Gu is the first action sports athlete to take home three medals (two of them gold) at the Winter Olympics, and she has written extensively about the vitality of fear in her life.

"For the last 10 of my 18 years, I've pursued a tumultuous love affair with fear," she says in an excerpt from her personal journal published in the *New York Times*.[7] "Instead of ignoring fear, we build unique relationships with it by developing a profound sense of self-awareness and making deliberate risk assessments."

––––––––

My parents, Sheida and Farrokh, who arrived in the United States in the late 1970s for better academic and job opportunities, taught me and my brother, Todd (yes, his name is Todd. I'll explain later), to be hypervigilant, proceed with the utmost caution, and play it "safe" in every respect. We were the children of Iranian immigrants in a country that wasn't always so welcoming of our differences, and as such, our parents encouraged us to see the world for what it was (and still is): a dangerous, booby-trapped labyrinth. The Torabi ground rules for living a "safe" life were simple: Stay home. Get straight A's. No dating until you're married.

My family's fearsome approach to life—while full of limitations—didn't upend me. Instead, it equipped me with ninja-like street smarts that later helped me cut through so much of the world's bullshit. From the ridiculing hallways of middle school to the beer-stained frat houses of Penn State to sexist and demeaning newsrooms, fear has been my guide, a steady source of wisdom, that has clarified my self-image and revealed my natural strength and power. It teaches me to respect myself and to live (happily!) on my own terms. **In short, fear has made me who I am today.**

The list of fears that I've dutifully confronted over the decades—

from loneliness to accidentally ingesting cilantro—is about as long as that CVS receipt crumpled at the bottom of your tote bag. I've faced rejection by peers, colleagues, and internet trolls, grappled with tens of thousands of dollars in debt, and still managed to become a go-to voice in personal finance, an award-winning journalist, and a sought-after speaker who appears frequently on some of the biggest stages in the world. In my personal life, I've been married to my incredible husband, Tim, for more than ten years and, together, we are raising two kids. I run my own business and benefit from calling my own shots, including taking the occasional afternoon nap. I am leading a big, purposeful life, putting one foot in front of the other, and making grown-woman decisions with conviction. Not every day. But enough of them.

And I didn't get here because I'm fearless. If my life had a theme song it would be . . . I don't know, the eerie opener to the *X Files*? The *"BOM BOM"* from the *Law & Order* title sequence? You get the picture.

I continue to be someone who has doubts about humanity and the safety of our world. I am the woman who irrationally suspects that the man parked outside her house taking pictures from his car is plotting a home invasion. (In reality, he was a real estate appraiser.)

But I choose to listen to my fears and respect their teachings to feel whole. I've decided to make fear my trusted partner in crime. And this book is going to show you how you, too, can become more self-reliant, financially invincible, and in control of your life. The stories and advice are designed to inspire a new way to see fear—an emotion often marketed as a flaw—as your flex. It's your superpower.

And anyone who tells you you're weak for being afraid is suspect. As Caroline Dooner says in the first chapter of *Tired as F*ck*: If you pride yourself on the fact that you are fearless, that you don't ever get scared, you're not brave or valiant. What you are, sorry to say, is a psychopath.[8]

BUT, WAIT. AREN'T YOU THE MONEY LADY?

The other morning, as I was dropping off my daughter at her ballet class, a mom turned to me and said, "Aren't you the money lady? I follow you on Instagram!" I nodded and smiled, simultaneously hoping my five-year-old didn't translate that as *Mommy has more money than she lets on!*

But yes, I am guilty as charged. For over two decades, I've dedicated my career to helping individuals make money decisions big and small. My journey began with an editorial stint at *Money* magazine, because nothing screams "dream job" like writing about Roth IRAs and no-load mutual funds in your early twenties. But very quickly, I grew to love simplifying complex topics and helping people get an edge on their finances. I've since written several money books, hosted a prime-time CNBC series, and was the money columnist for Oprah's magazine. I've been a recurring guest on the *Today* show and *Good Morning America*, and today, I'm the creator and host of the award-winning podcast *So Money*, with over 30 million downloads. But never mind all that— Drew Barrymore now follows me on Instagram.

So, why am I writing about *fear*?

Well, besides growing up a giant *tarsoo*, through my career I've come to realize that **the emotional underpinning of many of our financial questions is just that: fear**. Whether we're thinking about buying a home, getting out of debt, or investing for our future, few topics are more hair-raising than money. A recent survey found that three out of four Americans are anxious over their finances.[9] (The other 25 percent I guess are in denial?) We'd rather chat about death, our sex lives, and politics before sharing what's in our bank accounts.

When I'm answering audience questions on *So Money*, listeners invite me into their lives and share financial conundrums. Our fear of money often stems from real financial insecurities and thoughts of losing it all. We worry that our money and career choices may lead to setbacks, regret, letting ourselves down, and burning bridges with important people in our lives.

One audience member asks if it's okay to leave his well-paying job in tech to open a hair salon, his dream. He worries not only whether he can make more money as an entrepreneur; he is also terrified of betraying his immigrant parents, who sacrificed so much to put him through college so he could pursue a "secure" career. This shift may potentially impact not just his financial livelihood but also his relationship with his family. Because defying a tiger mom is no small matter.

Then there's the common question of how to crack open a conversation about money with a partner. The person is not afraid of talking numbers but is concerned about how the conversation will leave the two of them feeling. Will they argue? What if they don't see eye to eye?

And nearly everybody's interested in investing, often asking when a wise time might be to jump in. They admit they only want to start once they feel "ready" to take risks. But what if that's never?

While on the surface my listeners' questions may seem to be about money, they often reflect something deeper and more frightening: limiting beliefs about themselves and what's possible. They want reassurance, to know: How can I manage the risks? Will this work out? *Will I be okay, Farnoosh?*

Because **money moves are life moves and the stakes are high,** we're tempted to fight our fears, assuming they're trying to hold us back from achieving our greatest potential. But understanding our financial trepidations—as with other fundamental fears—can take us on a journey deeper into our motivations, values, and how we protect ourselves, financially and energetically. Soon, we're no longer discussing money. We're talking about our well-being, our pursuits, and the people we love. We're talking about life and our role in it.

YOUR GUIDE TO FLIPPING FEAR

You've arrived here because there's part (or all) of you that is intimately aware of fear. Perhaps you grew up constantly on edge because, like me, it was the script you were taught to follow at home. Or you've simply experienced a number of life's quakes and now anticipating the worst is your norm.

I'm so glad we've found each other.

This book is your permission to feel unapologetically scared. It is a map for how to go deeper with our fears, understanding why we're frightened and anxious—so that we can be more *constructively* afraid in our financial lives and careers and while facing life's toughest challenges. It will show you how to honor your fears and navigate this critical emotion so that you can feel empowered and keep fear from sabotaging your life. You'll be able to see and avoid disasters before they change your life trajectory. Taking a moment to stop, process, and figure out what your fear is trying to tell you—it is the key to being able to achieve your goals. And it is not a flash in the pan; it will sustain you long after the last page is turned.

These nine chapters are dedicated to the giant and relentless fears we've all experienced. We're not talking about the fear of leaving your house without your pants on, or escalators. These are rational and complex fears that affect us all, and drive us right into the collision course of making tipping-point decisions that can derail us—like cashing out all your stocks in a recession and compromising your retirement plan, or staying in a miserable relationship because being single feels just as scary, or fleeing to the Ozarks for refuge in a pandemic before remembering (regrettably) that you're not a *country* person. Also, Jason Bateman doesn't live there.

This book begins with the most primal fears that tend to emerge early in childhood and solidify as giant boulders in our adult years: the fears of rejection and loneliness. Once we learn to navigate and leverage these initial fears, we will have the tools to tackle the fear of missing out (FOMO), a wake-up call asking you: *What do you* really *want to experience?* And then, because we live in thrall to the dictum to be vulnerable in a world full of showing and telling every morsel of our lives on social media and beyond, we will talk about the ever-present fear of exposure, and how to flip it to create boundaries that can save you from embarrassment, hostility, and unfair setbacks online and off.

We then land on the fears of uncertainty, money, and failure (largely adulthood fears that just love a good hang when we're in the "real world"). These fears have so much wisdom to impart. I love how they breed self-reflection and instill a fierce sense of intention and direction in life, leading us to more wealth and other riches.

And finally, the fear of endings and losing your freedom are some of the most gutting out there, but I'll illustrate how they can help us find beauty in darkness and inspire a legacy.

Full disclosure: These nine fears do not live in silos. They sometimes buddy up and occasionally try to mimic one another. But each has a distinct identity, look, and feel. Assigning specific names to these fears was intentional. When we label that giant blob of discomfort just "fear," it is easier to dismiss it. When you give something a more precise name, you demystify it, stripping it down to its bare parts to see what hidden meaning it is trying to show you. And you can claim more power and agency over it.

Another announcement: **I'm far from the coolest, sexiest, or most adventurous person you'll meet.** You will not discover that I've crossed Niagara Falls on a tightrope. I have not ditched my husband for a backpacking trip through Bali at the end of which I joined a throuple. The most daring thing I've done in recent years was close on a house in New Jersey at the start of the pandemic.

But I've got some stories, *let me tell you,* including being stalked by an (imaginary) bird, shaving my unibrow, renaming myself more times than P. Diddy, accidentally saying a horrible insulting thing on the *Today* show, and sending my kids to a stranger's birthday party . . . for hours. My hope is that my odd-but-true tales will show you that we all stumble. And we have valid reasons to be fearful. But when life comes knocking and our decisions really matter, we can learn how to better read this feeling and follow it toward the most rewarding decisions, and lead the life that we may have only dreamed of.

Fear, as a matter of fact, is a loyal friend that keeps you not only standing upright but striding forward into your future. You no longer have to hide . . . or, worse yet, throw yourself onto a running vehicle.

1

THE FEAR OF REJECTION

and how it wants us to double down on who we are and go where we are loved

A S A LITTLE GIRL what I desired most was a sense of belonging, to know that I could be my weird, unconventional self and be accepted (dare I say, loved?), all while attempting to figure out the person I wanted to be. My classmates were often confused by the sound of my name, my lack of wardrobe pizzazz, and the potato-and-parsley sandwiches I'd unravel from loud tinfoil at the lunch table. Each time our family moved and I got the chance for a fresh beginning at a new school, I had high hopes of walking in and being met with bear hugs.

The night before starting first grade at Mary D. Stone Elementary in Auburn, Massachusetts, a quiet town five miles south of Worcester, I confidently laid out my black crewneck sweater, the one with tiny pink and purple polka dots, and a pair of black stirrup pants my mother had bought on layaway from Sears. Looking like a Broadway stagehand and thus blending into the background was usually the safest way to make an entrance as the new kid. I was walking into a brand-new class several weeks into the school year, after students had already formed their cliques. This was not the time to take fashion risks.

I was placed in Mrs. Burke's room with a homogenous set of rule-following, people-pleasing kids who also happened to test well on the reading exam. I must give the school props for knowing exactly where I belonged.

Later that afternoon, when Mrs. Burke called us to the circle rug for story time, I carefully chose a space next to Tara, a girl with a heart-shaped face, blue eyes, and deep dimples, dressed in head-to-toe pink. Catching my stare, she smiled. Could we become friends? Seconds later, I felt a light tug on my sweater; Tara wanted to talk. Leaning into the side of my face, she giggled, "Are you a nun?"

THE ROAD TO RICHES IS PAVED WITH MISFITS (AKA THE MOST DETERMINED)

My podcast listeners will sometimes leave generous reviews, describing me as "down-to-earth," "relatable," "unpretentious." If only they knew that the road to being seen as approachable is first being called a misfit and weirdo your whole life. Your fear of getting knocked down can be a recipe for humility and empathy if you're willing to recognize how, even when you are rejected, the world will still be tilting on its axis, once you pick yourself up off the ground. Your fear of rejection didn't ruin you, after all. It was there to serve you. Life is still waiting for you to grab at its opportunities.

But this is not how we've been wired to feel the fear of rejection in our bodies. As hunters and gatherers, we couldn't afford to be rule-breakers, let alone to be disliked. The laws set by the tribe were crucial to our survival. Nonconformity could mean being kicked out of the circle and needing to fend for ourselves in the dark against woolly mammoths.

We've evolved, but we're still social creatures who crave a sense of belonging, admiration, and support. Think back to a moment when you feared rejection: when you worried you wouldn't get the job, wouldn't land the deal, or would have your heart broken; when you feared your relatives would dismiss the idea of your unmarried (and thus seemingly unsettled) ways. You most likely felt terrible and wondered, *What's wrong with me?* We still look for acceptance from family, peers, and even total strangers on social media, to protect our sense of self-worth.

In a piece for *Psychology Today*, Dr. John Amodeo writes that rejection "confirms our worst fear . . . that we're unlovable, or that we're destined to be alone, or that we have little worth or value."[1] The fear of rejection pains us because we assume what is on the other side of this fear is a heart-shattered future.

In our hasty attempts to block this fear we may make moves that we think might win us social approval. "Adapting," playing by "the rules," and "sucking it up" may seem like a direct path to success and praise. For a short while, they might even work to our advantage, but they're hardly long-term plays. In my experience, we end up feeling more alienated down the road.

"Our aversion to unpleasant experiences prompts behaviors that don't serve us," Dr. Amodeo concludes. "We withdraw from people rather than risk reaching out. We hold back from expressing our authentic feelings. We abandon others before they have a chance to reject us."

Fearing being labeled as "too successful" or "too ambitious," especially as women, we downplay our goals, hide behind the success of a partner, and often fail to realize our own financial independence. I've seen friends who fear rejection for marrying someone outside a particular race or religion deny themselves the happiness that arrives with true love. They spend a decade or longer suffering through failed relationships for the sake of cultural approval. In short, we lose out on life's greatest wins before ever setting foot on the field.

And yet the hidden truth about the fear of rejection is that it can also work in our favor. In my younger adult life, I did everything to avoid rejection and never looked at what this fear could teach me: *to accept me for me.* I missed opportunities while trying to fit in. Initially too apprehensive to follow my dream of becoming a storyteller (are you going for broke?), I pursued finance, a more predictable path that my parents deemed "safer." Too afraid of being denied a job, I didn't negotiate my salary in the beginning of my career. Too assuming that my insistence on being financially independent and career-driven would repel young men looking to "take care" of a wife, I lied about my aspirations on dates and wondered why I couldn't find the right fit. Rather than befriending my fear of rejection and asking it questions to learn more about myself, I used it as an excuse to either stay silent or run away and hide.

But the fear of rejection is not here to show us how to be a coward, play by societal norms, or bend over backwards for everyone.

When probed and redirected, this fear can help us discover what matters most to us and how to be our own best ally. At times, this fear may be saying, *Look, you are afraid not so much because the rejection will sting but more because you know deep down that you need to put in more work, time, and patience to get to the yes.* Making the investment, especially if it isn't how you envisioned your path, can feel scary, but the fear may be simply telling you that if you improve your strategy, rejection becomes far less likely. You have a real chance to gain control of the ball.

When my newsroom coworker Sean worked as an associate producer, he was afraid to apply for an on-air role. He watched our manager turn away prospective talent on a near-daily basis. Initially his fear of hearing a no convinced him he should just "stay in his lane" and continue producing. But when he thought more about the rejection and the potential feedback he'd get, as frightening and uncomfortable as it was, he saw the right path forward. He anticipated what our boss would tell him—that he wasn't a "fit," and needed more experience reading the prompter and to develop a few more enterprising pieces.

Maybe he'd even need to go to a smaller market and come back with live reporting experience that proved he wouldn't buckle under pressure in the Big Apple.

Our station manager was tough, yes, but Sean was still a novice. Sitting with this fear, he was able to see and accept this truth. And while it wasn't an easy decision to relocate, that's precisely what he did. Besides, plenty of stations in smaller news markets hire beginners. You may need to supplement your small salary with a few shifts at the local diner, but it's how many top broadcasters get their start.

Fearing his boss's rejection offered Sean a revelation into what he needed to do, and if we're being honest, I think he must have also begun to fear settling and abandoning his goals without a try. This would have been an act of self-rejection, as well, and by fearing this, he'd seen the stakes even more clearly. It all gave him the determination to pack his car and move closer toward his on-camera goals.

My coworker didn't let this fear keep him stuck. He let it lead him to different cities outside New York, all with the intent to return as a seasoned broadcast journalist.

Today, he's one of the city's beloved reporters. Sean's fear of rejection was showing him he needed to use his time to invest more in the skill sets the top stations needed from him. He learned a no is not forever. **And rejecting yourself is sometimes the scariest.**

This fear, while it can feel like a speed bump on the path to success, is there to ensure you get to your destination, maybe a little more slowly, but prepared and ready to seize the moment.

PULLING YOURSELF OUT OF THE LIKEABILITY TRAP

The fear of rejection is ingrained in us early, often over aspects of identity that aren't even in our control. Your name, skin color, faith, your dad's rusty Toyota Celica with only one functioning door that was your ride to school each morning—the list is infinite. If only we'd known how little the rejection we faced back then had to do with *us*.

My friend Susie recalls the anxiety of eating lunch in elementary school in the early 1990s. Her meals were free because her family was on government assistance. But the daily experience of collecting her lunch token from the school office attracted much unwanted attention from classmates and substitute teachers. "It was really embarrassing and awful," she confessed on my podcast. "I hated it so much that sometimes I either wouldn't eat lunch, or I would wait until my friends had eaten so they wouldn't see me. I pretended I wasn't hungry."[2]

My fifth grade classmate Drew endured the quiet shame of collecting his free meal card in the morning from the edge of Ms. Tucker's desk, his head low. This ritual labeled him and the others he made the trek with as "poor." When it came time to pick teams in gym, it just so happened that Drew and these others were the ones chosen last. Then there was Jill, whose parents were struggling so hard that she went long periods without bathing, arriving in class with soiled clothes and hair in sticky tangles. I wasn't so brave then to stand up for her when kids gave her the side-eye. But I made tiny gestures, offering her part of my meal when I bought hot lunch on Fridays. I was obsessed with our cafeteria tater tots, but with Jill, I quietly shared.

Because kids can be so cruel, my experience of childhood rejection became an ongoing fear and traveled with me to middle school. By the sixth grade, this fear was so all-consuming that it prevented me from learning the importance of respecting and cultivating my own identity.

We'd moved to Shrewsbury, a new town in Worcester County that was richer than Auburn in both average household wealth and quality of school bullies. These were my awkward, ugly duckling years. I was so afraid of rejection, I became desperate to fit in. Just weeks before attending a too-important bar mitzvah, I begged Mom to help me tame my unibrow problem, but her response was a swift "*Aslan*," Farsi for "no way!" My forehead-scaping, she surmised, would be a siren call for pedophiles. And she'd be left with no other choice but to banish me to a tall, windowless tower.

But my fear of rejection made me oblivious to the risks of defying my mother. My friend Seth had invited our entire grade to his coming-of-age affair, one of the first events where appearances really mattered. The girls would be comparing their dresses and shoes. While I adored the green silk A-line frock I planned to wear, I was sad thinking I didn't have the face to go with it. *I wasn't pretty like them*. Unless . . .

"I wish I could pluck my eyebrows," I said to Layla, my best friend, who was sitting next to me on the edge of my bed. She understood my grievances. Her father was Iranian, which gave her an acute understanding of the sort of loudness and drama that came with being from the Middle East. But her mom's side of the family had been living in America for generations, and thus she and her sisters benefited from relatively liberal rules at home. Layla knew firsthand the confident life that came with having two sets of brows. She'd been tweezing hers for at least a year. I was deeply envious.

Layla jumped off the bed with an immediate and certain plan. The bar mitzvah was only a week away at this point. "We're gonna do this," she said. "Now."

I obeyed her instructions, sneaking into my parents' bathroom to grab my mom's pink Bic razor that rested on her shower caddy. A tweezer would have been more efficient, but in the rush I'd failed to locate one. I scurried back to my bedroom and quietly shut the door. Leaning close to my mirror, I surveyed the single brow. *So much hair.*

"Hold the razor sideways. Start in the middle," Layla demonstrated with her fingers.

I pretended to understand.

I raised the blades to the top of my face, imagining the smiles and flattery in my very near future. Even possibly being mistaken for a young Demi Moore.

Within a minute or two, the job was done.

I stood back from the mirror to look at what was now two distinct brows.

But also, razor rash, visible roots, and a few bloody nicks.

My attempt to be "normal" and *like all the other girls* hadn't turned out quite so neatly. I remember feeling that immediate regret, shame, and fear that comes with making an extreme, silly decision that lands us in hot water. That fear of rejection had made it so I couldn't even bear to look at myself. The self-loathing that followed was far worse than any rejection I'd felt from a classmate. And now I'd have to explain this all to my mom. For a moment I thought I might be able to dodge her, bury the damage with my bangs. But then, this wasn't exactly my lucky day. At dinner, while shoveling rice into my baby brother's mouth, she took one look at me and dropped her spoon. *"Ey voy!"* She hollered that Persian expression I must have heard a minimum of thirty times a day growing up. *Ey voy*, similar to *oy vey* in Yiddish, can be a standard, exasperated response after learning something surprising, like your second cousin Khosrow cheated on Roya or the fact that an avocado is technically a fruit. But that evening the term carried a more expletive, apocalyptic tone. Mom immediately grounded me for weeks, which meant the bar mitzvah was a no go. But by the morning she realized it would be rude to un-RSVP so late in the game. As much as she hated it, she let me attend the party, though to be clear, I was far from off the hook.

By the time the occasion rolled around, my brows were in recovery, but I still continued to wrestle with my fear of rejection. The bar mitzvah introduced me to the electric slide, which was admittedly awesome, but when a slow song would come on and kids paired up to awkwardly sway to Mariah Carey, I headed for the bathroom. On top of it all, I had the worry of what awaited me at home: a fiery mad mother and no TV or telephone calls for the foreseeable future. The moral of the story: trying to blend in because we fear rejection may seem like the natural next move, but it can be treacherous. You're left stuck between two worlds: the one you desperately want to please and the one you can't bear to face at home.

As blogger Janis Isaman writes, "Not being seen, heard, and held for who we are is a trauma . . . . It hurts."[3] Studies find that this fear has a tendency to linger, manifesting as low self-esteem, sadness, jealousy. We avoid conflict and aim to win approval. "Rejection trauma," as some psychology experts call it, is an often invisible pain that distorts your sense of self and can take a great deal of work to unpack.[4]

I was a tween back then; the risk of rejection meant discomfort at school, or not getting a phone call to hang out. But the stakes grow higher as we age. Research shows that our fear of rejection can amplify in adulthood in proportion with the stakes. Don't get me wrong, social rejection when you're a kid is excruciating and deserves attention, but when you're an adult, your fear of rejection can be as, if not more, costly. Sensing rejection, we may disengage or overreact in ways that can impact our health, relationships, finances, and careers. The fear of rejection can mean the difference between interviewing for a role that could pay your bills and buy you more independence or staying stuck in an unhappy job because you're afraid employers will reject you. You fail to apply and give yourself the runway for greater opportunities.

Unless we make friends with this fear, it can lead us down dark paths. We may self-medicate with drugs and alcohol. We may ditch an otherwise healthy relationship over our personal insecurities planted in the fear of rejection. We may quit a promising friendship or coursework at the first sign of conflict or tension. Without examination, this fear can make us self-isolate and become lonelier.

My unibrow massacre should have been the first inkling that I might want to look closely at my fear of rejection and make a pal of it, rather than cave to pressure because of it.

More than a decade later, in the winter of 2007, I received feedback that my forthcoming book, *You're So Money*, had been reviewed by the powers that be at NBC's *Today* show. They wanted me to come on the program when it debuted the following spring.

In some ways, this moment had been in the works for five years. While a junior reporter at *Money* magazine, I was sometimes tasked with urgent requests as part of our editorial collaboration with *Today*. I once triumphantly tracked down an exclusive, not-yet-on-the-market copy of the Hillary Duff prepaid debit card and rushed it overnight to NBC for the anchors to flash on-screen at 8 a.m. Then, five years later, while taking the crosstown bus in Manhattan, I bumped into Patricia, a *Today* producer who remembered me as that tireless, very eager young staffer. While we rode the bus, I told Patricia I had a book coming out. She was ecstatic and told me to send it to her office. And now, months later, here I was, getting the chance of a lifetime.

I was sitting in my cubicle at work when the good news arrived, and I immediately turned to my friend and then colleague James to share my excitement-slash-nervousness. He predicted this appearance would be a life-altering event.

"What do you mean?" I asked him, fishing for reassurance.

"I just think this is going to be a moment in your life when you look back and think this is when everything changed," he said.

In many ways, my friend's forecast would be correct. It would lead to more speaking opportunities, recurring press, additional book deals, and starting the business I have today. But the thing he didn't predict was how, during my first live network appearance, my fear of rejection would set off like a bomb. Humiliated, I'd be left picking up the pieces in front of millions of viewers.

The general feeling of being on one of the biggest morning shows in the country for the first time (and, honestly, still) is for me simultaneous excitement and horror. The most surprising part is how quiet it is around the set. Without a live audience inside, there's mostly just silence in between segments, which, as a guest, means I can hear—very acutely—the voices in my head telling me to not screw up.

In preparation for my debut, I clung to advice from Candace, my boss during a college internship at CNBC.com. She and I had shared a small office with floor-to-ceiling glass walls at 30 Rockefeller Center, a room that we called "the fishbowl." It was the summer of 1999 and one of the loneliest periods in my young adult life, a time when I ate no fewer than 192 inches of Subway sandwiches over a span of eight weeks. (More on this dietary triumph in the next chapter.)

Candace and I were trying to guess what it was about Katie Couric, who was a *Today* show co-anchor at the time and someone we occasionally spotted (okay, gawked at) around the plaza, that made her such a beloved star. Maybe it was her charm, her wit, her chic but effortless style, her ability to conduct revelatory interviews with everyone from celebs like Leo DiCaprio to presidents?

"I think people just *like* her," Candace concluded. "People just have to like you. You know?"

I nodded while squinting my eyes, the look I give when trying to pretend I have any sort of clue.

I wasn't sure how to achieve this "likeability" Candace spoke of, but I very much wanted to grow up and be like Katie. I wanted to be a respected journalist with adoring fans and massive financial power. I wanted *Glamour* magazine to say I, too, was the "best dressed" on daytime TV.

Fast-forward to *Today* Show Eve, when I rehearsed what might win me approval from the network executives and make me "liked" by the 5 million people watching. Up until that point I'd spent most of my career as a journalist being the one with the questions. I had the occasional experience being in front of the camera. While at *Money* magazine, the PR team booked me on local TV from time to time to share tips from the magazine, and at TheStreet.com, where I currently worked, I anchored web videos. But appearing on *Today* as a featured guest? This was a whole other ball game. And like baseball, football, and most major league sports, I had no idea how the scoring worked.

With the tables turning, I was afraid to face the light. I must have rewritten my talking points dozens of times. Tim and I were only dating at the time, but I tasked him to play the role of *Today*'s male co-anchor at the time (the one who shall not be named) and grill me with practice questions. I rehearsed my answers in front of mirrors, standing, sitting, and lying in bed. I channeled *Today*'s polished, re-curring guests who were fast-talking, soundbite-giving "conversation-alists." Those were proven, safe, and "likeable" moves, I told myself. I sped up the pace of my words and deepened my voice. I recalled how a moody boss once told me to refine my speech while on camera and stop saying things like "gotta" and "shoulda." (Side note: Women get a lot of stupid advice on how to sound and talk their way up the ladder. It was *the* Katie Couric who once said in a commencement speech that she was criticized for not having "gravitas" when she became the first woman to solo anchor the evening news, a word she decoded to mean "testicles" in Latin.[5]) I prayed I'd be seated on the right side of the host so as to easily hide the crater of an old chicken pox scar on my left cheek. I practiced how I might cross my legs. *Should* I cross my legs?

In the shower before bed, the hope was to relax. Instead, I chan-neled my stress into a new, sharp razor and accidentally slit the front of my right shin. Did I mention I was planning to wear a pencil skirt?

There was so much riding on this interview. My book was meant to establish me as an expert in personal finance. My insights would hopefully be a first step, a conversation starter in encouraging young adults to connect with one another and open up about the financial issues we experience. As someone who was embedded in this gener-ation, I wanted to be an empathetic advocate and friend to help us reach our financial best.

That's how our dialogue was *supposed* to go.

Here's the *real* rewind: Meredith Vieira, the *Today* co-anchor at the time, began by asking why I thought my new financial advice book would appeal to a younger audience. This was one of the first times that a twentysomething (who was also a woman) had attempted to simplify and demystify the financial world for her generation. "You probably are the best one to give them this advice because they might not take it from somebody my age," she said. She was clearly teeing me up so that I could easily drive home my message.

What I wanted to say was that young adults were tired of being told what to do by so-called "experts" who aren't living in their shoes. We wanted to hear from someone who personally understood our grievances.

Instead, I blurted out something to the effect of (and you can probably search for this gaffe on YouTube), "We don't want someone *who's three times our age* . . . telling us what to do."

"Now stop right there!" she replied with a look that said, "*I think I know what you mean, but do you realize what you just said . . . out loud?*"

My body tensed up as I tried to combat totally losing my grip on the interview. It didn't help that I heard the camera operators chuckling. I threw out a nervous laugh, and said, "No offense!" and immediately began speeding through the rest of my answer, desperate to distance myself from this mortifying moment. I wanted very badly to go home, but Meredith wasn't done with me. We had four whole minutes left.

When our segment ended, and we cut to commercial, I finally exhaled and apologized. I thanked Meredith profusely for understanding. She gave me a hug and a "nice job" before she was whisked to the studio upstairs.

While my blunder seemed to go over fine with the classy Meredith, I dreaded how others who were expecting more or better might be disappointed and lose confidence in me. How was I going to face my publisher? My colleagues back in the newsroom? I imagined some folks soaking up every second of my trip up. And, *ey voy*! What would my mother say?

Then, out of the corner of my eye, I saw Patricia slowly approaching.

My heart sank. She had taken a chance by booking me, had advocated for me, had encouraged her senior executives to feature this unknown, oddly named amateur, and I had word-vomited all over their exquisite set. I wanted to sprint out of the building but was forced to stay put and get de-mic'd by a crew member. I stood under the hot lights, roasting in shame until all wires were fully removed.

Patricia gently took my arm and said softly, "Okay, so . . . our executive producer wants me to tell you . . . we'd love to have you back."

What?

Patricia is polite but this seemed an egregious lie. Or, did the EP slip out and grab a muffin during my live catastrophe? And he had no clue?

Later, as Patricia and I went over the segment, I learned a big reason *why* they wanted me back: after tripping on my words, a wild thing happened—I was seen as someone who screws up . . . *just like everyone else.* I was seen as a woman who isn't perfect, but who shows up anyway. And attempts to recover as best she can.

Now, I can't take credit for understanding back then how to pivot and work my fear of rejection to my advantage on the spot. I was young and still needed to learn. But I do recall this: my fear had made me desperate to just stick my landing. When I could no longer trust the "scripts" for how I was supposed to behave, I turned to the one tool left in my arsenal: being me. I leaned on my professional listening skills, focused on my breath, and told myself to slow down. Maybe I'd perform unlike the "pros," but at least this way, I wouldn't trip on my words again. I showed my real, perfectly imperfect self.

In the end, my moves were far more likeable than donning a fancy outfit or using $10 words. Nothing spells *ratings* more than falling on your face on live television, amiright?

Reflecting on that messy moment, I see how fearing rejection can initially throw us into likeability quicksand. Misinterpreting this fear as a sign to model ourselves after others so that we can win approval can be destructive. When I began "posing" at the top of the interview with my mechanical talking points, my body got really confused. It's no accident that I said something inappropriate. This was fear's way of telling me to stop. Just stop. There's still a way to finish strong. But you have to start remembering who you are and trust that, like Rihanna at the 2023 Super Bowl halftime show, showing up entirely as yourself, without crazy dance tricks or a surprise musical guest, is more than plenty.

Something similar would happen again seven years later in a job interview with Lucy Kaylin, the then head of *O, The Oprah Magazine* and its editor at large, Gayle King. I caught my fear of rejection leading me down the path of self-sabotage. But this time, I was able to more consciously engage the fear and use the stimulus to course correct in the moment.

The role I was up for was contributing editor, and I was competing against over a dozen other money experts to write the new monthly financial column. In the meeting, when they asked what differentiated me from the other financial pros they were interviewing, I fumbled. I could only think of the strengths that the others had, their unique advantages over me. How could Oprah's team prefer me to some of these other candidates? One person I was up against had millions of followers. Another was an actual certified financial planner. I was thinking of the *others* when I should have been focused on me. I stalled. I even brought up a competitor's name to say, "Well, I may not have credentials like so-and-so . . ." *What? Farnoosh, why are you taking attention off of yourself? Why are you giving others a spotlight? This is* your *job interview.* My self-consciousness couldn't take the embarrassment, the self-inflicted wounds. And when I saw Lucy shift impatiently in her seat for a smarter answer, it was a wake-up call that an opportunity of a lifetime was slipping away.

At that moment, sensing that I was losing my way in the interview and failing to win any "likes," I harnessed my fear of rejection and shifted the adrenaline to excitedly talking up *my* work and what I knew to be true: that my podcast provided me with an ear to the ground to hear people's financial questions and problems like nobody else. If anybody were to reject that, I'd be its fiercest advocate. When I saw Lucy *and* Gayle lean in, I knew I was back in the game. We ended up talking for almost ninety minutes, so much that the next day I completely lost my voice. (My podcast was a seven-day-per-week show back then, too, so it was inevitable.) A month later, the team officially invited me on board.

When I've been afraid of being excluded, unfriended, denied, or ignored, I see both darkness and light. The fear in those moments, while excruciating, also led to wisdom. It was actually telling me not to focus so hard on assimilating and not to be so desperate for approval. Otherwise, things can spiral. **The fear of rejection was actually saying to start over and center myself. Relax and be real.**

Thanks to examining and ultimately befriending my fear of rejection, I've become the person who willingly and excitedly chooses to work in a male-dominated field. I appreciate how being different is an asset and a fast track to standing out. I am now that woman who offers her friends and followers the advice nobody else will. We shouldn't try to *not* be liked. But if people don't respect you for who you are at the core, why work so hard to convince them otherwise? Pretending to be someone else is fraught with challenges. What's most important is that you're being admired for your natural gifts and talents.

The truth is, we can't ever really escape or fight the gravitational pull toward our authentic self. We may struggle with who we are both as children and adults. We may assume life might be easier or better if we looked different (and, honestly, it might be, at least temporarily), but when we confuse the fear of rejection with a desire to be liked, we end up living a lie. We say things we don't mean. We lose connections. And in our efforts to *avoid* rejection, we live out a self-fulfilling prophecy.

GO WHERE YOU ARE LOVED

Evolutionary science reveals that human tribalism is baked in.[6] In Paleolithic times, your loyalty and allegiance to a group allowed you to live a longer life than if you went rogue or were ostracized. It's natural to want to be in groups that feel familiar or reflect who we are because, again, it's a survival mechanism. Tribalism, as one group of researchers at Durham University in England concluded, is "an ineradicable feature of human cognition . . . that no group—not even one's own—is immune."

That's why as a young girl my name was punishing. It was a constant reminder to myself and others that I was different. I'd never once met another Farnoosh. The name has various translations in Farsi—"joyful," "glorious life," or "a lot of drinks" (my personal favorite)—but for the other kids in school, Farnoosh only translated to one thing: *What?*

It felt like a mistake. Like *I* was a mistake. My name became this out-of-body thing that dragged me through an unkind world. People found the name confusing, confounding, and nutty. And all this was transpiring without my consent. Sheida and Farrokh had not planned to become parents a year into their marriage. Ill-prepared, they scrambled to give me a name. At least, that's what it felt like.

There's a phenomenon called the Dorian Gray Effect that finds strangers can, with bizarre accuracy, match names with the faces of people they don't know.[7] It's not just luck. There are cultural stereotypes at play. Researchers at the Hebrew University of Jerusalem evaluated how we perceive certain names to go with certain looks and personalities. Bobs are assumed to have rounder faces than, say, Tims. Katherines are more serious and reliable than Bonnies. Over time, the reality lives up to the perception. For example, Tim, my husband, has a great jawline, as one might expect.

While this study focused on adults, kids are not excluded from these preconceptions. As a Farnoosh raised in the closed-off, predominantly

Irish-Catholic Worcester County suburbs, there was no context or prec-edent for my name. Kids in my community often assumed I was an alien, unworthy of being included in their lives. My name could be demoraliz-ing at times, a permanent reminder that I was so very different.

Hearing my name mispronounced in public, especially when read off an attendance list from an unsuspecting substitute teacher, would sink me further down into my seat. "Furnish? Fer-NAHSH?" They all tried their darndest to get it right. I'd wait for a pause and go in for a gentle correction. "Um, it's Far-*NOOSH*?" I'd say, ending on a ques-tion mark, a way of suggesting that this wasn't their fault, even I didn't know. It's a name that really does deserve some probing. So, in my quest to fit in at school, I took on a few aliases.

In the fourth grade, I asked my basketball squad—kids from the surrounding towns who didn't know me from school—to call me Tina. Tina, to me, was the type A, religious girl from my kindergarten class who wore knee socks and threatened to tell the teachers whenever we used the word "God" outside of a prayer. She was kickass and modeled the intensity that I wanted to bring to my ball game.

Throughout the years, my parents, bless their hearts, never impeded any of my many attempts to swap out my name. In some ways, they sym-pathized. In the late 1980s, simultaneous to becoming naturalized citi-zens, Mom and Dad officially changed *their* names to Sheila and Adam. And when my brother arrived shortly after, they named him Todd, after the son of a wealthy and prominent Iranian couple from Bethesda, Mary-land. My parents deeply admired this couple. *Their* Todd had grown up to become a surgeon, and that's all my mom needed to know.

My parents left the door open for me to make a permanent name switch, too, but I was afraid to make the commitment without a few more experiments.

In the sixth grade, I introduced myself as Ashley to neighbors. Ash-ley was the whitest, easiest name I could think of, and by this time we were living in the very Anglo suburb of Shrewsbury, so I thought it would work like a charm. This name would win me some respect around the neighborhood.

But at school, my Iranian-ness was not something I could disguise. The curiosity from classmates concerning my origin story was beginning to peak.

"What's a Farnoosh, *anyway*?" Chris McMahon asked, hovering over me as I lined up the textbooks in my bottom locker. We were minutes away from the sound of our homeroom bell and he wasn't wasting any time in ruining my morning. This was the seventh grade, and as such, the kids had mastered a more sophisticated, psychological method of bullying. On the surface, Chris was asking a seemingly innocent question about my name. But the "what" in his question suggested that I wasn't a person to him. I was a thing.

"Farnoosh is a name and it's an Iranian name," I said, annoyed, as he stared blankly at me. "Iran. It's . . . a *country*?"

Holding on to my Trapper Keeper, I felt the comebacks bubbling up inside of him. He shot back, "Yeah, well, just go back to your *country*."

It was a predictable response that I'm sure he'd learned from ignorance at home, but it still stung. Asking questions, no matter how unenlightened, implied curiosity about who I was as a human being. But Chris was doing the one thing that was worse: giving up on me altogether. I was, to him, a lost cause.

I remained calm, turned away, and proceeded to take my seat in our homeroom.

The rest of my time as a kid in Shrewsbury was rough. I was getting certified in rejection and would come to understand why so many people feared it. By the ninth grade, my popularity had sunk to an all-time low. I didn't get elected to the Student Council. I didn't make the cheerleading squad or the tennis team. At every turn, I was refused entry. My hopes of being a part of something that might connect me with others, to feel like I belonged somewhere other than at my family dinner table, to something that was bigger than me, were dashed.

On a bus ride home one Friday in my first year at Shrewsbury High School, I cried a steady stream of tears. When the driver dropped me off at the edge of our home's driveway, I spotted my mom's mom, Mamani, waiting for me as usual. Back then, Mamani's visits from Iran spanned multiple months, and she would be the first to inflict anxiety and worry over our Americanized ways. She gripped my hand as we walked from the bus to the front door. Before we stepped inside, she hinted that my parents had big news to share: we were moving again. It would be our third and biggest relocation to date, to Bryn Mawr, Pennsylvania. While some kids might have resisted the idea of permanently leaving town when they'd only just started high school, I remember thinking this was some of the best news of my life. I began making a list of new names for myself.

A few months later, my family and I packed our latest-edition Camry (we were Toyota devotees) and headed south to an apartment rental on the Main Line, a high-net-worth suburban enclave that consisted of several small, upscale towns right outside Philadelphia. The Main Line had been named after the former Pennsylvania Railroad that ran along the district, home to some of the city's most prestigious families. And now, the Torabis. We weren't affluent like them, just ambitious immigrants making ends meet in a similar zip code.

In Bryn Mawr, I would attend Harriton, a tax-rich "Blue Ribbon" public school with only five hundred students. In this town, my parents had arrived with a goal to start a Persian restaurant with friends. My father, being highly risk-averse, kept his full-time job at a tech company in Shrewsbury and worked remotely from our new living room three states away, traveling back and forth every couple of weeks. Our two-bedroom apartment in Bryn Mawr overlooked the commuter railway stop. At first the vibrations and thunder of the SEPTA train that passed every forty-two minutes mere feet away startled us. But in time we learned to talk over the noise.

We settled in with only a few weeks until the start of the school year.

I'd be entering the tenth grade, the new kid once more. In a different state, I figured this was my moment to thoroughly commit to a personal rebranding and take on a fresh persona full-time. From my list, I picked a name that gave credence to the fact that I was now a young lady . . . possibly even rebellious. I wanted to exude an air of mystery, as I imagined strutting down the halls of my new high school. Sort of like Shannen Doherty's character Brenda in *90210*, the dark-haired Midwesterner who gave zero f's in the face of Beverly Hills mean girls.

To that end, I became Nikki with two *k*'s.

Nikki was a girl I knew from growing up in Massachusetts. She was beautiful, a little defiant, and a fashionista. She owned cashmere sweaters purchased from shopping trips in Manhattan with her mom. Her Persian parents doted on her. The other girls wanted to be her. And so I thought, entering a new town, a new school district, I could actually *be her*.

The American names I chose for myself throughout the years were all short-lived. The first two I selected—Tina and Ashley—didn't last because I simply outgrew them. I fell out of favor with their ordinariness, I guess. Besides, basketball season ended, and I had no new kids who didn't already know me as Farnoosh to practice with and call me Tina.

And although I was adamant about being Nikki, the ruse only lasted for a week or two. Students and teachers couldn't get my attention. They'd call on me in class or shout "Nikki" across the gym to no avail. Turns out, I was oblivious to Nikki. My reflexes were not accustomed to the change. I was fourteen years old going on fifteen. By then, I'd been living my life mostly as a Farnoosh, albeit begrudgingly. My subconscious resisted this radical shift. It's almost as if my fear of rejection was begging me to wake up to my own preposterousness and make friends with what it was trying to tell me: accept yourself, the person you are at the core, your *true* self.

I was misusing my fear of rejection as a weapon against myself, to change aspects of my identity. I'd become the biggest culprit of my own rejection. What would have happened if I had just remained *Farnoosh*? Would the basketball team have passed me fewer balls? Would I have felt sadder on that first day of school? I'll never know because I was too busy pointing arrows at myself.

High school was a formative time for me, when I began to not only discover but *decide* who a Farnoosh could be. Over the next year, my relationship with my name would transform. I was able to step into my genuine self more safely, due in large part to the fact that my classmates in the suburbs of Philadelphia, while beyond wealthy, came from more diverse backgrounds. I was given the inviting space and support to explore my identity, thanks to classmates and teachers who encouraged our individuality. Kids started to call me Noosh and Nooshy, both terms of endearment. I couldn't believe what was happening.

My new start in Bryn Mawr taught me that our fear of rejection can be sneaky. In the beginning, this fear may stem from hostility and denial from the external world, prompting you to turn against yourself. You begin to like yourself less. You doubt what you're capable of accomplishing. You long to assimilate. And even when circumstances change, it has this way of sticking around. This fear, that you initially sourced from the outside, becomes part of your identity. You see yourself as *less than*.

When I landed in a place that was more inclusive, I felt more at peace with who I was. I became more courageous. I spoke up in our English class more often and debated the other students, even the popular ones. I tried out for the tennis team, despite having been rejected in Shrewsbury, and actually made the cut. (I was still awful, but the coach was patient.) I auditioned for the school musicals and landed both comedic and dramatic roles I didn't know I had in me to perform.

My move to Bryn Mawr found me asking, *Who's doing the rejecting?* It was me and solely me. I'd allowed the previous bullying in Massachusetts to get to me so much that I began to believe the rejection was justified, and so I'd started to be dismissive of myself. Moving somewhere new, where I could express myself more freely, taught me a lesson I would remember in times of loneliness, insecurity, and rejection: Appreciate what makes you . . . *you*. Be yourself and see the doors open. And as I got older, that move to Bryn Mawr suggested another lesson: **you don't have to spend your whole life surrounded by people who don't understand you.**

This surprising journey of my relationship with my name inspired my college personal statement essay, in which I defined what it meant to be a Farnoosh. It was a story I was sure would win over college admissions teams everywhere.

I illustrated the early torment, my countless identity crises, and finally the acceptance and peace that arrived with just giving up, letting go, and leaning into what set me apart. I wrote about how I discovered that the most challenging part of my name—that it was unprecedented and unfamiliar—meant that I also had a blank slate to do anything and become anyone. With no cultural expectations of what a Farnoosh should be, I had a unique opportunity to blaze a trail for myself and any other Farnooshes who wanted to be as unpredictable and weird as I knew I was.

I mailed variations of it to about ten different schools, all the top ones my counselors said I ought to try, so I'd be including some fancy private universities. My father also insisted I apply to Penn State, our in-state college and the most affordable option, as my backup. There was no special higher ed fund set aside for me, and wherever I attended either needed to grant me a scholarship or be inexpensive enough for my father to cash-flow the cost out of his paycheck.

That following spring, the admissions letters began trickling in. One by one they arrived, mostly in standard four-by-nine envelopes, the kind that only meant one thing. Every sentence started with those five awful words: *We regret to inform you . . .*

To imagine rejection is one thing. It is another to see it addressed to you on official letterhead.

In all, I'd gotten rejected from 80 percent of the schools I'd applied to.

I thought I'd conquered my fear of rejection in high school, but now that persistent dread rushed back. It was a sinking feeling, tangled up with self-pity, foolishness, and the fear of facing my friends (and their parents) when they asked, "So, where are *you* going to college?"

Penn State it would be. My parents were proud. They said I was making the best choice, not just because it was the most affordable, but because the school was rolling out the red carpet. And they were right. Penn State was *into me*. They'd accepted me into their honors program, which meant more intimate class sizes, exclusive study abroad programs, and a partial scholarship. In my slow attempt to make peace with the fear and insecurity surrounding all the college rejections, I grew more optimistic and focused on what this acceptance—while underwhelming at first—had in store.

And you know what? Attending Penn State led me to some of my best friendships. And most importantly, to Tim, a handsome, smart, and funny classmate who totally friend-zoned me at the time. Unbeknownst to him, I was quickly convinced he'd be my life partner one day. (More on this soon!)

Your fear of rejection can be an all too important Spidey-Sense telling you that certain people or places don't deserve you. It's not worth the effort to make the situation work, to get accepted or become one of them. In my college admissions process, and in so many other instances, I've seen how a *no* can be life's way of steering me toward a place of *yes*, where I am meant to belong. To freely share yourself with others is of tremendous value, and some audiences, some people, some places don't want you. And frankly, they don't deserve you. **If you've put in all the effort and still the fear of rejection keeps looming, let it be your cue to move on with your head held high.**

Podcast listeners sometimes write in with questions at similar crossroads. They don't feel valued at their jobs, but the idea of going elsewhere frightens them. They fear burning bridges with their boss.

"Should I stay at my company where they haven't given me a raise and keep dragging me along?" they ask. "I feel loyal to my manager." My reply? Where is *your manager's* loyalty to you? Do you really fear leaving more than the fear of languishing at a job where your talents aren't valued enough? Whether you work in corporate America or at a nonprofit, teach in a fifth-grade classroom or drive Lyft, your allegiance is admirable, but if the feeling isn't mutual, don't fear rejection so much that you don't try for somewhere else that may recognize and compensate you for your talents. I've been laid off more than once in my twenty-year career, interestingly enough just weeks after glowing quarterly reviews. Workers are dispensable, as we've all learned from many cycles of layoffs in the past. Don't hesitate to start applying to other jobs if you know you can advance better somewhere else.

Aim to go where you are loved.

When I lost out on all those private school dreams and landed at Penn State, I learned that rejection is not always something that happens *to* you. **A rejection is a move that might be made *for* you.** It's a *no* that's leading you to your *yes.* All those times I attempted to change my appearance or name, to say the right things so that I could fit in and be liked, were ways that I was rejecting myself. And it always came back to bite me in the ass.

Later, in my thirties, when I circulated the proposal for my last book, *When She Makes More,* the feedback from publishers was mixed. One editor rejected me because she was turned off by the idea of giving female breadwinners "advice." She assumed I was suggesting that being a higher-earning partner was problematic for women. (When in reality, being the poster woman for female financial independence is my full-time hustle, okay?) She replied that my idea was built on a false premise and that I was naive. I was crushed, of course, but my very experienced literary agent was kind of jazzed. An interesting and irreverent book will have lovers and haters, she said. Some rejection, in this case, was not something to fear. It was something to desire because it meant there would be debate and discourse. If everyone agrees with your book, what's there to talk about? Friction breeds energy. In the end, the book had multiple bidders.

When someone rejects you, or you feel like they might turn you away, they may be doing you a favor. Go for the opportunity anyway, then feel thankful that you were spared the time and effort in trying to make something impossible work, especially when there are so many other avenues worth traveling that will bring love, encouragement, and a welcome sign. **Sometimes in life, we must trust the rejections.** We must not try to force, twist, or pressure rejection into acceptance. I wish I'd known years ago that not everything has to be a fit. Remember this when, say, you hear someone is not or no longer into you. Thank their rejection because, by giving up on you, they've opened the door for you to leave and go to where there is alignment and growth and where you will be met with the embrace you deserve.

LET YOUR TRUTH FLIP THE SCRIPT

At twenty-six I had worked my way up to being an online video reporter for TheStreet.com, a site that caters to stock market enthusiasts and Jim Cramer devotees. Jim was cofounder of the company, and at the time, he was hosting CNBC's top-rated investing show, *Mad Money*. I joined TheStreet.com after failing to convince my boss at NY1 News that I deserved a raise and promotion. TheStreet offered me nearly double the salary that I earned at NY1, as well as the opportunity to build their online video domain from the ground up. To be the channel's founding reporter was too hard to pass up. I was even tapped to host a daily show with Jim himself. I was extremely nervous at first, as this was someone I revered, a man with an encyclopedic knowledge of all things financial.

It was around this time when Elliot, a colleague who sat a few desks away in our open newsroom, started firing off microaggressions. He'd say things like: "Do you even read the *Wall Street Journal*?" and "Hey, maybe you ought to start learning some Wall Street lingo." At first, I engaged him. I told him that yes, I read a lot of related material. And no, I didn't care to pick up Wall Street insider language and use it in my work, because my job was meant to demystify the world of money. Time after time, he would slip in these backhanded remarks or questions. Time after time, I would let it slide.

I don't think it is a stretch to say that Elliot's annoyance with me was due to jealousy and resentment. He was probably bitter that someone younger than him—and a woman at that—had gotten the coveted role of working closely with Jim. His passive-aggressive quips were not a huge surprise to me.

Then one day, months into the job, we were both standing on a Midtown corner, waiting for the walk sign. We were heading back to our offices from an off-site meeting when he began his usual unsolicited rant about how I could "improve" as a journalist. "You know, I'm *trying* not to be an asshole . . . ," he said. And, friend, I don't know what came over me in that moment. Maybe it was the vigor and loudness of New York City behind my back that pushed me to the edge. Whatever it was, I turned to Elliot and said, "You should try harder."

His jaw dropped. Either he hadn't realized just how much of an asshole he had been, or he'd never thought I'd have the guts to talk back to him.

"Okay," he muttered. "Sorry."

I'm positive that our exchange did little to improve the way he felt about me, but at least now Elliot knew that coming at me with insincere advice and suggestions was no use.

I tell you this with the full recognition that I was lucky that day. It should never be assumed that when you speak truth to power, especially as a minority in the workplace, it will lead to favorable outcomes. Talking back to Elliot was not without risk. He could have continued to make my life miserable at work. He could have spoken ill of me the next time he was in a meeting with our CEO. And who knows? Maybe he did. But I felt okay with talking back at that moment because Elliot was kind of known for being the office loudmouth. If this were to blow up into a "he said, she said" battle in the newsroom, and he attempted to berate me to others in retaliation, I was confident he would not win. I knew my position, too, as an experienced professional who had the trust of senior management. I had some currency, as well. That all factored into my calculus and gave me the confidence to give him some lip service.

What's riskier? Voicing misgivings and possibly rocking the boat at work, or staying silent and allowing the microaggressions to build up to the point where you begin to doubt your own capability or undermine your value? Speaking up to bias and unlawful rejection may create short-term volatility in your career and life, but your silence will also exact a price. The question becomes: How soon do you want it to stop? How badly do you want to move on? And how sure are you that you can do it without creating much bigger problems for yourself? If the animosity only grows and creates more stress and possible setbacks, will you look back and wish you'd said something? **The more anxious you feel about speaking up, the more your fear of rejection is begging you to stand up for yourself.** I'll never forget the advice *New York Times* bestselling author Luvvie Ajayi once gave my audience on *So Money* about how to get over the edge and speak with more confidence in these moments when we are afraid of potential backlash—especially in the workplace. Luvvie says we should ask ourselves this one question: Will my silence convict me? In other words, as a witness to this harassment, bias, and injustice, will my silence make me a culprit down the road? To my own unfair demise or someone else's? Will I disappoint myself and others by staying quiet? If the answer is yes, let this be your catalyst to use your voice loud and clear.[8]

In her book *The First, the Few, the Only*, author Deepa Purushotha-man talks about how, after two decades, she managed to climb the ranks at Deloitte to become the first Indian American woman to make partner at the global consulting firm.[9] It didn't come without some serious trauma, however. She took on insurmountable work, which, as a woman of color, is not atypical in a corporate setting. You are often working harder than your male colleagues, and your white colleagues, just to prove you're worth it. And it's not only you. Everyone—men and women—has bought into this falsehood and unconscious bias. "For me, there was a growing sense that I was responsible for a lot of people around me . . . and that's part of the burden of being a woman of color in these spaces where you are first or an only," Deepa told me when I interviewed her on my podcast. "There's all this extra work."[10]

Deepa knows firsthand the challenges that come with calling out bias to someone rejecting you, especially if it is a person in power. "We don't necessarily feel empowered to confront the person in the mo-ment. So, part of it is understanding that it is going to happen to you. Be prepared for it. Have prepared commentary or prepared things you can say," she says. "So often I was caught flat-footed."

When she felt unable to speak up or quit in her role at Deloitte, Deepa's health began falling apart. "It started as skin rashes and infec-tions and small things," she said. "Then it started to mount and mount and mount. Then at one point, it was full-blown shingles and neuropa-thy and pains in my head and my hands and my feet." The illness led to an eight-month sabbatical and, eventually, her resignation.

People often ask whether it is my gender or my Iranian background that has been the taller hurdle in a world that can be at times sexist and xenophobic. I never know the definitive answer. In some moments in my career, when I have been rejected for the raise or when I've sat in a job interview while the recruiter didn't even pretend to review my work (instead, he played Solitaire on his desktop), I've asked the ques-tion myself. It's probably been both at different times. And perhaps I've too often given people the benefit of the doubt. That day with Elliot, he'd used up all my benefits.

Now I'm quicker to call out bias, especially if it's the sort of rejection that stands in the way of me and my integrity and success. I don't think we can afford to stay quiet. We must call out rejection that has no room in our lives, the type rooted in discrimination. A woman I mentored once asked me if it was strange that a male team member was rerouting the minutiae of his work onto her plate, things like scheduling group calls and building slide decks for his clients. Deep down she knew what was going on, but part of her didn't want to believe it. He was taking advantage of her and would never ever have done this to a male colleague. I told her that she was within her rights to say *no*. It may be uncomfortable but could be as simple as "Sorry, I won't be able to do this. I suggest an administrator handle this for you." It may have caused her some rejection later down the road from this man . . . or maybe it wouldn't. Maybe, like Elliot, he'd just be more inclined to quit being a moron.

The biases I've encountered haven't been exclusively from men, either. Women have been conditioned to expect less from society and the workplace than men, and sometimes, as women, we place those expectations onto other women and police each other for breaking laws set by patriarchy. We've been made to feel that just having a job should be "enough," even if we make less than our male counterparts. We should be happy with mediocrity because it's better than nothing. At least then, we're not getting rejected. But as Alexandra Carter, a friend and author of *Ask for More*, has told me, if you're not somewhat scared, Farnoosh, if you're not somewhat uncomfortable in a negotiation, you haven't asked for enough.

While I was renegotiating a yearlong consulting deal with a financial institution, a female account manager said that the increased fee I'd asked for my services was too high because "Don't you make enough money already?" To which I responded, half-jokingly, "Are you sure you want to go on the record for saying that . . . to a woman?" She apologized and eventually upped my fee. Watching a woman be ambitious is just too much for some people to bear. This manager falsely assumed she could take advantage of my fear of being rejected, in order to offer me less than the value of my contributions. But my fear of rejection showed me I could not sell myself short.

And let's not forget that I wasn't the only one afraid of rejection there. Months deep into this negotiation, I was certain this woman was not going to call it quits over my reasonable fee increase (which should not have surprised her after I'd delivered above and beyond the first time). I could tell that she wouldn't want to go back to her boss and say that they'd lost the deal over what was a relatively small amount of money for them (but significant for me). They, too, were invested in making this partnership continue.

Sometimes our fear of rejection is signaling us to sniff out what's fishy. Maybe someone's disapproval or bias toward us is unfounded and has the potential to stand in the way of what we deserve or what we've worked hard to earn. It might compromise our well-being or mental health. Ever get that feeling? In these cases, you owe it to yourself to dig deeper. Don't succumb to it. Examine it. Use this fear to fuel your next best step.

The Fear of Rejection Self-Inquiry

- Am I fearing rejection so much that I am neglecting myself and not staying true to who I really am?
- Is my fear of rejection a sign that I'm not ready yet? Is it an instinct to invest more in myself and my skills to earn my spot?
- Am I sacrificing my own values for likeability?

- Is it safe to speak up? Is there a way that I can use my voice to shut down the naysayers and their biases?
- Or is it time to shift my perspective? Might this fear be about them and not about me? And might it be best to find a new place where I can grow?

2

THE FEAR OF LONELINESS

and how it promotes strength,
resilience, and creating
community

A COUPLE OF MONTHS BEFORE my brother was born, my mom and I spent those cold winter nights leading up to his delivery nesting and watching old-timey movies together. Our favorite was *The Little Princess*, the 1930s classic starring the awe-inspiring Shirley Temple.

My mom has a thing for *oldness*. She loves black-and-white movies, antique furniture, and grandparents. If she finds out that a friend's mother is visiting from Iran, she'll eagerly invite her over for *zereshk polo* and then back for chai the following afternoon. I remember being puzzled as to why she longed to spend one-on-one time with women thirty years her senior. I guessed it was because she enjoyed their wisdom. But looking back, I believe it had more to do with missing her own mom, my Mamani. These visiting elders showered my mom with praise and affection for the life she'd built since arriving in the States at a young age. They understood the sacrifice and courage it took for her to leave her own family in Iran and arrive here with nothing of her own. These older guests provided the presence and attention of someone who *seemed like her mom*. And it made her feel less alone.

My mom has many gifts that I sometimes wish more people—beyond the elders that came and went—knew and appreciated. Her advice, while comically intense at times, can be quite profound. She is wildly generous, cherishes her friendships, and has massive willpower. In any dispute, even if she's lying through her teeth, she'll be the last one standing. Just ask anyone who's ever worked in the returns department at Nordstrom. Without a doubt, my mom could have been a top-ranking executive or entrepreneur, had she been provided the access, resources, and encouragement. But nobody ever asked her, *What are your dreams, Sheida?* and the key follow up to that, *How wonderful. I'd love to help.*

Almost out of necessity, my mother became the hero in her own life's journey. She respected and championed herself, all to fill the void in a life where others may not have been so encouraging, supportive, or aware. This was important to witness. My mom modeled how to treat yourself with kindness like nobody else can or will. "Do you think you're beautiful?" I asked her one morning when I was in sixth grade and was watching her get ready for work in front of our bathroom mirror. Back then my mom had a mane of curly brown hair that fell past her shoulders. She liked to tease her tresses for a fuller look. And then, as a finishing touch, she'd use her medium round brush and a Conair blow-dryer to style her bangs. A lot of hair spray was involved in this 7 a.m. ritual. "Yes," she said, making sure to make eye contact through the mirror's reflection. How someone could feel so lonely at times and remain resolute and proud was something I still needed to learn.

Maybe my mom's story is what drew me to *The Little Princess*, the story of Sara, a girl who was left to fend for herself in a challenging new place. Sara, played by Temple, enrolls in London's Miss Minchin's Seminary, the "most dignified and exclusive school for girls" while her father, Captain Crewe, fights in a South African war. She and her dad had been inseparable, especially after her mother died. And shortly after settling in at the seminary, Sara receives the tragic news that her father has been killed in combat and all of his assets have been seized by the opposing army. The headmaster banishes the now penniless Sara to the attic, where she will reside indefinitely as a servant. Her bright, handmade wardrobe is garnished and replaced with rags. This, the headmaster says stoically, is Sara's way of repaying her father's debts to the school.

Through it all, this young girl keeps an unshakeable faith, insistent that her father will somehow return. She creates calm in the chaos by keeping her tiny room neat and cozy. She befriends a bird outside her window, a fellow maid, and a sympathetic neighbor. Similar to my mom finding comfort in the visiting grandmothers in the neighborhood, Sara leverages her fear of loneliness to seek refuge within the understated beauty and warmth that surround her, and to trade solitude for solace. In her loneliness, she turns to herself as a source for strength.

LONELINESS: AN EPIDEMIC

The fear that belonged to that lonely Little Princess is real, and it's in all of us. A recent Harvard study found that one in three Americans, including 61 percent of young adults and over half of mothers with little kids, express "serious loneliness."[1]

Fearing loneliness is part of our nature, as social connection has always been a critical part of human survival. In fact, brain studies prove that the need for interaction with others is woven into our biology.[2] Feeling excluded triggers activity in the part of the brain that processes physical pain. We become frightened, and the brain releases chemical responses similar to hunger, in which we can sense deprivation, stress, and depression. Researchers in 2020 examined the fear and confirmed it can lead to lower self-esteem.[3] It can be harmful to our well-being, as well as to our overall sense of identity.[4]

We ought to be afraid. An often cited study led by Julianne Holt-Lunstad, a professor of psychology and neuroscience at Brigham Young University, found that the health risk of loneliness and social isolation is equivalent to smoking nearly a pack of cigarettes a day, and that people with strong social connections had a 50 percent higher likelihood of survival.[5] Being alone for too long can be problematic for our health and longevity. It can lead to depression, anxiety, and disconnectedness.[6]

Loneliness, it turns out, is a matter of life and death.

Because the fear of loneliness is so common, most of us were already used to covering it up with quick fixes of immediate connection and busyness. And then COVID hit, and many of us had to finally come face-to-face with our fear of loneliness. Suddenly schools, social clubs, and parties were no-fly zones. Loneliness was the hottest topic on all the media channels. At the same time, frontline workers were showing signs of extreme exhaustion, suicide rates were skyrocketing, and over a million deaths associated with COVID were being reported. These times of crisis are often when we need one another the most. But amid all this negative news, we could not escape into friendships, cocktail parties, book clubs, and moms' groups. Behind many closed doors, people were suffering. Loneliness, and our fear of it, became its own pandemic.[7]

That terror of being alone, of not having anyone there to listen to you or hold your hand in the dark or—at its most extreme—be there when you are on your deathbed, was all too real during the pandemic, but it can creep up on you at any time. The fear of loneliness can rise from the stories we tell ourselves, or when we break out into new territory, take on a new job, or move to a new city where we don't know anyone. Like the fear of rejection, loneliness can emerge when people are overlooking you because you don't look or act like them.

The better news is that your fear of loneliness is not trying to ruin you. It's reminding you to find the connection you need. That connection may be to your self, the goals you want to reach, the culture you abandoned in a rush to assimilate, or the fear may be leading you to a brand-new friend. Either way, the fear of loneliness is one of the best ways to cultivate patience, resilience, and empathy for your self.

HOW TO INSPIRE A BRAVE, NEW STORY

In order to make our fear of loneliness a friend, we first need to ask questions about the story we're telling ourselves. Those internal dialogues can make all the difference. I learned this young, from my little friend Mina at one of our many *mehmoonis*.

Mehmoonis are Iranian parties where families gather to eat, dance, play cards, and brag about their kids' college test scores. Ours technically began at 6 p.m., but guests trickled in much later, as late as 9:30 p.m., which meant dinner did not get served until well past my bedtime. *Mehmoonis* ran beyond midnight, probably so parents could sober up before driving home. While other kids were snug in their beds by 8 p.m., following a *mehmooni* my parents would find me passed out atop a pile of coats in their friend's house around 2 a.m. and toss me like chopped wood into the back of our car before commencing the hour-long drive back home.

Upon arrival, children were quickly sent to the basement to fight over the single Nintendo console. Kids were not permitted back upstairs until the smell of *fesenjoon* and *ghormeh sabzi* (popular Persian dishes) had made their way toward the dining room. When I was a kid, *mehmoonis* taught me the virtues of patience and humility, and a tolerance for hunger.

At one such party when I was six or seven years old, I met a little girl named Mina, who'd arrived with her dad. After about half an hour of playing, I asked her, "Where's your mom?" "She went on a shopping trip," she promptly said, continuing to comb her Barbie's blond locks.

"So, is she coming *after* dinner or . . . ?" I pressed. It was unfathomable to me that her mom was missing in action, since East Coast *mehmoonis* were mainly coordinated so the ladies could show off their newest suit coordinates from Jordan Marsh. What was this necessary purchase that just couldn't wait?

A few seconds of silence passed before Mina looked at me and said, "No. She's not coming. My mom went shopping in Iran."

But everyone knew that post-revolution Iran in the early 1980s was hardly a fashion destination. This was clearly the story this little girl had practiced and prepared to tell nosy people like me. Later at home, when I asked my mom about Mina's situation, she told me that her parents had divorced and that her mom had made the incredibly tough choice to move back to her home country by herself.

As the years went by, I never forgot about Mina. Finally, when I was a teen, my parents told me more: Mina's dad was abusive. Knowing his wife wanted a divorce, he gave her an ultimatum: Leave the marriage if you must, but you'll get no support from me. You'll have to leave your daughter, too. As a mom now, I wonder how desperate things must have been for a parent to decide to leave without her child. Penniless and lacking any other resources or knowledge to fight for Mina in a foreign country, her mother flew back to her family's home. From there, with her family's support, it was assumed she might have tried to win custody or visitation rights. But we never found out.

The fear of being separated from someone I loved and depended on—as Mina had experienced, as I'd seen play out sometimes in movies, and as my mother had lived through with her own parents at a very young age—became a fear that I carried for years. My parents, too, had a turbulent marriage, and I witnessed too many of their verbal matches. They often threatened to leave each other, and I was convinced that in a divorce, I'd find myself seeing less of them. And if I had to guess, it would mean fewer hugs from my mom, who for years had been solely dependent on my dad for money. Without Dad, how would Mom be able to afford to raise me? My fears of loneliness as a kid stemmed from dark stories I crafted, a series of terrifying what-ifs.

Remembering Mina today, I don't know if her tale about her mom's shopping trip was what she truly believed—if she was trying to cover up the truth and protect her parents, or maybe her dad just fed her the lie? Perhaps she committed to the story because it was the only thing she could control at a time of uncertainty. I still can't believe that she managed, in that state of loneliness and missing her mom, to engage with me, play with me, talk to me. All I can think is that this story was what this innocent girl needed in order to put one foot in front of the other and keep going. She couldn't bring her mom back. But could she rewrite the narrative detailing her absence?

I'll never know. And I don't ever want to glorify or appropriate Mina's story. I am only fascinated at how the mind works when we experience fear. As adults, the stories we tell ourselves about fear of loneliness can do us good, like they might have for Mina. But they can also do us harm. They may suggest that we're always going to be alone, nobody loves us, we're loners and destined to be by ourselves. Stories like these don't deserve space in our lives. We don't want our tales about the fear of loneliness to cast us as victims. If I'd maintained my childhood theory that loneliness meant danger and an inability to take care of myself, I would never have survived living in New York City as a young woman.

When I interviewed author Tara Schuster of the acclaimed books *Buy Yourself the F*cking Lilies* and *Glow in the F*cking Dark*, she discussed how she learned about her own resourcefulness during bouts of profound loneliness as a child, when she was abandoned as a kid by her parents or a babysitter.

"One of my first memories is wandering down a paved path, screaming for adults, because I was just home alone. The memory had always been so shameful to me," she told me. "But . . . I realized, wait a minute, that part of me was so healthy. I could have played with matches. I could have gone out to the pool where there was no protection. But instead, I sought help,"[8] she said. As adults, we must give ourselves more credit for the many times we worked through our own periods of loneliness and be willing to throw a splash of cold water on a personally undermining story tied to that fear. If we think that loneliness is our fault or that we're not worthy of connection, well, who taught us to believe that? How is whatever story we're holding on to about our personal sense of loneliness helpful or true?

If you are fearing loneliness or already living in it, create a narrative that elicits hope. This might include suggesting that time alone is just part of a journey, and that we might still have a brighter ending. Or we can turn a story about someone leaving us into the idea that this is a step toward the right person, friendship, or community that's arriving next. We can tell ourselves that loneliness is giving us the time to collect our emotions and find some peace in the chaos. Be sure that whatever narrative you choose gives you the space to prove victorious.

Katie Sturino, founder of Megababe, body acceptance advocate, and a media and fashion favorite, said that once upon a time she was a "real asshole" to herself: "Nothing set me off on a self-shit-talking spiral more than when I felt physically inferior to other women." Back then, when she talked to women in her high-octane career in fashion, she felt like a "bear in a tutu."[9]

Katie decided to change her life. She didn't change the externals; she flipped her story. When I invited her on *So Money*, she said she used that fear of alienation and loneliness about her size to create a new narrative.[10] She realized she must not be the only one having these feelings and decided to trade fearing loneliness for feeling empathy. She decided to empower other women just like her. She went from being ashamed of her weight and feeling inadequate and scared about her prospects for connection to running a brand that helps other women feel proud of their bodies. She is now connected to millions of women *because of* her size.

When actress and entrepreneur Suzanne Somers asked for equal pay to the men on the sitcom *Three's Company*, studio management demeaned her by isolating her from other cast members and, finally, firing her. She shared the full story on my podcast and talked about that voice in her head, which allowed her a whole new story.[11] It insisted she focus on what she had, as opposed to what she'd lost. She took stock of her high-profile position as a studio actress and beloved household name and got busy connecting to what she loved. She became a lifestyle guru, sharing her knowledge about health, beauty, and empowerment. And she paved the way for celebrities to create their own brands.

It's sometimes hard to figure out what stories we are telling ourselves. The mind can keep them turning like an old record player. Bob Litwin, world tennis champion and author of *Live the Best Story of Your Life*, says that if you write the story down and look at it from all angles, you can see where it is dragging you down.[12] Once you know the bad story you are telling yourself, flip it. See if you feel better with the new story than you did with the old. This exercise can give you the motivation, energy, and direction you need to move forward.

RISKING LONELINESS TO ACHIEVE BIGGER AND BETTER

In recent years, the team-building firm Wildgoose found that one in four people under twenty-five felt lonely at their jobs. About 44 percent said they had no work friends.[13] I'm not a member of Gen Z, but I know everyone has to start somewhere. When you're breaking out professionally, loneliness often feels like wearing a backpack full of rocks. The more you take risks, set goals, challenge yourself to grow, and meet new versions of yourself, the more you may also encounter that old friend: the fear of loneliness.

During these growth stages, loneliness can be the cost of moving toward new horizons with ambition. This is only a bad thing if you do a U-turn because you are afraid of the fear. If instead you follow your fear of loneliness to where it is leading you next, it may be nudging you to connect with your goals and higher ambitions. **When you can't find resonance with the people in your new environment, look for it in yourself.**

Fifteen years after I met Mina, I experienced my fear of loneliness during my first college internship in New York City. The fear arrived as the scent of a foot-long turkey sandwich, drizzled lightly with honey mustard. I opted for this $5 meal on many weeknights throughout that summer of 1999; it was the best I could afford as an unpaid intern who relied on a limited weekly stipend from her parents. I'd close my work laptop in the sales and marketing department of CNBC.com around 6 p.m., zip from midtown to Canal Street on the R train, and pop into the nearby Subway franchise to grab dinner before crashing in my room.

That summer, I lived in short-term housing in a modern New York University dormitory on a narrow, trash-lined street in Chinatown. It was New York at the height of *Sex and the City* fandom, where dining in chic restaurants suddenly became a sought-after *experience* and women thought it wise to trot along cobblestone streets wearing $600 stilettos. I engaged in none of it because for one, I didn't have that kind of money. I was also just nineteen years old. The nightlife was virtually nonexistent for someone my age without a convincing fake ID. Plus, I was cautioned against taking the subway by myself after dusk.

One of my loneliest nights happened while hovering over my small wooden desk, staring at a Subway sandwich resting on its green-and-yellow packaging. My twenty-six-year-old roommate (a continuing education student from overseas who was randomly assigned to share a room with me) stood facing me by the doorway in her gym clothes, arms crossed. "Are you going to eat the whole sandwich?" she asked. She wasn't curious because she was hoping I might share. She was expressing disgust. And in that moment, I felt not only lonely but rejected for the simple choice to eat a lousy sandwich while alone. "Yes, why?" I looked up at her, prepared for judgment. And then it happened: "It's so . . . much," she said. Nothing quite like being food shamed while you're already suffering through loneliness.

My New York summer had begun with a glimmer of hope. On move-in day, as I awaited the elevator's descent to the ground floor, I spotted two familiar faces approaching: Aria and Carina, two former high school classmates who had always been perfectly nice, always lovely, but not friends who would invite me to the movies or pool parties. But seeing them, years after graduation and here on neutral ground, I perked up. In the absence of our school's social hierarchy, I thought maybe we could hang like the mature women we were. Maybe they wouldn't any longer see me as "the new girl" at Harriton who had much to learn about popularity contests, boys, and vodka, but instead as the cool, independent girl who'd scored an internship in New York *just like them*. Maybe we could all go out and have brunch and build a long-lasting friendship.

Of course, that never happened. While they seemed delighted to run into me and we even exchanged phone numbers in our flip phones, we never connected. Over the next eight weeks, we shared a few more elevator rides filled with fake pleasantries, but that was it. It's easy to ask now why I didn't just reach out. But I was still a teenager and easily intimidated. I didn't know yet how to initiate a hang out or if I should. I didn't trust that I wouldn't embarrass myself. Or maybe I was afraid I would still feel lonely in their company.

During the week, I commuted to 30 Rock to sit at my desk and quietly format Excel spreadsheets. I also grabbed lattes for the sales executives, who weren't that curious to get to know me. There was one other intern like me, but he wasn't friendly. Come to think of it, he wasn't there most days. He was the son of someone important at the company, so maybe he didn't feel the need to prove himself?

There were moments in the beginning of living in a city with over 8 million people when I felt strangely isolated. I could have let this fear convince me that New York wasn't right for me. But the more I experienced it, the more I saw it urging me to widen my eyes. After all, the New York connection I longed for was much bigger than just roommate to roommate or intern to intern. By the middle of that summer, my fear of loneliness was pleading with me: Soak in the city before you leave. This place is famous for bringing people together. Okay, sure, your roommate's a drag, but New York is by and large a non-judgy melting pot, Farnoosh. It's why you were drawn to this city in the first place, remember? **If you're willing to lock arms with your loneliness and get lost here, then you will eventually find your way.**

Trusting that my fear of loneliness had more to show me, more for me to experience, was transforming. I stopped pitying myself. I saw this fear as an unmet craving to explore, discover, and find myself in the city. Alone, I took long walks after work and learned my way around Manhattan better than most cabdrivers. I visited museums along the East Side and trekked north to Columbia's campus to explore its graduate programs. In Central Park, I observed families playing with their young children. I smiled at the elderly Upper West Side couple pushing a grocery cart back to their apartment. I did this all alone . . . and gladly.

Surrounded by the raw and bountiful energy in New York, the time by myself led me to discover what I didn't want to do (work in sales or finance) and what I did (be a journalist who could afford tastier takeout). I became convinced I could not only start out here after college—but build a successful life here for many more years. The city beyond the walls of my dorm and office had a lot to teach me about what was possible, as long as I was willing to see my fear of loneliness as a companion. **It's fine to fear loneliness, but it's not okay to sit in your dorm and take insults from a mean girl who's going to make you feel bad for eating.** Get outside. Draw inspiration and connection from the world around you.

And these epiphanies can be the real, long-lasting derivatives of your fear of loneliness. They are treasures that will turn into launching pads for the career, life, and legacy you will someday soon build. I may not have left the city with a collection of new friends, but I did leave with a better understanding of the directionality of my life, and meaningful professional relationships that would offer me a leg up in my career. It underscored my priorities and where I saw myself thriving. I returned to New York the next two summers. And eighteen more years after that.

As it did for me that fateful season in New York, the fear of loneliness can arrive uninvited and can catch us by surprise, just as we're about to relax at our table for one. It can sneak up on us when our job relocates us to a new city. It's a creep, and we're not sure how to immediately handle it. We're at first excited by the idea of venturing to somewhere new, but then the possibility of having to start over in a foreign place keeps us up at night. We may even let this fear derail the trajectory of our lives. It can sabotage important moves forward. We may email our boss to say we've made a mistake and stay in a position that we have outgrown, just because it's familiar.

Remember this when the fear of loneliness takes you by surprise: there's beauty in examining this fear and seeing what it may be telling you about possibly forging something new or moving on from where you are. Life isn't meant to be lived in stasis. Connect with what the larger ambition is. If you have a goal you are trying to reach, the loneliness won't last. It's conditional. **Strength arrives during some of the worst bouts of loneliness when you are trying to move the needle on your life.** That strength will outlast the fear.

Loneliness is a challenge, a dare, an opportunity to show off your risk-taking abilities and find sweet comfort in the discomfort.

Use the fear to redirect your focus to what matters. You may not know anyone in this new place, or the people you meet may not yield friendships no matter how much you want them to, but the leap has the potential for faster growth in your career. It may mean a warmer climate or access to more nature. It may be the chance at a fresh start or a bridge to a future you can't see yet but have always imagined. And maybe, in the midst of all that, a friend will arrive. But if they don't, you know why you came and what you were meant to get from this moment in time.

SITUATIONAL LONELINESS: USING YOUR FEAR TO SET YOU IN MOTION

My summer months in New York taught me that the fear of loneliness doesn't exclusively mean being in the absence of others. You can be in a marriage, on a team, sitting in a crowded cafe with your baby asleep in her stroller, and all the while feel like you are on your own, with no shoulder to cry on or friend to share a laugh with. The feeling shows up when we find ourselves being an *only* or *other* at work, school, or on the playground.

Loneliness expert John Cacioppo, the late director of the University of Chicago's Center for Cognitive and Social Neuroscience, said this can be one of the riskiest types of loneliness, the one to really fear. "If you're in a crowd and that crowd is perceived to be antagonistic, then that's more dangerous than being alone," he said.[14] In other words, in the company of people who seem to lack empathy, who are unkind or untrustworthy, is one of the scariest places to hang out. This fear is one to befriend. It may be the only thing you have during that tough time of feeling alienated, and it may be telling you to take stock, find fruitful connections, and figure out where your resources are and how to use them to build community.

Perhaps the people who are most successful at doing this are those who haven't been included in the overarching culture's narrative of who belongs and who doesn't. Sometimes the crowd around us is so foreign, we don't know if they are antagonistic or friendly, or who we can trust. When my mom got married to my father, she was promised a whole new world, but when she got stateside, it was anything but *this land is your land, this land is my land.*

She was nineteen, didn't speak the language, couldn't drive, and had no network. Her story may not be unique in a room full of immigrants, but living in an apartment in Worcester with me, her little human appendage, while my father spent his days at the university, all she felt was lonely. She was not only new to the country but also to marriage and motherhood. And I didn't exactly cure her loneliness either. For my mom, some of her loneliness may have stemmed from not really wanting to be a mother, at least not so soon. I mean, she didn't even want me to call her "mom" in those early days, preferring me to use her first name, Sheida, followed by Joon, a common term of affection in Farsi. So, for many years, she was not my mom, she was my Sheida Joon.

Our home in the early 1980s was a two-bedroom apartment located in an affordable housing community called Washington Heights. What we lacked in space, we made up for in coziness and the constant scent of fresh basmati rice, herbs, and saffron warming over the stove. I had my own bedroom, from which I could see the community pool directly outside my window. We, of course, never swam in it.

By the time I was three or four years old, my mother had earned her driver's license. On commutes to the Worcester Center Mall, a friend's house, or the grocery store, I heard stories inspired by her pilgrimage to the United States, a journey filled with equal parts hope and resentment. Just as she was about to turn seventeen, her parents sat her down and explained that she needed to get married. And quick.

College was not an option, nor was living with them indefinitely. My mom was the last remaining child in their house, and rather than encourage her to take the necessary time to create a plan and design her own way, as they had with her siblings, my grandparents introduced her to my dad to arrange a union. Maybe they treated her differently because, as the baby of the family, they underestimated her potential? Maybe they were just growing older and tired from dealing with her higher-maintenance siblings? These were also very unsettling times in Iran with rumblings of a revolution underway. I have no doubt that the fear of an uncertain future prompted their sense of urgency. And so the decision was clear: the first viable suitor who checked enough boxes would earn her hand in marriage. My dad came from a well-to-do family in Shiraz. He was educated and already friends with my mom's brother-in-law. So that was that. A year later Mom was on a plane to the United States with her new husband, and an overstuffed Samsonite handed down from her sister.

Mom missed the "normal" life back home. She missed the days of worrying about very little except preparing for an exam and making herself some lunch. She missed focusing on her own passions. Her life in America left her afraid, distrustful of the world around her. And while I didn't always understand her anger and controlling nature, or the depths of her sadness, looking back, I see that beneath it all she was scared of being alone.

Sometimes when you are lonely, you can try to change your story, but my mom's loneliness was not a state of mind. You can move to a place with more community, but my mom didn't have the freedom to come and go as she wanted. At first she couldn't drive. She didn't have the means to call a cab whenever she was bored and wanted to go somewhere new (which was often). She couldn't just walk out of the apartment and try to meet people; they wouldn't have understood her. She was facing too many barriers to connection, including mobility, language, and the lack of a shared cultural foundation. And it wouldn't be until much later that she and my father engaged with local Iranians. So what should she have done?

This is a big question that we need to be able to answer because loneliness doesn't play around. In the absence of being able to create human connections, we need to reach for something else safe that makes us feel alive, even happy. My mom's way of creating solace in her solitude was connecting back to who she was through dancing. Dance was an activity that she'd brought with her from her past life in Iran, and it gave her a way to tap into her culture. Weekend mornings, while my dad was still asleep, she'd softly turn on the cassette player in our living room downstairs, close her eyes, and begin moving to and through the sounds of Iranian singers Hayedeh and Moein, on classic tracks she had brought over from her childhood bedroom in Shiraz. She did this alone, freely expressing herself without judgment. As a kid, I studied her from a distance. I often felt a bit "in the way," a wedge that stood in between my mom and her freedoms. I got the feeling that she didn't want me around all the time, something I can relate to now, as a parent who hides often in the basement bathroom. Even I occasionally need a break from my children, two humans I willed into the world.

Persian dance is a delicate art form, a series of small, carefully crafted moves, engaging your entire body: toes, hips, shoulders, wrists, and even the eyebrows. Back then, I perched on the stairs, peeking below the handrail and watching my mom be the most relaxed she'd be all week. I knew not to interrupt. She performed without ever asking for permission. It was something nobody could take away from her; it was hers to keep and share as she chose. And she loved it. Her passion for movement empowered her. It brought her joy, and for a little under thirty minutes every Sunday morning, it made her feel less lonely.

When you anticipate loneliness, when you feel the fear moving in, ask yourself what it is you need to connect with. **What are you missing? What can help ease that fear for a stolen moment?** For my mother, letting music take her back to when life felt more familiar was a way of connection to a self that felt free, and part of something bigger. Poet Laureate Maya Angelou coped with loneliness through music. She wrote, "Music was my refuge. I could crawl into the space between the notes and curl my back to loneliness."[15]

When you are in a place where you cannot find a waiting community, let the fear of loneliness set you in motion. **Discovering the move that can untangle you from loneliness may mean replaying a time when you felt at ease or at your freest.** Were you a child? Was it last year? There's no expiration date for bringing back that feeling. What's an activity that can take your mind off the present? A pivot that can take you to your happy place, even while the world around you is standing still?

LONELINESS IN A CROWD: WHEN TWO *TARSOOS* ARE BETTER THAN ONE

As I sat buckled and strapped in the back of my mom's car on those trips to the mall, I became schooled in many of her fears. She loaded me up on life's scary truisms. I learned that people aren't always who they seem, that some strangers love to prey on little girls, and that I should not trust anyone but my parents. This was her way of keeping me out of harm's way. "Making you afraid of things . . . that's all I knew how to protect you," she told me on my podcast decades later.[16] "I was growing up, myself."

And thus, my fear of being left alone—or left behind—was cast on me by my mother's own trepidations and insecurities, alone in a country she did not yet understand and had no agency in. Her thoughts became focused on her fears about raising a child—a girl, especially—in this foreign place that nobody could pronounce (why wasn't it WAR-cess-ter? we often wondered). The fearful tales about strangers and kidnappers she fed me were borrowed from rare, outlier stories seen on the local news that she had internalized during her hours alone.

For others the fear of loneliness results in low self-esteem. We fear abandonment, or a lack of support; we miss someone we once loved and fear there will never be another. Loneliness comes in all forms, and it feasts on silence. When we are in stillness, the mind can travel back to those darker times when we were by ourselves, unguarded and vulnerable. It can trigger feelings that we try hard to bury. I once asked my friend Lynn, a successful television producer, one of the youngest to land a senior role at a major network in New York, what she was most afraid of. "To be alone with my thoughts," she said. All these years, I had assumed she enjoyed staying out late because she had lots of energy. But left by herself with no distractions, she was afraid her mind would venture back to memories of growing up in an unstable home. The negative thoughts that loneliness brings often arrive when the party is winding down and we must return to our empty homes.

But fearing loneliness can be a landscape of possibility. It leads you to search for support and friendship in the most unlikely of places. It can open your mind (and heart) to people who may not at first seem like people who are *your* people. But, they so are.

On a campus with over fifty thousand students, it was easy to feel alone at Penn State, even when I was never *really* alone. The culture then centered around football (it still does), and I know this might shock you, but I wasn't a fan. As I lost a sense of connection to the school, my fear of loneliness started to make me question whether I'd made the right choice to come in the first place. I'd dared to arrive on campus that freshmen year without season tickets to the home games, unlike nearly all the girls on my dormitory floor. On fall Saturdays, while my roommate and her new best friends packed into Beaver Stadium in head-to-toe blue-and-white to cheer their beloved Nittany

Lions, I, alone, headed in the opposite direction. Fearing loneliness—as well as rejection—I could have easily bought some tickets from a scalper and stuck a removal paw tattoo on my cheek and pretended I was a die-hard fan. And, admittedly, for the first home game of the season, I did just that. But leaning into the fear initially made me feel like a phony. I didn't understand the game or the feverish fandom that overtook spectators. I cry watching the film *Rudy*, but not a real-life touchdown.

But you know what? Eventually game days became my favorite because for the first time all week, with so many students and staff up at the stadium, the campus would be quiet and still. I could choose any seat at the local coffee shop, even the coveted one closest to the wall outlets. I could stroll down College Avenue with the entire sidewalk to myself. The fear of loneliness was still within me, but I coaxed it by immersing myself in what felt familiar: caffeinated drinks, window shopping, and looking after myself. That may sound boring to some, but these became some of my most cherished hours in college.

My fear still wanted me to make real connections with others at school, but it wanted to first ensure I was secure in my loneliness. It didn't want me to force it. Because that can happen all too often, right? To cure the emptiness we may feel inside we risk building false bonds. We rush a sorority because everyone tells us it's an immediate way to make friends. It's fun until the recruiters threaten to deny us because of our "presentation," which is a technical term for how you look. And now suddenly your fear of loneliness is in a cocktail with the fear of rejection.

The fear of loneliness is giving you the gift of telling you to go way out of your way to make a *real* friend. It was only when I became secure in my loneliness, in this strange, new place, that I could strike up authentic relationships. Those game weekends alone, oddly enough, helped me to reach that point. I was ready to develop friendships in maybe even the unlikeliest of places, in lieu of wallowing in that loneliness. And that's how I met my best guy friend, Dustin.

Shortly into the fall semester, we met in the middle aisle of Chemistry 101. I was one of the last to arrive one day and had a tough time finding an empty seat. Think: flashbacks of being the new girl on the bus or holding my tray of food before a noisy high school cafeteria, figuring out where to sit. In those instances, it just takes one person to change the trajectory of your day, to say, "Hey, you can sit with me." That morning at Penn State this person was Dustin, as he waved and flashed his endearing smile in my direction. On the surface, we were an unlikely pair of buddies. My aggressive, type-A-ness wouldn't have guessed finding such a calm friend in the chill, soft-spoken Dustin. I was a finance major while he was pursuing film. I came from a nuclear family that had moved its way up to a wealthy suburb, while Dustin had been raised by a single mom in rural Pennsylvania. Furthermore, he was an ice skating pro, while I'd never been at the mercy of a toe pick. On purpose.

And, my friends, he was a diehard Penn State football fan.

But we became fast friends because we saw how each one of us, despite sheltering the fear of loneliness inside, was trying to make the best of things. I began to admire Dustin for his ability to see so much good in people. He was quick to trust strangers, something I still can't easily do. The world can be kinder than we think it is, he constantly reminded me. Dustin was the first to say thank you, and even if things weren't his fault, he never hesitated to apologize. He was braver than he knew. And while he was laid back and giggly, there was also a real depth to Dustin. He had big dreams and a bold vision for life that included writing screenplays and winning Oscars.

I knew he was afraid, too. Growing up in an ultraconservative part of Pennsylvania, my creative friend did not always feel understood or safe. What he often felt was loneliness. He experienced bullying at school and at home, and even some death threats. He was constantly on alert, always scanning to make sure he wasn't a target. In the high school cafeteria, he told me, he usually ate lunch by himself. "I spent a lot of time in fantasy. I spent a lot of time alone, a lot of time in my bedroom," he would say. To distract himself, he became hyper-focused on schoolwork. His way out was through achievement.

One summer we lived together in a house with a few other room-mates in downtown State College. After a full day of work, classes, and bouncing around campus, we played tennis on the school courts and went for nightly runs. We spent evenings after dinner listening to Radiohead and having drawn-out conversations about big life things (religion and love, mostly) and our super-sized goals. We would assign each other the impossible:

Dustin, you are going to run a studio!

Farnoosh, you won't need a last name when you're older. You'll just be Farnoosh with an exclamation point at the end!

We had dreams of what we were going to accomplish, and we didn't hesitate to reveal them.

I noticed that many nights, after the rest of us had turned in for the night, Dustin would take long walks by himself. While I worried about his safety (because God knows I wouldn't be walking by myself at 1 a.m. *anywhere*, especially not in a place ironically named Happy Valley), for Dustin these lonely laps were essential. They were his med-itation, his way of clearing his mind, building emotional strength, and readying to show up fully as himself in a world that wasn't always so hospitable.

Then later that summer, as he and I waited for our dinners to arrive at the Ye Old College Diner downtown, he told me he had a secret to share. For the first time to another person, he said out loud, "I'm gay." I told him that I was honored to be his friend and happy that he felt comfortable telling me his truth. That night we ate every bite of our burgers and split a brownie sundae.

Years later, on my twenty-third birthday, Dustin wrote a long, handwritten letter to me, as he often did, always lovingly and in his perfect penmanship. By then he was out West pursuing his Hollywood dreams, taking writing classes, working at a studio, and waiting tables on weekends. I was on the East Coast crying in work bathroom stalls over humiliating fact-checking mistakes that had almost gotten me fired. (Keep turning the pages for that one!)

His beautiful card arrived in the mail, and in Dustin's signature fashion he didn't hold back. He described the bond we shared and what it had meant to him:

> *I think that we have gotten along so well these years because we are the only ones who could talk to each other about the future, and not with the least irony or doubt. And as much as I know how much you hate the touchy, feely stuff, I just must tell you, I love you, kid.*
>
> *Love,*
> *Dustin*

Loneliness may have brought Dustin and me together, but it's not what locked our bond. Our friendship was able to blossom because we had learned how to self-soothe in our loneliness. This fear, while an impetus for creating friendships, has the potential to run you straight into vacuous relationships just to assuage your fears. Be careful of that.

That we were *the only ones*, as Dustin wrote, is for sure. But we *got* each other because we knew ourselves.

John Cacioppo once said, "Loneliness . . . helps us think about other people's perspective and empathize and care and go beyond our personal interest."[17] Yes. Leveraging loneliness to build friendship doesn't have to mean crying in your soup together, it can mean mirroring each other's strengths and being the one who's there to listen and dream big for the other.

My friend, find yourself a Dustin. An individual who, like you, might also be struggling on the inside in their own way with a sense of aloneness, someone who understands what it means to be unsupported, isolated, unsafe, or misunderstood, but instead of dwelling on all those challenges, they choose to connect with themselves . . . and you. And lift you up. A fellow person of color at work, the only other woman in your department, a friend you sense may be struggling to come to terms with who he wants to be. They may be a text message away or seated next to you at the next family gathering or work dinner. You don't have to search far.

Look for that one *tarsoo* who can mirror back your strengths and remind you that there are bigger roads ahead about to open to you.

Loneliness might be a pandemic, but it is also a huge opportunity. Grab it.

The Fear of Loneliness Self-Inquiry

- What is this fear wanting you to do next?
- Do you have a chance at a community that you may not be taking?
- What is your personal narrative about your loneliness saying to you? Do you need to flip it?
- What are the big-picture goals you are trying to reach right now?
- If you can't find community, can you find peace in your own company? Learn how to contently be with yourself?

3

THE FEAR OF MISSING OUT (FOMO)

and how it begs for self-reflection and signals you to do you

M Y DEAR FRIEND KATE never judges me for my impulse to promptly leave situations I find unnerving. But, oh, how she tried to bring me out and about in college.

We met as neighbors in the fall of 1998 in McKean Hall and became instant friends. We shared an appreciation for Eddie Murphy's comedy, Ani DiFranco's music, and Philly's soft pretzels. I was especially drawn to her because, in addition to being a tall, gorgeous redhead resembling a young Susan Sarandon, Kate was quick to compliment you for things that you didn't even know were particularly worthy of praise. For example, she appreciated that I was an early onset careerist with no chill, and that I could often be found applying for internships under a desk lamp at 1 a.m. She saw me choose work over fun many times and found my pragmatism endearing . . . maybe even a little inspiring. She made sure to mention this when giving the maid of honor toast at Tim's and my wedding reception dinner in the summer of 2012. "Whenever I'm at a crossroads in life," said Kate, "I think, 'WWFD': What would Farnoosh do?"

One fall evening, during our first couple months on campus, she convinced me to join her at a fraternity party, an activity that even the most introverted students took part in in those early, bleary-eyed days of freshman year. For many students, this would be a typical social outing. In a single evening, there would be fifty or so such fêtes starting at 8 p.m., within a ten-block radius. But to me, these debaucheries symbolized then (and now) much of what is wrong with the world. You're telling me it will be okay if we go to a random, dark mansion off-campus to hang out in a dank, sticky-floored room, outnumbered by fraternity brothers who've been drinking since 11 a.m.? Is that R. Kelly playing in the background? *I know how this will end.*

Kate, a more optimistic and forgiving human than I am, was eager to meet charming young men that evening. I was not as hopeful of making such connections, but I tagged along anyway because I genuinely didn't want to let her down. Plus, I was curious to see what all the hype was about. I didn't tell Kate, but secretly, I worried that if I didn't go, I might miss something special. I wanted to believe that I could enjoy myself. Maybe make a new friend.

Alas, upon entering the frat, we were accosted by the stench of Natty Light beer soaked throughout the estate's creaky oak floors. Beyond the front doors, freshman girls wearing an array of pink and red tube tops stood alongside nervous young men in popped-collar polos.

In the central room, the brothers of the house had decorated the otherwise empty space with countless ice buckets filled with beer. "It's a case race," said one wearing a blue belt with pink whales on it. Kate served as my translator for a language that, too busy being responsible in high school, I'd failed to learn. This, she whispered to me, would be a timed race to see which "couple" could be the first to finish a full case—or twenty-four bottles—of booze.

Kate could sense I was uncomfortable and eager to leave, both because she was a close confidante and because of the fact that I'm cursed with an exceedingly expressive face. Without question, she and another friend walked me outside and to the corner bus stop that would safely take me back to the dorms. They apologized for my sub-par evening. But I was fine, I told them. Trust me. I was heading back to my happy place, eager to throw on some pajamas.

THE DNA OF FOMO

Like many fears, FOMO is something we can catch from the world around us—a sting from family, friends, and Facebook. Like a bad cold, FOMO can leave us down for the count. It can leave us with a false sense of urgency or concern. It's like that time I fell upon a carousel of photos on social media taken from a friend's baby cel-ebration held at their home. All their loved ones and friends were there . . . except me. Tears started to well as I scrolled past photos of guest after guest holding the babies, looking at the babies, kissing the babies. I'd known this friend and his partner for almost a decade, surely long enough to have been included in this momentous event. Right? We'd been to each other's homes, shared many meals, and gone on trips together. I began to make up stories in my head about why I'd not been invited. *Maybe they didn't want me in their lives any longer. Maybe I had it all wrong about our friendship. Was it something I'd said? Had I offended them?*

My FOMO drove up real fast with the fear of rejection sitting shot-gun. At first, I cowered. Rather than reach out and say something, I just clicked "like" on all the photos. It was my way of passively saying, *I still love you. Will you forgive me?* For what, I wasn't sure.

A few weeks later I was in this friend's office building for a meeting and passed by his desk. We hugged as usual. Then he said, "We missed you at our baby shower!"

Wait. What? "But I didn't get an invitation!" I said.

"Oh, we definitely mailed it," he replied. "Did you not get it?"

Of course, I hadn't gotten it. I had recently moved to a newly constructed building and the post office didn't always recognize the address, which caused mail to sometimes be returned to the sender. Here, my friend had thought I'd bailed on an important occasion in his family's life, while I'd thought he'd left me out intentionally.

And in the frenzy of being new parents, they hadn't followed up with me to see if I was coming or not. They just assumed it would be a yes. "We were wondering why you didn't show up! We were like, 'Where's Auntie Farnoosh?'" Their invitation bounced back to their mailbox weeks later.

And that's the thing about FOMO sometimes. It's a joke. You were meant to experience it, to be there, but life got in the way. The wires got crossed. It wasn't intentional. The mail courier screwed up.

Despite that baby shower brouhaha, when it comes to my social life, I now rarely experience FOMO, the nagging "fear of missing out" on experiences that could, according to others, improve my well-being or offer a leg up in life. What I mostly fear is being pushed into things I don't want to do. In college, that meant participating in Greek-life functions. Now it's succumbing to Botox injections, buying NFTs, and performing karaoke. **My unrelenting fear of going against my own desires and values is usually bigger than my fear of missing out on what others deem "cool." And it grounds me.**

But the truth is, FOMO is a complex and deep-rooted fear. According to a Baylor University study, about three out of four young adults say they've struggled with it.[1] We know this fear as the uneasy, threatening, and sometimes all-consuming feeling that you're not doing what's expected of you or what society, friends, and family deem righteous.

Others appear to be experiencing something wildly life-changing while you're home, cleaning grease off your stove. FOMO hits where it hurts: our sense of self-worth and accomplishment. It makes us wonder if we're actually living life to the fullest . . . like everyone else apparently is.

"It's in our DNA to compare ourselves with others," said Patrick McGinnis, who coined the acronym in 2004 as a student at Harvard Business School. "We now live in a complex world where we're overwhelmed with choice and information. We're constantly bombarded with opportunities to compare ourselves with what other people are doing and evaluate how we're doing in comparison," he shared on *So Money*.[2] "But . . . we're idealizing things and that's where the FOMO happens. **We create a narrative in our head that something is way better than it is in reality.**"

FOMO tends to flare up when we witness or hear about others doing things that we find intriguing but mistake our fascination for *I want that thing—and now!* We can experience a perceived scarcity, which can create pressure to live up to a false sense of what success means to you, says Chantel Chapman, cofounder of the Trauma of Money, a program that certifies professionals in trauma-aware and trauma-informed financial strategies. Her advice applies to FOMO of any stripe. "What happens is you tunnel on that scarcity thought and you inhibit your ability to basically play out your long-term goals because of the perfectionist and shame narratives," she said on my podcast.[3] A remedy for this, she says, is to focus on the feeling you want to inhabit, rather than the thing you want to have that seems so popular. We want to be happy, to be immersed in something cool, to be investing in ourselves *just like them*. And how we pursue that feeling ought to be different because, put simply, no two people are identical.

FOMO isn't a modern-day phenomenon. It traces back to the Stone Age, when going astray might have meant getting devoured by a Eurasian cave lion. Julie Coultas, a researcher on conformity, explains, "A conformist tendency would facilitate acceptance into the group and would probably lead to survival if it involved the decision, for instance, to choose between a nutritious or poisonous food, based on copying the behavior of the majority."[4]

Even though I seemingly beat FOMO that night at the frat party, FOMO and I go way back. On February 15, 1980, my nineteen-year-old mother delivered me at UMass Memorial Medical Center after several hours of unmedicated labor and gallons of blood lost. "I almost *died*," Mom has reminded me on at least a few occasions.

I'm not sure if it was my near-tragic and untimely arrival into the world ("Who vants a baby at nineteen?" is also something that my mother has said out loud) or the fact that Worcester's crime scene of murder, rape, robbery, and assault was worsening by the day, but soon after my parents' flight from Iran landed on American soil, a move that itself was a huge leap of faith, they proceeded to stop taking chances. Instead, they took risks that were calculated and safe. My dad would attend the local Clark University on scholarship and achieve a PhD in physics. My mother would first learn basic English by watching *Sesame Street* seated next to me. Soon after, she'd attend the local college part-time, and later, while working and raising us, she'd complete a bachelor's degree.

While we Torabis are movers and shakers in our own right, we did not run toward life like our free-spirited, more privileged American neighbors. We spent our days running from death. **Missing out? That's how we self-preserved.** Growing up, I missed out on so many things, all by design. Each time I attempted to engage in Western culture and needed permission, FOMO showed up. Whether it was my request to attend a sleepover, watch *Punky Brewster*, or go see a PG-13 movie with friends, I was met with a strong and surefire "*Aslan!*"

On early-release days in the sixth grade, it was common practice for my twelve-year-old classmates to walk together to Dean Park Pizza for lunch. But my mother, concerned that walking the 0.4 miles un-chaperoned would lead to my swift abduction and entry into a sex trafficking ring, denied me this outing. *"Aslan!"* Each time, my Persian parents came to my rescue to teach me about all the things in life I *ought* to miss out on.

Like many Iranian immigrants coming of age during the Islamic Revolution, my parents were determined to swap out tyranny for the American Dream. My mom and dad never let me forget how lucky we were, especially me, someone who was born in the States with green card–carrying parents. To receive an unrestricted education, ride bikes with the boys, and wear tank tops without consequence—without ever knowing anything different—was beyond privilege. To be able to hang a poster of New Kids on the Block over my bed was a divine order. Those ear-pierced boys never would have made it through clearance at the Shiraz Airport. And so, the unequivocal mantra in our family became: *Sit still. Don't tempt fate.*

When I was a new kid at the start of middle school, making friends continued to be difficult, as I spent most of my free time in close proximity to my parents. The FOMO I felt had everything to do with wanting to feel involved in the external culture. I was afraid that I'd never feel like I was a part of something cool.

Was it temporarily crushing to have to tell my friends that I couldn't tag along? Certainly. But as my mother likes to point out, *it all worked out, didn't it?*

As much as it pains me to admit this, my mom wasn't wrong.

Because the funny thing about FOMO is, if you can learn not to give in to it and follow the herd, this fear can lead you inward, to tap what is already inside and leverage it in a purpose-driven way.

When I couldn't join the other kids, it gave me the opportunity to ask what it was that I *could* naturally do and be good at. Back in my parents' house, the answer was to double down on my studies and extracurricular activities. I worked harder, turned in assignments earlier, and fed my sense of self-worth through what I loved to do—get those A's. I joined the theater club, where even if you didn't get assigned an actual role, you'd at least get added to the chorus. Eventually, focusing more on what came naturally, what was within my control, and what made me unique, I began to feel like I'd finally found a way to connect to something bigger that was simultaneously meaningful— the point at which any FOMO you have felt sits back and says, *My job here is done.*

In the absence of doing all the things *the other kids were doing*, while I always feared missing some life-enhancing experience, not giving into FOMO led me to a fierce sense of individuality. What other choice did I have? Sitting with my FOMO, I discovered that the "enoughness" I was seeking, that sensation that comes with feeling as though I'm doing the "right" thing or the "best" thing . . . this was something I could only achieve from within. FOMO helped me see that missing out on other people's "fun" is not the worst thing to fear. Instead, be scared of missing out on something more special—a calling, a talent, that's within you.

Of course, if you're drawn to an experience and it just so happens others are into it, do it. But still do it *your way*. If FOMO arrives and all you feel is pressure to conform, fear becoming a follower and letting someone else take control of where you're going. That GPS isn't always trustworthy. One time, I set the destination to a HomeGoods on Long Island, and it led me to the edge of a lake. Even then, I wasn't convinced the store wasn't tucked somewhere in the surrounding woods. All my common sense had gone out the window in favor of this fraught navigation system.

We assume the person or ideology leading the way possesses some grand compass to a world where we will be met with joy, adrenaline, and discounted furniture. In reality, we may very well be giving up our control to a broken guide.

When you catch the FOMO bug—but something inside you says the thing in question is not really for you—it's more than okay to refuse, bail, or disengage. Respect yourself and grab the next bus out.

LET FOMO LEAD YOU TO THE *WHO* AND *WHY*

Sometimes FOMO is your own (misplaced) fear of missing out, like me at the baby shower earlier, but sometimes FOMO is someone *else's* fear of missing out entering your orbit. If that's the case, we need to stop and ask: *I'm sorry FOMO, who brought you here?*

Chelsea Fagan, a money expert and founder of the Financial Diet, or TFD, explained to me that she never had the urge to have kids. "Every year and with every person around me having children, there was such a strong feeling of like, 'I'm so happy for you. I love this for you. Absolutely not for me,'" she said.[5] She stopped by my podcast in 2021, in her thirties, happily married and running a thriving media company. She talked about the journey to becoming resolute and at peace with decisions that others around her didn't understand. Friends and family would impatiently probe. They would dangle the fear of missing out on children and having a more "settled" life. "I used to always kind of be on the back heel when it came to justifying. It wasn't just the motherhood stuff. It was working online for a long time before TFD seemed legitimate enough or choosing to stay in New York City, as opposed to getting a house. I used to feel like I really had to defend myself," she said.

When FOMO arrives or, in Chelsea's case, shows up uninvited from others in your world, the healthy next move is to examine the source. Who's serving up the FOMO? Why?

Questioning the *who* behind FOMO can lead to a critical reframing that takes the attention off of you and puts it back where it belongs. The influence of family and the outside world exists in many of our FOMO-related pickles. *So Money* audience members write in wondering whether they should buy a house, and I often learn that pressure comes from a parent's constant pushing. The parents are afraid their son or daughter will miss out on something they believe is the "right" way to build wealth, without factoring in that their grown child may have more student loan debt and a higher cost of living than they ever did. Still, the FOMO is relentless: *Don't you want to be financially se-cure?*

People who push FOMO are often struggling with unresolved mat-ters of their own. Part of their subconscious is wondering, *How can someone make a different choice from me . . . and still feel successful?*, and, maybe worse, *Could things have been different for me?* (We will talk about regret in another chapter.)

Chelsea and I discussed how many people, especially women, are taught that big life choices are binary. Good vs. bad. You get married (good). You stay single (bad). You buy a house (good). You rent (bad). You have kids (good). You stay childless (bad). You breastfeed (good). You use formula (bad). You become an entrepreneur (good). You work for corporate America (bad). Pressure to be "good" makes us defend the choices we make against the status quo. "It can't just be the right choice for them," Chelsea said. "It also has to be the correct one, the proper one." And Chelsea had a choice! Many people who don't follow the herd don't have the money to buy a house, or they have fertility is-sues, or they need the steady income and benefits corporate America provides.

Today, when facing FOMO-inducing questions over her decision to be child-free, Chelsea says she knows it has nothing to do with the validity of her choice, but more to do with the person who's puzzled by it. "I've had actual moments where the conversation is like, 'If you're having some feelings . . . I'm always here to listen to them, but I'm not going to justify my own life to you.'"

Michelle Obama is a pro at this. When friends have insisted that she pursue politics, she's gently pushed back. "That's not my story," I heard her share on an NPR interview in 2018.[6] "That's what people want, but what do I want for me?" she told the reporter. "Sometimes you can get swept up in other people's wants for you when I know in my heart that my skill set, and my desire and my passion, doesn't lie in that arena." She's right. (No matter how much I would like to see her run. Sigh.)

WHEN FOMO FEELS LINKED TO MONEY AND SURVIVAL

When so many online entrepreneurs started making massive dollars by selling digital courses, I questioned my own business model. Up until that point, my company had been mainly built on writing, speaking, hosting programs, and working with brand clients. And then these online entrepreneurs—some of them my friends—made the virtual course world seem so simple, so rewarding. If you weren't selling digital workshops or online courses, then you were leaving money on the table. Or that was my fearful inference. These friends boasted six- and seven-figure course launches that left me feeling behind and sort of embarrassed that I hadn't created a passive income stream. Was I missing out on an obvious financial opportunity? *And . . . if my friends can do it, why can't I?*

The better question I should have asked about my FOMO was: *Is there something else I'd rather do with my time to make money?*

But I didn't. I skipped the Q&A and attempted to create a goddamn course.

No surprise, I despised every minute of it. It was not easy. It was not a four-step process like all the courses on how to build courses had promised me. In the end, I spent many hours and dollars buying said courses about courses, buying website domains, hiring overpriced marketing "experts," and ultimately giving up.

The nail in the coffin came one afternoon at a meal with an entrepreneur friend who'd just sold over a thousand units of his virtual course. His online program was priced at $2,000 a pop, a sum of over

$2 million in revenue. I asked him to lunch to learn his secrets over sushi. But before our edamame had arrived, he turned to me and said quite frankly, "Don't do a course, Farnoosh. It's . . . exhausting."

My friend was very tired and stressed. While the headline read that he was a millionaire, the bottom line was that he had to burn through a ton of marketing and affiliate dollars and time to cross that seven-figure sales threshold. He confessed that the behind-the-scenes grind and gruel, which I'd experienced, was not because I was doing anything wrong. That's what it took to get to the finish line. With thousands of paying students, it was way too late for him to back out, but it wasn't too late for me.

Some people have truly found a way to turn a passion into an online business. For me, and many others caught in the trend, it's been painful. But they were too afraid to admit it publicly because . . . *What might that say about them? That they weren't cut out for it? They weren't talented enough? No pain no gain, right?* I thanked my friend for his honesty. This good man had just explained that my FOMO stemmed from a giant holographic portrayal of an untruth. I appreciated him so much in that moment that I let him have the last piece of my spicy tuna roll.

Don't get me wrong. Some make boatloads of money selling online programs and have teams in place that manage everything. But when FOMO came calling, my gut was telling me I was not going to thrive sitting behind a computer drafting aggressive emails that triggered scarcity in my readers' minds. Nor did I want to be responsible for a team of workers to get it done.

My fear of missing out on this "wildly" lucrative business strategy was simply the insistence from some very loud online voices saying their formulas were a slam dunk.

Isn't that suspicious? They were selling a course about how to build a course and trying to dangle a carrot wrapped with Benjamins. They had become cheerleaders for this business strategy to justify their own participation. Meanwhile many were secretly afraid of not being able to sell enough of their own courses to break even that year. They were caught in a vicious cycle.

Why does doing this thing that seems so popular, so cool, so on the money make me feel so terribly unhappy? I realized what had attracted me to this course idea was the concept of being more in control of my income. That was the part that really spoke to me and got me excited.

My business had been largely reactive up until that point. I would get a request to speak at an event, and I'd take it. I'd get a call that a brand was interested in working with me, and I would create a proposal. This felt like a vulnerable business strategy. What I was missing was not an online course but optimizing my time and revenue. I wanted to go straight to my audience and consumers and decide the pace, the schedule, the approach, all of it.

Once I had the happy ingredients that my initial FOMO encouraged me to gather, I designed a business idea that addressed those desires but was more up my alley.

The answer was a high-touch, in-person workshop for a limited number of guests, the antithesis of an online course that relies on having scale. I'd leverage my skills as a producer, director, teacher, and hostess and connect with highly motivated individuals over two days together. That intimacy, as it turns out, was what many people were craving.

With everyone and their grandmother starting an online program, we were all missing the IRL engagements. And when I did the math, my profit margins were better than building a course. My participants were willing to pay five times more than what they would online and I filled the event mostly through word of mouth—no need to spend thousands on Facebook ads. The workshop was the perfect Farnoosh move. Use FOMO to ditch the trendy script and do what you do best.

If you ever feel yourself not wanting what everyone else is doing—getting married, having kids, pursuing a "stable" career, opening an Airbnb, etc.—question the FOMO to unearth your actual intent. See what it's like to stop following society's GPS and ask yourself what you really want.

I've written about how the Financial Independence, Retire Early movement, or FIRE, has, in recent years, become an idolized goal for many.[7] But the pursuit of saving a million dollars or more by your forties and "retiring" from your full-time job can require intense frugality or major sacrifices. It's not for everyone. Even when you've "arrived" at FIRE, things can backfire.

I've spoken to FIRE followers who've needed to return to a nine-to-five, as their financial and health insurance demands grew and made it ultimately impossible to solely live off their investments. They felt defeated, embarrassed, and a little misguided by their fear of missing out on this popular financial trend.

A good question to ask when FOMO intersects with your finances is this: What is it about this FOMO that's calling my name? It may be that sense of accomplishment you're after. That's fine, but be gentler to yourself. Stress less about lofty, financial goals that push for perfection over progress. Instead, appreciate your shorter-term wins, like saving for a rainy-day reserve or making an extra principal payment toward your student loans. If it's the praise and recognition that comes with being a part of the FIRE community or other trend you don't want to miss, then form your own squad of supporters, friends, and family who will definitely cheer you on to the finish line.

Bottom line: Engage this fear in some healthy interrogation. Find a more personally aligned alternative. What activity, ritual, or way of living is more rewarding and meaningful to you?

It's like that quote that popped up in my Instagram feed the other day because the algo knows me so well: "You're not missing out on anything when you're getting your shit together."

BIG FOMOS WON'T GO AWAY? CREATE SPACE

In the same way that we have to flip the loneliness narrative to move ahead, we can flip the FOMO narrative to see that what we believe we've been missing has been there all along.

Catherine, a twentysomething living in New York City, wanted my advice on how to transition out of her corporate job and pursue her passion for acting full-time. Each day she felt as though she was missing out on the chance to properly build a theatrical career. Being busy with her day job meant skipping important auditions and chances to connect with fellow performers. But without it, she'd lose a steady paycheck and health insurance. Her fear of missing out on a more creative life was competing with her fear of becoming financially insecure. What were her FOMOs telling her?

"Why not do both?" I suggested. "Keep your job *and* work on your performing career."

She told me that many auditions happened during business hours, and it would be difficult to attend tryouts with a full-time job.

Were there other ways to make inroads as a performer besides midday try-outs? I wanted to know. New York City seemed like a performing arts mecca. Could she network online and during her off-hours? Could she carve out time to produce her own shows? Could she follow both paths, at least until she had enough in savings to pivot entirely to acting?

As it turned out, the answer was yes. One year later, Catherine wrote to me with this update:

I've done a lot of auditioning and building relationships with casting directors. This past spring, I acted in a short film and will be producing my own later this year.

On the corporate front, I was promoted to Associate Director with a small raise in November 2021. Just this week, I negotiated *another promotion with a $42,000 increase. Thank you again for the excellent advice. I've been able to continue moving forward in both careers and look forward to the day my acting career kicks my corporate career to the curb.*

Catherine's FOMO had been keeping her stuck, telling her she couldn't have her dream because she had a day job. But her job wasn't a roadblock, it was a bridge. She flipped the story. Her paycheck allowed her to stay in NYC, the performance hub of the world. And being valued at work and trusting her role there was relatively secure gave her the confidence to move forward into acting and producing more intensely.

"There's this whole mentality of 'either you make it big at twenty-five or you struggle and have a million part-time jobs' that is fed to young actors and artists," she told me. "It makes a lot of people give up the arts entirely to get a full-time job . . . or be miserable just scraping by during those prime savings years."

Sometimes we assume that pursuing the big FOMOs in life—fear of missing out on a career path because it isn't "safe" or predictable, never having kids because you have yet to meet the right partner, not moving to a new place because it would mean leaving everything that's familiar to you—requires a cost or trade-off that's too much to bear. But FOMO isn't always asking for that.

When FOMO comes calling, persist. Poke holes in the conventional wisdom that's holding you back or giving you absolutes and either/ors. You don't have to be all in with one solo pursuit in order to be successful. You don't have to save *or* pay off debt. It may be more challenging, but you could find a way to address both at the same time.

We fall into this trap because binaries are everywhere. As a kid, I hated when someone asked me what I wanted to be when I grew up. I felt like it required a single, absolute answer. No one I knew had started side hustles, let alone multiple businesses. Few women in my town were even paycheck-earning mothers, pursuing a career outside of the home and raising a family at the same time. I imagined life as a single-track road. It's anything but. Today, I'm sure to ask my kids, "What are *all the things* you want to be?" My daughter Colette's list stretches from being a vet to a math teacher, and I couldn't love it more.

There's no pamphlet for how to live your best life; we stitch it together on our own. I majored in finance because I didn't want to miss out on job security. But I also cherished the idea of working in the media because it spoke more to my inquisitive personality. **You can combine unlikely ideas as long as you don't let FOMO talk you into limitations.**

Give this fear some space in your life. Don't assume you have to follow an ultimatum. It's here to inspire you to create an out-of-the-box strategy or a killer combo. Sometimes the right answer to your FOMO is *both/and*.

WHEN FOMO ENCOURAGES BOUNDARIES

In the summer of 2014, when our firstborn, Evan, was about to arrive, my mother didn't want to miss out on being present for this momentous occasion. A couple of weeks before my due date, she flew in and waited patiently until go time.

Finally, on June 21, we woke her up a little after midnight to let her know my water had broken. We needed to get in the car—fast. Mom had her bag ready by the door next to mine, packed to the rim with *ajil*—Persian trail mix—and, of course, a prayer book.

It took courage for my mom to join us in the delivery room, given that she had such a hell of a time bringing both me and my brother into the world and the trauma remained vivid. To this day, she has a hard time watching birth scenes in movies. Still, she didn't want to miss out on being by my side. To reconcile, she assigned herself to a hidden spot in my hospital room. Behind drawn curtains, she sat in a padded chair, listening to me shout during intense contractions on the other side of the partition. It was her way of being there, but only so far as she could handle. Behind the drapes, she would sit, listen, and crack open pistachios.

Occasionally she'd join me and Tim to see if we needed anything from the commissary. Or maybe some dark chocolate protein bars from her backpack? My poor mom, so shaken by the day that at one point, she mistakenly pressed the button to increase my epidural dosage. What I had asked, instead, was if she could help elevate my bed. *The other button.*

I am my mother's daughter. Like her, I have also learned how to healthily lean into certain FOMOs by creating *boundaries*. Despite making all efforts, I am not a beach person. And those who say they are, obviously haven't experienced the ripping waves of the Atlantic Ocean while looking after small, carefree children. I can swim, but I don't enjoy the constant terror that a crashing wave will wash us away. That, and sharks.

The walk from the car to the beach, pulling your wagon full of chairs, umbrellas, the cooler, and sand toys is the equivalent of a fifty-minute HIIT workout. It's ninety-one degrees. Your sweat has melted the sunscreen off your face before you even toe the water. The only entertainment is the occasional single-engine plane dragging a Geico insurance banner. You take solace in the little patch of shade you created for your family, as you watch your four-year-old pour sand into her bikini bottom. You can't help but think, *I chose this. The beach was just sitting here and I, somehow, chose to engage.*

And so, during a recent summer vacation, my forty-something-self mustered up the confidence to elegantly say, "Je refuse." Instead, I swam in the comfort of a shallow, heated community pool while the rest of my family ventured to the edge of the Delaware coastline. I didn't say no to the *entire* trip. I just said no to this one aspect of the trip that had a clear, easy alternative. I drew a line.

It was no surprise to Tim when I finally stood my ground on this, but for me it was a triumph to tell him and my in-laws (with whom we were vacationing) that I was going to hang back while they all went to the beach. Would they think I was too precious? Too high-maintenance? Not adventurous? A coward? Of course, they never thought those things of me, but I imagined them in my head. I'm not always as confident as I like to think I am when working through my FOMO.

In my attempts to make peace with this fear, I've learned the importance of protecting my energy. It has encouraged the use of the full and complete sentence: *No.* I enjoy declining at least a few events, asks, and goings-on per month. It's part of my self-care routine. The beauty is that saying no requires zero qualifying. I will say, however, that turning down invitations gets easier with age and practice.

Now, I can't tell you if missing out on marriage will work out, or if having a kid will be the best decision of your life. I don't have absolute answers to life's FOMOs. But with my more than four decades of life experience, I know with certainty that no matter what FOMO tells you, you should avoid these precise things:

- Starting a business with people you barely know, even if the idea sounds really great. *Definitely don't mix your finances with them, either.*
- Going on an elimination diet because the hottest fitness influencer swears by it, and you might drop pounds quickly. *You might, but they'll return even faster.*
- Waking up at 5 a.m. because all the productivity experts say it leads to happiness. *Really, they're just stressed and can't sleep.*
- Agreeing to speak for free at a major company because they promise "exposure." *Last I checked, exposure doesn't pay my mortgage.*

I imagine what some might say to this: *If you want to grow, you need to test yourself and get "uncomfortable" from time to time, Farnoosh. Challenge your boundaries!*

Trust me, I do plenty of that when I attempt to make a reel on Instagram lip-syncing to J.Lo. But I'm here to tell you: don't underestimate the joy of resting in your locked house wearing sweats on a Saturday night. As Wharton professor and popular-science author Adam Grant once said, "It takes integrity to put your personal values above social approval."[8] And I would add that it takes guts *not* to compare your life's journey to someone else's. It's fine to observe. It's fine to care . . . *but not that much.*

The FOMO Self-Inquiry

- What's the source of your FOMO? Who is telling you that you are missing out?
- What are you really afraid of missing out on?
- How can you experience the feeling you're after without following the herd?
- Is the FOMO even real?
- What is FOMO telling you about your desire to belong to something that feels bigger than you?
- Is there something you can almost effortlessly be a part of because it is what you love to do and speaks to your core interest?
- What can you actively join that is entirely your choice?

4

THE FEAR OF EXPOSURE

and how it heightens awareness
and draws comedy and
connection

"MOM, WHAT IF I'M *not* good today? How will you know unless I tell you?"

As we headed up to his bus stop, my then six-year-old son and I had been discussing that if he was "good"—meaning kind and polite—we'd take a special trip to Target after school to spend the tooth fairy money he'd saved to buy a Bakugan, a toy that kids his age were obsessed with collecting. We'd high-fived on the deal at breakfast, and now he was turning to me with this cute question.

Here I was worried that a midweek shopping trip would spoil him, and instead, it had led to a crisis of conscience.

"Well," I replied. "Don't worry about that. I'm sure you *will* have a good day."

I knew how my little guy felt. I remembered expressing those same anxieties at his age. My mother, however, did little to calm my nerves back then. Instead, she enjoyed telling me about a bird named Tooty, who loved to spy on me during school. It watched me from the kindergarten classroom window, and this winged operative, she said, would fly home each afternoon with the singular goal of exposing all my misdeeds. This was her genius way of ensuring I was "good" at school and that if I wasn't, I'd be guilty and spill my guts to her.

The thought of this bird gave me some agita, as you can imagine. Afternoons during "quiet time," when the other kids dozed off on their mats, I would nervously lie awake, recounting all my damage from the day. In response to the question "How was school?" I was afraid of omitting key details. My mother would be expecting me to share a full replay, including something—anything—mischievous that I had done, or else my story would not be convincing. Should I come clean and say that, for instance, we'd harassed our substitute teacher so much that she literally stormed out of our classroom, never to return? That I took a bite out of Felicia's strawberry Pop-Tart at lunch, a strict no-no because my mom said, "Other kids' food might have drugs inside"? What to reveal?

In Farsi, the word *tooty* can also be a pet name. Like when I call my kids my "tooties" for being so very adorable. But this early 1980s Tooty did nothing but scare the bejesus out of me. So, I would spill *everything*. I overshared and overdramatized my confessions. I began to see even the good parts of the day as problematic. I assumed that revealing all and risking punishment had to be better than keeping some details close to the chest.

And although my mother rarely got upset when I told her about the day's low points, exposing myself hardly ever sat well with me. It left me heavy with emotions ranging from self-doubt to regret and guilt. The night of my Pop-Tart confession, I got so sick I threw up every bite of the toaster pastry.

As a kid I lacked the skills to harness my fear of exposure and rein it in, to appreciate it as a signal to possibly hold back, not drivel. I mistakenly let it push me over the edge and expose everything to my mother, assuming there would be some giant reward at the end of it, when often there wasn't.

If I could travel back in time, I'd tell my younger self to listen to this wise fear. Proceed with caution. It may be telling you that, yes, some details related to your personal life are *personal*. Not everybody—including your mom—needs to know your business or that you once nibbled on a tempting snack.

TO BARE OR NOT TO BARE?

The fear of exposure arrives, as it did for me as a kid, when we worry about sharing aspects of our lives and identity that may be unpopular, confusing, or punishing. This is a primal fear that dates back to biblical times. We have been severely warned about exposure since Adam and Eve took a bite of the forbidden fruit and tried to hide behind the trees in the Garden of Eden. When they were found out, Paradise was lost. And while that story is misogynistic and pejorative, as with any ancient cultural myth it holds a grain of truth.

On one side of the spectrum, reality stars like the Real Housewives, who risk huge exposure, occasionally get investigated by the IRS for fraud. They go to jail. Or they just go too far by airing, as one annoyed reality star spouse said on camera, "our dirty laundry." The show—and the pressure to bare all for ratings' sake—turns family members against one another. The kids stop communicating with their parents, divorce is almost inevitable. This is hyperbolized, but I'd be lying if I said it's not the reason I've steered clear of posting too much on social media about my family and posting every detail of my income and spending online, like some of my fin-fluencer peers do. I am afraid of the risks, the costs, and the unwanted distractions, and that's okay.

This fear can rear its head whenever we think about sharing

ourselves or our ideologies, financial realities, or life circumstances. We worry if we are discovered for who we really are, we could be banned from opportunities or ostracized. And I know this may sound like the fear of rejection, which we previously explored, but this goes far beyond that. **The fear of exposure may be telling you that you need a better balance between baring all to the people you can trust, in situations that warrant it, versus exposing too much to the wrong person at the wrong time and risking a threatening situation or missing opportunities you truly deserve.**

The fear of exposure is universal. Essentially, we have various pieces of our lives that we perceive as weaknesses and vulnerabilities. If others find out about them, we are afraid we won't be appreciated and respected for all that we have to offer. We may be judged for just a small part of who we are. And there's so much more to us than that. We are afraid that if we reveal too much, we can wind up ashamed, underestimated, and laughed out of the room.

A study at the National Institutes of Health, which brought together the leading experts on guilt and shame, defined shame as an emotion characterized by a sense of shrinking, smallness, worthlessness, and exposure and a "helpless concern that the self will be revealed as defective."[1] J. P. Tangney, a doctor of psychology and professor at George Mason University who has studied shame for over thirty years, has said that feelings of shame "often give rise to a range of potentially destructive motivations, defenses, interpersonal behaviors, and psychological symptoms."[2] Shame is difficult to come back from and is often the result of saying too much to someone you can't trust. In response, this fear is in fact telling us that we must proceed with caution.

This issue has become complicated. While historically we were warned against telling all and exposing our most private secrets, society has shifted dramatically. Our impulsiveness to overshare in all circumstances is encouraged by the onset of reality TV and social media. There's a cultural insistence that we be fully transparent with the world. Some sociologists have offered compelling evidence that vulnerability can lead to success in our personal and professional lives. And the internet has taken this to extremes, telling us to live life with "no filter," bring our "whole selves" to the web, work, school, and social gatherings. Telling all has become a way to rage against conformity and break barriers.

The fact is, promises about how we can live our best life by being wide open books don't always come to fruition. On the one hand society is telling you to go there, live loud, be "authentic," while on the other hand it's slapping your wrist with the threat of cancel culture. Putting it all out there may make sites like Facebook and TikTok rich as they earn more subscribers, views, and engagement. All this further lines the pockets of Mark Zuckerberg and Chinese billionaires. But what's in it for us? How do we decide when we should hold back and when we should go full frontal?

Most online influencers who talk about how to master the art of putting yourself out there are not teaching how to navigate making those tough decisions. While I want to believe we can be ourselves and be totally unapologetic about who we are, that's a privilege. To be able to expose all in front of any audience without risk—that's a promised land that many of us won't get to. Sharing everything about yourself can affect chances at social engagement, job advancement, and how the media portrays you. If someone is still figuring things out, our culture doesn't have a lot of patience for nuanced beliefs and gray areas.

Nowadays, many people have absolutist views on parenting, feminism, racism, politics, and finances. And it can be tricky to expose who you are and exactly what you think to those people. A 2020 study by the National Bureau of Economic Research showed that the US is polarizing faster than other democracies.[3] It frightens me to think of how divisiveness can weaken our desire for exploration and limit our sense of empathy and patience. People are alarmed by others who are different. You may be okay exposing your ideas in NYC, but in Kentucky it could mean a threatening encounter. I've been in the Deep South and had to grab something to eat at the only place available: a country store with a Confederate flag in the window. That might not be the place to question the racist decor or strike up a conversation about how my parents are Muslim immigrants, let alone that I believe in equity and belonging.

It can also be risky to expose what happened to you and what you know. According to a Spredfast analysis in September 2018, the hashtag #WhyIDidntReport was tweeted more than eight hundred thousand times. The viral comments were in response to former President Trump's doubts over the sexual assault allegations against Brett Kavanaugh, his pick to be the next justice on the Supreme Court.[4] People are afraid of retaliation. Can we blame them? In this cultural push to share everything, our livelihood could be in danger. I am not condoning silencing yourself. We ultimately want to live in a world where we don't feel coerced into signing nondisclosure agreements or gag orders. We want police forces and administrations to be held accountable. Until then, when the fear of exposure rises inside you, take your time. You may find yourself in situations where if you speak your truth, you will not be protected. If you feel wary and skeptical of *going there*, you may want to listen to this fear and take a beat.

The fear of exposure may not be one that we discuss with others—because *what do you have to lose*, society says—but what you lose is very real. **I'll be the first to say that there's a gift in being guarded sometimes.** The fear isn't always telling you *Don't engage*, it's merely encouraging you to pause, to share only if it's appropriate and you feel safe, to confide in those you trust—and strictly those you trust—and to take a minute (or longer) to consider what you want to share and why.

WHEN FEAR OF EXPOSURE WANTS YOU TO READ THE ROOM

Over the years, being the new kid at school many times over brought me face-to-face with this natural fear. In early years, I'd impulsively cover up my family's ethnicity because I didn't feel safe. True story: I once stood up and shared that I was Italian to my entire third-grade class on "where are you from" day. If I said the truth, I feared the kids would cringe just as they did when my mom occasionally spoke to me in Farsi in public.

My fear of exposure was tied to concerns about rejection, shame, and being "othered." Later, my training as a journalist educated me on how to travel with this fear with better directionality, to examine my environment and try to understand the *who*, *what*, and *why* of this fear to discern the best way forward.

In a *Harvard Business Review* article entitled "What's Wrong with Asking People Where They're From?" the writer Rakshitha Arni Ravishankar describes the problem people of color navigate when it comes to exposure better than I ever could: "For those of us who already feel 'different' in a given space, being asked where we're from carries implicit assumptions about our race, caste, ethnicity, nationality, etc. Often, it translates into: You don't *seem* to (already) belong here. It validates existing beliefs about social identities and can be quite patronizing."[5]

Nowadays, this question is still a trigger. When I'm asked, "Where are you from?," nine times out of ten, I'll say that my parents are from Iran (or they're Persian) and that I was born in the States. But depending on who's asking (and their intent), I'll provide one of many other accurate answers: Worcester, New York, Philly, or New Jersey. If I'm getting bad vibes over that question, I might say, "What do you mean?" Because I'm well trained in recognizing a xenophobe.

At the end of the day, this fear isn't pushing you to bare all to anyone. It's often guiding us to reveal yourself only to those who can respect and value your truth. **It's saying quite literally: before you share, read the room.**

I'll never forget sitting on a panel at an industry conference, when one woman rose from the audience and asked me in front of a hundred people, "How much money do you make?" I had to give her credit for asking. The topic of the panel was how to negotiate your fees as an entrepreneur, and I had just finished advising the audience to reach out to those in their fields and ask how much they earned or charged for projects. Touché! But I refrained. I hesitated because revealing how much money a creator like me makes comes with nuances that need explaining or can otherwise be misconstrued. You may be exposing your annual income and inadvertently causing stakeholders in your company or industry to feel uncomfortable or become judgmental and retaliatory. It's also why many states now ban employers from asking candidates their salary history. While I believe pay transparency is mostly a positive thing, in my self-employed world, there is a risk in being wide open about your earnings, especially as a woman, because it can have unfair consequences when it comes time to getting hired for a future project. Potential clients may base their offers on how little or how much you earn; they'll either lowball you or not even come to the table with an offer. That's a big reason why when companies want to know my fee, I will respond with my own question: "What's your budget?"

Back at the panel, with that inquisitive audience member, I listened to my fear of exposure and resisted sharing something as personal as that on the spot and in front of a crowd. Instead, I answered, "Let's you and me get a coffee after this and talk." I saw the value in transparency and helping out a female peer and figured sharing some personal financial details in private was the smarter, less risky route. But even then—before revealing all at the Starbucks in the hotel lobby downstairs—I'd first ask my own questions, including what her goals were and if there was a specific reason she was curious about my earnings. The hope is to establish a rapport, gain trust, and gather information before sharing the goods. And since then, she and I have kept our conversation going.

This fear reminds us to be selective. The choice of with whom to share aspects of our truth—be it about our finances, ancestry, religion, sexuality, political leanings, or that we're half-naked under a jacket by accident (also true story: a malfunctioning dress once left me exposed from behind and almost jeopardized a major interview)—should require pause and consideration. **Scope out the scene, and then decide for yourself whether you want to stay and engage or fast-walk toward the nearest exit.** If the fear is telling you it won't be worth it, won't lead to more acceptance, and may only lead to more annoying questions, do the latter.

While I watch colleagues benefit from being far more open with their followers on social media, earning more fans and money, I choose a different avenue. I save deep reflections, insights, and tell-alls for my podcast and books, where I know my audience has chosen to show up for me with purpose and openness. On these platforms, I feel safer sometimes sharing controversial opinions. Or bursting into tears over a listener's heartfelt review. The cost of exposing what I believe and feel on the show and in my books is not high. If anything, it mostly brings rewards, as I know what the community came for. In these places, my brutal honesty—even when it's an opposing view—is what keeps followers coming back for more.

For example, I let my audience know I have a hard time promoting stay-at-home parenting as a long-term practice. Do we sometimes need to take time out of the workforce to care for loved ones? Absolutely. Does it cost us our financial security? Sadly, it can. And that's why I hesitate to encourage people—in particular, women who are, on average, far behind men financially—from indefinitely forfeiting a paycheck. Off-ramping from a full-time job to be a full-time caregiver of any kind can be a tremendously rewarding and worthwhile experience, I've shared with my audience, but the longer you're away from the workforce, the harder it becomes to get back in. All the while, you're missing out on earnings, an ability to contribute to Social Security, and potentially a workplace retirement account.

Even as I expose my opinion with facts, figures, and strong anecdotes, I'm prepared for the anger and backlash that sometimes follows. While most parents who respond say they're grateful for my message, I'll get an occasional negative review or a mean email because of it. But, for me, exposing a controversial opinion in these select forums is a small price to pay for encouraging even just one woman to not give up on her financial independence.

I feel relatively safe being candid on my podcast because the individuals who subscribe to it are keen to learn—not troll. They got a recommendation from a friend, found me after typing in key search words, or read my work and wanted to discover more. They intentionally signed up to hear my opinions. Same goes for my books: my readers paid money at a bookstore or checked out a title at the library. There's an undivided attention and a deeper commitment from the audience that signals to me they are here for all of what I have to say, and while I know they may not always agree with me, they're ready for a meaningful exchange. Nobody's bringing pitchforks.

Reconciling with our fear of exposure is still hard, though, because we're told again and again to speak up, especially over critical topics like abuse, racism, discrimination, or the corporate crimes we witness. While living in a perfect world means that you have an impactful voice all the time anytime, there needs to be some compassion and understanding for those who choose to survey the scene first and decide it just isn't a great idea to tell all—at least not loudly or right away. Emily Ladau, a disability rights advocate and author of the book *Demystifying Disability*, believes in the value of disclosing your disability to an employer, but she also understands the fear that comes with disclosing, particularly if it's not visible.[6] This includes things like a mental health condition, diabetes, or hearing loss. We might benefit from disclosing this on the job so that we can receive the support we need, but should we always? Employers cannot force workers to share personal medical information, so it is entirely our choice. And as much as we'd like to think that the world is open to our differences, the workplace remains a tough audience in some cases.

"Employers have not exactly demonstrated that they're welcoming to people with apparent disabilities. So why would you want to put yourself on the line by opening up about a disability that people can't see?" Emily told me on my podcast.[7] But staying fully silent and exposing nothing isn't the solution, either. The key is to strike a balance between supporting your needs and protecting your privacy as it feels necessary. Consider just sharing the *parts* of your story that focus on the accommodations you need to perform your best at work. No need to get into all the details if you don't feel comfortable.

MAYBE JUST GET OVER YOURSELF?

I once suspected a coworker was out to get me. I assumed she was setting booby traps around the newsroom *just for me*, trying to expose me for being unqualified.

Serena and I had both applied for a producer position at NY1 News, and given that she'd been filling in as the interim producer while managers interviewed new hires, she had presumed it was just a formality and that in the end she'd get the gig. But then I seemingly strolled in and unseated her. Based on her intense side-eye as she passed my cubicle on the way to the cafeteria every afternoon, I knew she wasn't pleased. Nor were her band of close work friends, who were also wondering how on earth I'd usurped her.

I understood this. I was new. I was twenty-three, younger than most producers. I hadn't paid my dues, so to speak, and hadn't advanced to this role like others at NY1. And I'll be the first to admit that I was learning a ton on the job and afraid that I wouldn't be able to keep my head above water in this very intimidating New York City newsroom. I felt that at least a few people in addition to Serena's friends didn't want me there either. On my first day, while I was washing my hands in the restroom, a colleague introduced herself and asked how my internship was going. When I corrected her, she gave me a death stare. She slapped on her lip gloss and left without saying goodbye. Good times.

I guess you could say that my first few months at NY1 were ... interesting. My overwhelm and fear were messing with my focus and follow-through, and I was making a lot of mistakes. But rather than trust I could get better and improve, I suspected Serena was secretly plotting my demise and that I was being set up for doom.

Inexplicable things were going on. My stationery and sometimes important documents would go missing. And my news pieces, written for the overnight anchors, would disappear from ENPS, the internal software we used to load scripts into the prompters.

In the mornings, I'd arrive at work to furious emails sent from the tired 3 a.m. producer. "Where is the copy for the business report?! We had to scramble to write something before going live!"

Hmm. I was positive I completed those scripts because I'd scratched it off my dang list. *Serena! She must have gone into the system and deleted my work*, the voices in my head repeatedly told me.

When it happened several times within a span of a few weeks, I explained my conspiracy theory to an older, wiser coworker. Serena, you see, was attempting to get me to fall on my face, and then the entire newsroom would see how much of an illegitimate hire I was. She wanted to reveal that I didn't have staying power and that I was in over my head.

My sage colleague listened the whole way through, took a pause, and then said something I'll never forget: "I doubt it, Farnoosh. You're not that important."

At first, I was taken aback. It was kind of a hurtful thing to say, no? What did she mean I *wasn't important*?

She went on to say that I wasn't important in the context of Serena's ability to be successful. My winning didn't mean Serena was losing. She was not targeting me or carefully strategizing my fall because, as disappointing as it may have been to not get the job and while she wasn't my biggest fan, I wasn't that important *to Serena*. She was over it, working with a new team, continuing to make money, and gaining the respect of her colleagues. She was fine. She'd moved on. I, however, was stuck in a weird sitcom.

My kind colleague was effectively telling me to get out of my head, to stop making myself the main character in some imagined story and see the reality in plain sight: I was a woman who'd been selected to take on the role of producer. This didn't happen by accident. I had earned this job after several rounds of interviews. I had every right to be here. If things were going wrong with my performance, maybe it had more to do with me trying to work a new software system that was glitchy . . . and not a menacing colleague.

Perhaps one reason I was so upset by what I thought Serena was doing was that she had touched a nerve. I feared being exposed for not really being as competent as they thought I was as a producer, and the more I dwelled on it, the more additional fears like rejection and failure surfaced. What I was experiencing was some straight-up *imposter syndrome*, defined as lacking the confidence to see yourself as skillful and valuable. The underlying fear of imposter syndrome is that you might be exposed for being less talented than you think you are, which you then fear will result in a demotion, being fired, or never actualizing your potential at work. Ironically, this "syndrome" often impacts high-achieving women and people of color. (Thanks systemic discrimination!) And you often experience it in silence.[8] I never ventured to learn why my reports weren't saved—assuming that it was just my fate.

The fear of being found out for our mistakes is universal. I didn't want to be thought of as a hack at work. But when I paused and recognized my thought spirals, I found that I was just letting my own insecurities about being new and young get in the way of really committing to the job. **Becoming obsessed with the fear of being an imposter can cloud reality to the point that you don't see the opportunity that lies in front of you.**

At NY1 News it was only after weeks and many restless nights that I was able to take a few (mental) steps back and see that my fear of being found out as a fraud could be used to show my coworkers and colleagues the greatness I was capable of.

As I advanced in my career, the fear of being exposed as an imposter never dissipated. It became a steady companion. But when the fear rose, I didn't let it diffuse my spirit of can-do-it-ness. Instead, I took it as a cue to lean out and see the bigger picture, as my dear coworker had taught me to do with Serena. This not only relaxed me, it led to a lot of laughs. And this was nowhere more apparent than fifteen years later in 2018, when I met Suze Orman in person for the first time.

Suze and I had been invited to film a discussion about women and money. The event was moderated by our mutual friend Adam Auriemma, who was then the managing editor of *Money* magazine. By this time, the world knew Suze to be the Queen of Personal Finance. She was the Financial GOAT. Me? My podcast was big in Germany. I know, I'm selling myself short, but you get the picture—and how I walked into it.

I was nervous to meet Suze. I was afraid she wouldn't like me, because I was used to being let down by some more experienced women in our field. I remembered, decades prior, scheduling a lunch with a female boss I admired, only to get stood up with no explanation. And then there was the female financial expert who said straight to my face, "Farnoosh, I was *you* ten years ago. Enjoy it while it lasts!" It was as if she was implying youth was the only thing that merited success, and I was to blame for the fact that she wasn't getting as many opportunities as she once did. So, when I finally got the chance to meet Suze, I was prepared for a bit of a snub.

I remember the moment she walked into the hair and makeup room. I was early and already seated, receiving some touch-ups. I smiled hello and waved from my seat. She said hello back. But then . . . nothing else. The silence, as the saying goes, was deafening, and it endured until we were both in our interview chairs and getting mic'd. I couldn't help but assume that she was *trying* to psych me out! Was she going to take me down in the interview? Was she preparing for battle? While I'd been inspired to follow in her path (one that she paved), I was afraid she might think I was trying to be a copycat or step on her "turf," the same thing I'd felt from other women in my industry. Would she try to expose me as a fraud?

But as I'd meditated on those thoughts in the makeup chair, I realized once again that my fear of being found out as an imposter was begging for a zoom out. I ultimately did care to have a positive experience with Suze, so the fear was telling me to lean back and see the reality that was before me. I did this with both my mind and my physical presence.

From my previously hunched position I sat in the interview chair and rolled my shoulders back and sat straight up. And then I assessed with clarity, the *facts* rather than the fears: Suze and I were two accomplished women. We had both been invited to speak with the top financial magazine to be in service to an audience. We were not here to prove our worth.

With the new, clearer perspective that leaning back gave me, I was able to tame my anxiety and relax. This was a physical technique I had learned practicing theater in high school and college and spending all that time in front of a camera as a broadcaster. Being "natural" before a crowd was a conscious effort of harnessing my fear and getting out of my own mind. I stopped making myself the center of my attention.

As it turns out, there is a real physiological science behind what I was practicing. When we lean back—mentally and physically—in moments of raised anxiety, as I did here, assessing the facts and calming our mind, we quickly feel more confident because we're no longer constricting comfort.

What happens next is a radically helpful hormonal response, says Lee Bonvissuto, a communication coach who uses science and dramatic training to help clients lay down their fear of exposure and boldly trust who they are, which, by definition, means having confidence. Lee teaches a physical change in posture and an assessment and shift in what we are mentally telling ourselves. "Leaning back, we are going to feel hormonal confidence. . . . The biggest benefit to that is we are changing our habitual behavior and forcing ourselves into the present moment," they said on *So Money*.[9] And from that we provide ourselves with presence, power, and agency in the midst of anxiety.

When the interview began, I purposely kept my answers concise to give Suze more of the floor. I was accomplished in my own right, but I deferred to her because, for one, she commanded the room and, two, it was the polite thing to do in the presence of an icon. I knew my place there. It was to bring in a perspective that maybe Suze didn't have, the perspective of millennials and mothers. I stuck to my wheelhouse.

All was going well. I was satisfied with my contributions to the conversation. But then, things took a startling turn. It happened right after I finished answering a question with "It's important to put your oxygen mask on first before helping others."

That's when Suze shot back, "You got that line from *me*, girlfriend!"

She said it with a smile, and yet in that moment, my heart attempted to go where it normally would—to the pit of my stomach. But thanks to the little bit of self-coaching I'd done earlier, my anxiety was now a source of healthy adrenaline. And it led to one of my finest moments as an amateur comedian. "Actually," I said, "I think I got it from American Airlines."

The room burst into laughter. I am pretty sure everyone had been feeling the tension, and that comeback cut through every layer of it.

Leaning back meant working through my own fear of being found out as a fraud, decentralizing myself and my worries, relaxing and just being myself. This helped me break through the nerves and calculate an appropriate response that was part self-protective, part performance theater.

That meeting with Suze wasn't anything like I'd thought it would be. It was better. I got out of my own head and got comfortable with who I was in the context of what I was delivering on stage.

The next time you're in a high-pressure moment, experiencing stage fright, a fear of public speaking, or anxiety in the presence of someone you admire, remember this: we're all afraid—at one point or another—of being exposed as less than we seem to be. We don't want to feel ashamed if we make a mistake. We don't want others to think less of us. We don't want to narrow our opportunities for advancement. We don't want people to think we are just that one performance; we want them to see our whole selves and admire us. How you're feeling is not unique to you. We're all walking around with tiny fig leaves covering our private areas, and the winds are racing at forty miles per hour.

Let the fact that you are one in a crowd calm you. Let it remind you that getting worked up will only make you more miserable. Instead, let your fear signal the importance of putting your mind and body at ease. **Remember to breathe. Remember your gifts. Listen for cues. And let your natural magic flow.** On the other side of that, who knows, maybe you will be met with both a renewed faith in yourself and a barrel of laughs.

At the end of the interview, as we were collecting our bags and saying farewell, Suze came in for a hug. She said something to me I never expected. "I want to tell you something, Farnoosh," she said. "You are a strong woman."

Another surprise gift in leaning out and getting over myself was an unexpected kinship. Were Suze and I best girlfriends now? Please. We were, however, closer than we were an hour earlier. What began with silence ended with selfies.

HOW RISKING EXPOSURE CAN BE A SPRINGBOARD FOR CONNECTION AND INTIMACY

In my mid-twenties, I reconnected with Tim, a great big love, the man I'd eventually marry. If you recall, I initially felt the spark at nineteen years old while seated next to him in a business class at Penn State. I was so taken aback by this man, I remember thinking (and whispering to myself when I saw that he arrived, like he said he would, to the opening night of my college play), *"I'm going to marry him."* But, before we could become a couple, I'd need more time. I'd need to experience the lows of dating and, maybe more importantly, reconcile my complicated relationship with the fear of being exposed.

As I would discover over the years, to arrive at a deep, meaningful life partnership with someone, I would have to get comfortable with aspects of this fear and its rules of conduct—chiefly, loving yourself and valuing your own boundaries first. I'd need to learn to be comfortable with all my "wobbly bits," as the wise Bridget Jones once said. Only then would I, an independent woman, be ready to embrace an interdependent love and appreciate the ultimate gift that comes with working with and through the fear of being found out for who you really are. **That gift is intimacy.**

No matter how off-putting you think it may be for the other person, when you are unequivocally willing to share your values and desires in the context of a relationship, only then can you welcome immense love into your life. In this pursuit, you may have to pre-pare for the fears we just covered: rejection and loneliness. But your fear of exposure in the context of finding your "person" wants you to take the risk. What's on the other side will be worth it. "A lot of people have a barrier to interdependence," says clinical psychologist and podcast host Dr. Morgan Anderson. She stopped by my podcast and confirmed my own experience.[10] "It's because they're lacking self-trust and they're lacking the relationship tools that they need. If I don't know how to communicate . . . how to set boundaries, I'm not going to feel safe being vulnerable with people and building re-lationships."

After hearing your truth, some potential partners won't be into you. They won't love your boundaries, or how, say, you don't want to have kids, or how your greatest desire in life is to start an amphibian rescue. But someone very special will. And as I've always thought, if someone wants to break up with you over something that is nonnegotiable to you, while it can be painful, just let them go. Release them. Thank them for their honesty. Thank them for not wasting your time any further since there's no point in making it work by changing yourself or them.

In New York, exposing my truth (and the why behind it) to the men I dated was never easy or fun. Many had not seen this level of financial feminism modeled in their lives. And some dating advice I received made me even more insecure. A married, male colleague offered what he considered his "best" tip for me on how to attract men. "Don't tell these guys that you own your own apartment or that you have a big job in the media," he said. He thought it would crush their ego and be a romance buzzkill.

While my fear of exposure had protected me in other realms, in the dating field, it left me exhausted. I held my tongue and didn't talk about my financial and career ambitions, my side hustles, that I was working on my first book, and that I planned to work and make money . . . forever. Exposing all of this made me fearful of never meeting a man who'd tolerate me, let alone be my soul mate. But *not* sharing didn't feel like progress, either.

In truth I wanted to find a partner with the same foundational values, someone who was a feminist and did not see my success as a threat or challenge. But I didn't trust that man was out there. Even in the marriages around me that seemed to be "working," I saw power struggles. I saw men who believed that money was strictly a "husband's domain" and women who were left picking up the pieces when their spouses left or passed away. When my mother's friends became widowed, they had no idea where any of their supposed *shared* money was sitting.

My parents raised me to be strong-willed, which has its benefits. But the challenge of being a girl who was groomed to be fiercely independent is that you have a hard time letting your guard down and inviting in the love you deserve, the love that might not be the same as what your parents and the culture envisioned for you.

After a while, I wrongly interpreted my fear of exposure as meaning I should put up a front and hide the fact that I did want (and deserve) to have a big love and to be in a real relationship. It was a defense mechanism that we all sometimes deploy when trying to protect ourselves from being hurt. But here's what I also learned: the sooner you have had enough with holding back your truth in the dating field, the sooner you can lay down your shield, put up your hands, and say, "World, this is me! I can't anymore." This is the moment when you finally experience what the fear of exposure was nudging you toward in your pursuit of romance: getting crystal clear about your values and honoring them no matter who's across the candlelit table. You've arrived at a place where you're making peace with the idea of being *outed*.

More importantly, you've come to terms with your fear of the consequences of being exposed, and what might be on the other side of that exposure, including criticism, rejection, and being single forever.

A year or two before Tim reentered my life, after a lot of strikeouts, I remember thinking, *I may never get married. I may never meet my person. And that's okay. I'll be okay. I'd rather that than live a lie.* My fear of being exposed was a blessing; it made me protect and stand up for the real woman inside. In this way, it's like the fear of rejection. When you're no longer willing to silence or compromise your truth, what may feel like a desperate moment of "giving up" is anything but— it's actually an inflection point where happiness and connection can finally arrive. **Because *you've* arrived. No holds barred.**

It's not just romance. It's friendships, too. When I run into a mom from my kids' school at the library on a Saturday morning, I some-times think about the fear of exposure. I've left the house with a food-stained shirt, messy hair, and flip-flops in thirty-five-degree weather. After my efforts to look presentable in public during the week, another mom suddenly catches me in a moment of relative weakness. On this day (like many weekends) I'm the woman who can barely see straight after a week of rigorous deadlines and bad sleep because her children kept sneaking into her bed. I'm here with my kids so they can roam and search for books (free babysitting) while I attempt to finish writ-ing my own. Being found out for who I really am in that moment could mean inviting judgment and pity from the outside world . . . and who wants that? Or it could mean that this other mom who sees me in my frazzled state relates to the feeling. I decide not to hide behind the tiers of Mo Willems books. Instead, I come forth and say hello, and she doesn't pity me. She may even see herself in me. In that moment, we experience a connection that only being exposed could have afforded. The next day, she and I will grab coffee.

And just like with friendships, romantic partnerships can thrive when we lay down our fear of being exposed and risk revealing the full reality of our lives.

By the time I'd reached my mid-twenties, I'd been reflecting quite a bit on what life might be like without a partner. I saw how other women were leading fabulous lives without being in long-term, committed relationships. I decided I, too, could be a woman willing to risk being exposed as career-loving and financially in charge, and one who might even have a baby on her own. I was more than fine with that.

With that acceptance, it got easier to stop hiding. Plus, not telling men what I really wanted was not a sustainable play. You can't lie or censor your way to a healthy, lasting relationship. I let the fear of being exposed while dating lead me to take the risk and stand up for who I was—and connect me to the person with whom I was meant to be.

Not long after I quit worrying about being seen as the woman with the uncompromising ambitions, and led with transparency, love arrived. Tim and I reconnected five years after college, when I'd just been through the misery of dating but not really being ready for true intimacy. I never got the playbook, so I didn't always feel confident I could learn. But I didn't need instructions for intimacy. I needed to be willing to share everything with Tim, from the way I grew up to how much I earned, the apartment I owned, all my ambitions, and even my fear of being found out for who I really was.

Tim made this easy because he was genuinely trustworthy. And even though I sensed this, I didn't tell him everything all at once. I offered pieces of my story to see how he would react. At every turn he was interested, supportive, and accepting. As opposed to the previous times when I was uptight, close-lipped, and judgey on dates, Tim invited me to be relaxed, confident, and curious. There were no red flags like the time that one guy asked me how much I weighed within minutes of sitting down to eat. Or the more senior coworker I went on *one* date with (big mistake) who thought paying for dinner (he really insisted) would necessarily mean there would be a second date and some kissing. When I declined, he became passive-aggressive and a little punishing around the office. Which, in retelling the story now, I can see was textbook sexual harassment.

Tim and I married a few years after we got reacquainted. My marriage reinforces my faith in the divinity of the universe, for intimacy is not something I always excel at. But with Tim, it's easy. We are not at all the same, but we balance each other out in the ways that matter and mix well. I am with him now because I risked sharing my whole self with him. You can't do that every time in all situations with every person, but occasionally if you meet someone who is disarming, who feels personally secure, you could find that it is a catalyst for falling madly and deeply in love.

By the way, the fear of exposure doesn't stop just because you are in an intimate relationship. Throughout it, you may be afraid of exposing your views, opinions, shortcomings, and so on . . . because you don't want to disappoint the other person, break a vow or a promise about living in a certain place, having kids, or wanting or not wanting a career.

Exposure in relationships is hard if you are afraid your vulnerability could be used against you. You may worry that if you tell all, your partner will leave you. But this fear is still on your side. It is calling you to champion yourself first and foremost. It's nudging you to ask that all-important question: *What is more important: to love myself or please the other person?* You may need to reevaluate whether or not this relationship works for you.

The stakes could be high. If you realize telling all would put you at risk, that isn't true intimacy. Because in true intimacy, being found out is where you find support. It's part of the fun.

The Fear of Exposure Self-Inquiry

- What am I willing to share with a person or group of people that may bring value?
- What will be the cost of what I am about to share?
- Why do I want to share this?

- Is this the right place to share it? The right audience?
- Is my fear of being exposed related to imposter syndrome, in which case, I shouldn't trust it?
- What will happen if I don't share?
- What is the connection I'll experience if I do?

In the perfect world, you will know all these answers. In the real world, you will guess.

5

THE FEAR OF UNCERTAINTY

and how it inspires new pathways and helps us find order in the disorder

O N A RANDOM THURSDAY in March 2009, the fear of uncertainty crept up beside me in a downtown New York salon chair. It became known as the morning I would lose far more than just a few inches of hair.

As water dripped from my split ends, I felt my work BlackBerry buzz under my robe. It was my editor in chief at TheStreet.com and he had company. "Hi, Farnoosh, it's David and I've got HR on speaker," he said.

My first thought was that I was in deep doo-doo for scheduling a haircut during business hours, even though it was protocol for the website's video reporters to get a quick trim before heading into the office. My appointment had been cleared with my executive producer for weeks. *I can explain!*

But they didn't care about any of that. In a scripted tone, my boss proceeded to say that the media company had made the decision to lay off 10 percent of the newsroom staff. A few seconds of silence later, he confirmed my fears. "This includes you."

I've never been punched in the gut, but I imagine being told you're fired—for no fault of your own—is just like that. In the past when I left a job it was by my *own* doing. I'd leave with another role lined up to avoid a gap in pay. But here, I was being terminated immediately, with about three weeks of severance and no other full-time role in sight. It was the Great Recession, after all, and companies were going belly-up overnight. The media industry, like so many other sectors, was shrinking and consolidating.

I went home on the uptown 2 train in tears. I cried when I phoned Tim and my parents the news. I cried while eating my Chinese dinner. I cried the next day when I rode the elevator up to the office where I collected my belongings and handed in my badge and BlackBerry.

At TheStreet.com I was an on-air senior financial correspondent, a promotion I'd recently negotiated. Giving up that title was painful. I felt an existential crisis approaching. This job was supposed to be my stepping stone to reach the next echelon in broadcast news. My next stop was hopefully at CNBC or another national network. Who was I now in the absence of a real title at a real media company? Would anyone take me seriously once they knew I'd been canned? I was left stressed, anxious, and desperate. Thankfully, I had some savings to tide me over, but my ego and self-confidence were decimated. What could possibly be next for me besides moving back home with Sheida and Farrokh?

FROM DIVORCES TO DEAD ENDS, YOUR FAMILIAR (FOREVER) FRIEND

Uncertainty is the only certainty in life. It's a fundamental law of nature that the level of disorder in our world is steadily increasing. As the daughter of a physicist, I feel this in my bones.

No matter how hard we try to maintain our routines and stick with plans, life simply won't allow it. It is constantly in motion and evolving. From recessions to regime changes, divorces to dead-end deals, we never know with certainty how things will pan out. In the 1960s, the decade that gave us the civil rights movement, the Vietnam War, and a presidential assassination, American author Ursula Le Guin wrote, "The only thing that makes life possible is permanent, intolerable uncertainty; not knowing what comes next."[1]

The what-ifs of the modern world resemble a nuclear mushroom cloud. As I write this, we are emerging from a devastating pandemic that upended so many lives, we're still grappling with the new normal world and our place in it. Globally, there's tremendous political unrest and intolerance for differing ideologies. We also have the ongoing threat of other medical and health uncertainties. There's an ever-widening wealth chasm. And as technology evolves, we're afraid of what that means for the future of our relationships, money, employment, and more. Will the rise of robots, artificial intelligence, and crypto be the downfall of civilization? It has crossed my mind.

For someone who spends her career answering questions, I never know with certainty whether things will work out. People want to know: *What if I get laid off this year? What if my house loses value? What if I can't get my business off the ground? What if I don't have enough money to retire or send my kids to college? What if my marriage ends in divorce and I can't support myself? What if I fall sick and my health insurance won't cover my bills?* More than anything, my audience wants reassurance. They want someone they trust to tell them, "It will be okay."

Not knowing the future frightens us—and naturally so. This fear of uncertainty is fundamental to the human experience. Research shows that *any* aspect of unpredictability makes us painfully uncomfortable. One experiment showed that when people knew, with certainty, that they would be electrocuted, they exhibited less stress than when they knew there was a 50 percent chance of receiving a shock.[2] That's dark, I know. But it illustrates just how determined the fear of uncertainty can be and how it can fuel anxiety to the point of illogic.

This fear runs deep for most of us. For me, the fear of uncertainty has been a longtime companion with a surprising upside.

This fear signals us to pause, reflect, and gather information, and then diligently work our way through the fog. This fear can also tell us it's time to do something bigger: make a serious decision or a change that will mitigate risks. The challenge when we're young is that we may lack the agency to do either of these. But as we grow, this fear can instill determination, a quench for finding solutions, and a penchant for being able to count on the self above anyone else. This fear can help you harness and grow what you have worked so hard to cultivate: your resourcefulness and instincts.

CALCULATING IF AND HOW TO MOBILIZE

During the last big recession, Rebecca came to me as a twenty-two-year-old college graduate with this whopper of a question: Should I go to law school?

She was terrified of entering an uncertain job market, and law school seemed a respectable way to make the most of the next couple of years. While she wasn't in love with the idea of becoming a traditional lawyer, she figured it couldn't hurt to have a law degree if and when she decided to work in public service. She didn't have her whole life mapped out (because who does?), but after speaking with her parents and professors, she thought attending law school seemed like the wisest strategy to ride out the uncertainty. It was not as though the labor market—with a high unemployment rate at that time—was going to present her with any sort of dream job.

Rebecca had come to me for my thoughts. She knew I'd be honest because I didn't have a stake in the matter. I could be objective. But before I shared my opinion, I had my own questions. Chiefly: *How was she going to pay for law school?* She already had $40,000 in undergraduate debt. Was she going to borrow more to attain the graduate degree? "I guess," she said. She admitted that she hadn't quite thought that part through. So then I presented her with the average cost to attend law school—$100,000 to $120,000. Those six figures stopped her in her tracks. "Hearing these numbers—it makes me feel like I'm about to walk myself into my own grave," she said.

I explained to her that it's one thing if you know you can and want to leverage the law degree right away by making a high salary at a law firm. But to rack up six figures' worth of debt for the possibility of maybe, someday, utilizing the degree? The math doesn't add up. As I told Rebecca, taking on debt to attend law school is a too-costly way to hide from uncertainty, especially since a return on her academic investment just didn't seem plausible.

I offered her a couple of alternate pathways to ride out the uncertainty. One, she could *still* go to law school, but be more financially strategic. Could she go part-time, while paying for the degree out of pocket? Or apply for grants and scholarships with the goal of borrowing only a fraction of the cost of law school? That would be my preference. Or option two: ride out the uncertainty of the next couple of years by taking on a job that might not be her "dream job," but hey, she'd be working, exploring, advancing, and making money to help pay off those undergrad loans. No job in your twenties is ever really a "dream job." It's a time to conduct all sorts of career experiments and count on being disappointed in (many of) the results. What's important is that you're constantly learning about yourself, the world, and your place in it. Heck, I'm still doing this in my forties.

And I had one more question for her, and for anyone in a similar predicament: What is it you're really afraid of? Is it the uncertain job market? Or the pressure to be "successful," which you're not quite sure how to define yet? If it's the latter, don't be too hard on yourself. Defining success is something you can only do by *doing*. By applying yourself. By sometimes winning and sometimes failing. By learning your likes and dislikes. It takes time and patience. I could sympathize with Rebecca because I, too, had thought that law school might be the next step for me when I was a college student and had no idea what I wanted to do with my life. It was a prestigious move that would make my parents proud, to say the least. But carrying a huge financial burden can lead to a whole new level of uncertainty.

Before you make a costly choice to ride out uncertainty—whether it's debt-financing college or graduate school because the degree might afford you some clout, buying a house because renting feels unstable, or quitting your job because you're not clear on how you can advance at the company (or you're not sure how much longer you can take it!)—run some calculations to figure out what's really at stake if you make the jump. How much will this transition cost you in time, money, and stress? Is the nature of what's happening around you cyclical or is this the sign of a whole new world? In other words: Is the uncertainty going to pass?

Fun fact: there's this thing called recency bias, a New Agey behavioral science discovery that says we tend to incorrectly place too much emphasis on recent events when making decisions.[3] If I get into a car accident, I may hesitate to drive again because I don't trust that I won't sideswipe a food truck parked on Bloomfield Avenue and need to get the entire front side of my car replaced (true story). Even though this fear may be totally irrational. I see this a lot in the financial world, too, for example when people fled their 401(k)s in the 2008 market crash, assuming stocks would never rebound.

On the other hand, it may be that the situation you are in is only going to get worse and affect your well-being, your finances, and your prospects. Perhaps you just will not be able to manage if you stay put. In this case it's probably time to consider a big change.

Like many Americans during the pandemic, a friend of mine quit his job because of severe burnout. Waiting for things to get better was not a solution. After five years (two of them working overtime during the pandemic), he resigned as an editor at a news organization without a full plan for what would come next. He wasn't afraid of the uncertainty of what lay ahead because he was almost certain that staying would destroy his health. "I reached a breaking point," he told me. "I said, 'This is what I need to do for my own mental health, and to make sure that this burnout doesn't turn into a serious, actual crisis.'"

For everyone else using this calculator to determine whether to stay or go in any uncertain situation, assess your goals. How do you plan to take advantage of this shift to propel you to a better, more secure place? In my view, if what's on the other side is going to provide you with not just more confidence and stability, but possibly more financial capacity and a chance for growth, it's worth it.

Deciding to leave our nineteenth-floor Brooklyn apartment for a single-family home in Essex County, New Jersey, during the pandemic was an uncertain move for us. I was leaving behind a life that I loved. And what if we got to New Jersey and hated it? I was not at all sure I would enjoy the new home, the new neighborhood, or the lifestyle as much. I didn't know if my kids would be happier being raised in the suburbs. I wondered if the house we had bought was going to plummet in value because the world did seem, after all, like it was ending.

But we knew *our* values. We knew what was most important to us: our family's safety—both personal and financial. With that we concluded that the move was right for us. We were parents of two small children living in a city that was becoming increasingly unsafe. Social services like hospitals, police, and fire departments were overwhelmed and understaffed. We weren't comfortable staying there because in our own assessment, our uncertainty over living in New York wouldn't be resolved after the pandemic. We'd still be living in a city where public schools were a mixed bag. Would our kids get reliable educations? We weren't sure. We'd tried out one private school, and it just wasn't the right fit for our son. But our suburban public school district was more accommodating and better resourced. We estimated that leaving the city would save us money and provide us with a stronger and more reliable infrastructure in the pandemic and for many years to come.

But me being me, I knew that the move could still be a bust. Before loading the moving truck, Tim and I committed to pivoting if things didn't turn out to be "perfect" in Jersey, either. Making a bold move amid uncertainty, I've found it helps to have a fallback, a Plan B (and possibly C). Staying open-minded and flexible takes some of the pressure off. Maybe we'd move again. That's all right. If nothing else, my childhood had made me a pro at fresh starts.

We were very fortunate to be able to afford this move. For many during the pandemic, a full-time relocation wasn't financially feasible. But you (or your dollars) don't have to go far to reclaim calm and sanity during an uncertain time. For some who remained put in 2020, feeling more in control meant committing to a steady routine of to-dos that included making their bed, journaling, and exercising, even when it felt pointless many days. They rearranged their homes, converting dining rooms into offices to compartmentalize work from personal life; they turned their backyards into private escapes with zen gardens and hot tubs purchased on Facebook Marketplace—all to feel more relaxed and take their minds off the chaos, even if just for a short while. Others, who flirted with leaving, rented short-term Airbnbs five miles away. This gave them the breathing room to make clear, more conscious choices about how they wanted to pivot long-term.

Making a high-pressure change amid uncertainty can be problematic; there's always the risk of throwing the baby out with the bathwater. In 2021, a year into the pandemic, millions of Americans quit their jobs with the hopes of finding more happiness someplace else. This has been termed the "Great Resignation." Many understandably had felt uncertain at their jobs. Would the workload ever get easier?

Would they ever get that raise? How would they manage to juggle life at home with the constraints of work?

Researchers at Harvard and the University of Oxford found that uncertainty and the fears surrounding it can lead to burnout.[4] The burnout that fueled the Great Resignation was, in some cases, related to an overwhelming fear of uncertainty. Many weren't sure whether the stress they felt at work would die down or if their boss would become more accommodating over time. It drove a large number of them to quit. And while this was the right move for many, a study one year later by career platform The Muse found that three out of four of those who left their jobs—particularly younger workers—experienced "Shift Shock," a regret of the move because the new position or company did not meet expectations.[5] The grass wasn't any greener.

Cait Donovan, the host of *FRIED: The Burnout Podcast*, and someone who's experienced her own bout of severe overwhelm, said that while we may feel the impulse to quit to remove ourselves from the shackles of burnout, it's usually better to first pause and reflect. "To me, quitting your job just to get away from things is not always the answer," said Cait.[6] She joined my podcast in 2022 to offer some advice to younger workers who were struggling to manage their massive fatigue at work. "If your job is extremely toxic, and you're being bullied and harassed, and you're in a hostile work environment, get out. But if you're just trying to deal and you don't know how, get some help. Stay in your job," she recommended. "I think the hidden cost of burnout is that recovery time and that loss of work time, right? I know people that have been out of work for eighteen months just recovering. That's a year and a half of your life's salary. That's 401(k) payments. That compounds over time. Missing that much time and that much income is hugely impactful for the health of your financial future."

Rather than take this fear as a sign to make a ninety-degree turn out of the job, Cait recommends clients take smaller steps, what she calls "life pruning." After all, quitting without another job lined up is not something most of us can afford. Examine your life and see what you can cut back on; what can you take away to help ease the uncertainty? "What's happening in your life? What responsibilities are you holding on to that are not actually helping anybody?" she said. "Notice all the places where you don't have to say yes in the first place because nobody's asking you anything, and stay out of them."

You may think that everything you're doing is important and necessary, but what if you stopped doing something you think you "need" to do? Coordinating all the office social outings or getting too emotionally involved in a coworker's problems can lead to big stress. "I promise you, 10 percent of the things you do, if you stopped doing them today, no one would ever even notice . . . . So let's life prune. Let's get rid of all that stuff," Cait says. Overwork, overdoing, and overproducing can feel very unfulfilling, and can make you question your value and whether a job is sustainable . . . when really, there may be a far less stressful way to approach your work.

KNOWING WHOM TO TRUST (HINT: IT'S NOT GOOGLE)

As I grew older and experienced more uncertainty, I got better at asking this fear some key questions and discovering the best people to trust for guidance in any consumingly precarious time. This was never more apparent than during the days and weeks after having my first child.

As Tim and I approached Evan's birth, in some ways we felt extremely prepared. Leading up to his arrival, we'd taken all the suggested baby classes and had bought hundreds of diapers and an overpriced stroller. But as soon as he arrived, I came face-to-face with a huge and unexpected battle: breastfeeding. Nobody had told me how painful breastfeeding would be. Nobody had said I might not produce any milk for the first few days. And as time passed, and Evan needed to be fed, I didn't know what to do. Formula was the easy fix, staring me right in the face, but every time I reached for it, I felt incredibly guilty.

I kept replaying the many conversations I'd had with mom friends who'd waxed poetic about the virtues of breastfeeding. "It's challenging, but so worth it," they all chimed in harmony.

It didn't help that a "breast is best" campaign had engulfed New York City back then.[7] The rumor was that Mayor Michael Bloomberg had instructed maternity wards across the city to lock up the formula and only provide it in dire circumstances. I was afraid of asking a nurse for a bottle of formula in the delivery ward, that it would be a sign of defeat, laziness, and cruelty.

Besides, I'd *wanted* to breastfeed and had planned for it. I had all the stuff! A state-of-the-art breast pump (free with insurance), plus nursing bras and easy-to-open shirts. I was going to be that cool mom at the Brooklyn playground, effortlessly whipping out her boob (under her chic nursing cover) to feed her baby.

But within hours of Evan's delivery, my plan was going to hell in a receiving blanket. We tried everything to get him to latch, everything to get him to nurse. We even hooked up a giant breast pump with a four-foot-long suction tube to my nipples to try to squeeze something—anything—out of my barren breasts. It was an absolute joke. But I played along with the dedicated nurses and lactation consultants. They told me it might take a few days before my milk would arrive and, in the meantime, to just be patient.

Really? Deprive a newborn of nourishment in those critical first few days of life?

After the first night, when nothing seemed to help, I finally asked for the dreaded formula. Thankfully, there was a nurse on duty who didn't judge and she brought it immediately. Within seconds Evan was chomping away at the bottle, and all was as it should be. A hungry baby being fed, a tired mom resting.

Even so, when we headed home from the hospital, I wasn't convinced that I should totally give up on breastfeeding. My milk was slowly coming in, so now was my chance, I thought, to give this a real go. But it only became more painful with my now swollen, engorged breasts and Evan's wailing at the sight of my nipples. He refused to latch. Had he already experienced something better and easier in that latex nipple, and was he now refusing the *actual* nipple on purpose? Could we blame him?

Worried that I was setting up my child for poor SAT scores and professional failure, I hit up Google a lot in that first week, for reassurance. My main search: "Should I breastfeed my child?" The results: "Of course, you should, how dare you even ask!" all the top mom blogs yapped back.

I cried desperate tears in between bottle feedings those first few nights. I wondered how I would keep it a secret. I couldn't imagine what my mom friends would think if they found out. When I texted one for advice, she didn't say, *Do what works for you, Farnoosh*. Instead, she instructed me to "not give up" and lay cabbage leaves on my breasts to help with the pain. I tried. It did no such thing.

As the days went by, one thing was proving certain: formula was working like a charm.

It not only satisfied our growing son's appetite, but it also allowed my husband to feed our baby throughout the days and nights. I had more time to take care of myself and recover. *Sue me.* And by the end of the first week, I had made the decision to feed him formula—exclusively.

Then, of course, the fear of uncertainty morphed into the fear of exposure and being labeled a "bad mom" who was selfish and putting her needs first. How could something that I really, really wanted to do and that felt critical to my ability to parent well . . . feel so wrong? How could I feel so certain and yet so uncertain at the same time?

My fear was telling me to seek answers from "experts." Like, when

I'm on a plane and there's severe turbulence, I don't take cues from the terrified passengers around me counting their prayer beads. I look directly at the flight attendants who've flown hundreds, maybe thousands, of times in recent years, and unless they're screaming and praying for dear life, I'm back to reviewing the in-flight menu and contemplating spending $8 on a tube of Pringles.

In times of uncertainty, as my friend and executive coach Stef Ziev says, avoid consulting with the naysayers taking up space in your head, also known as the "shitty committee." "Clean out any of the cobwebs in your mind," she told me on my podcast, "and fire some of the shitty committee that's not aligned with your true value and abundance."[8] Whether you're making decisions related to your career, health, relationships, or family, be careful with whom you consult. Everyone will have an opinion, but only a few will be invested in your well-being and/or have the proper expertise to provide you with the right guidance.

I decided that my committee would consist of Tim, our baby, and our pediatrician. Evan, we could tell, was a fan of formula. Tim? He was wonderfully supportive and never pressured me one way or the other. Then came our doctor. At Evan's first checkup, soon after we left the hospital, I was nervous to admit that I was contemplating going full steam ahead with formula. But surprisingly, the doctor didn't even blink when I told him what we'd been up to. Instead, he shared how a couple of his own children had also been raised on formula. "You do what's ideal for your family," he said. I asked him what brands he thought were best. I'd heard of the organic European baby formula that was illegal in the US but that some were smuggling in. "I like whatever is on sale," he replied, not even a little jokingly. At that moment, I knew we'd picked the right doctor.

It took me a beat, but after all of that, I realized a very important thing: I didn't have to breastfeed if I didn't want to. Why? **Because last I checked, I was a grown woman, and a mother at that.** If nothing else, the certainty about those two facts afforded me the right to choose my own path. Beyond all my fear of uncertainty about breast-feeding, I knew for sure that every mom is permitted to choose for herself and her family. And despite what the mommy industrial complex will say, I learned that sometimes choosing what's easy *is* best.

Fearing the uncertainty of the experience taught me something else we learn the hard way (if ever): **our needs matter.** Honor yourself and your instincts. You may be afraid to stand up for yourself lest you be seen as "hormonal," "dramatic," "unstable," or "histrionic." But staying silent in the face of uncertainty can be the beginning of something even scarier: the demise of your mental and emotional health. As the primary caregiver to a newborn child in those first few weeks and months, my self-care had never been more vital.

In moments like these, where the noise and haze of uncertainty takes over and you want to curl up in a ball, let the fear turn your focus on what *is* certain: your health, your needs, your happiness. When seemingly everyone has an opinion and thinks they know what's right for you, it can cloud your judgment. This is when your fear of uncertainty wants to remind you that *you* matter. Protect yourself. Take the time you need. Our fear of uncertainty might make us panic, freeze, or make impulsive moves. But listen to what this fear is trying to say: tune in to your instinct; trust yourself to know how to make your next move.

This isn't always easy. Mercii Thomas and I met on the one-year anniversary of the day she left the chains of a frighteningly uncertain life. It was the spring of 2021, and she was joining me on my podcast to talk about how she'd managed to escape her abuser. She and her ex-boyfriend had met through mutual friends shortly before the pandemic, and like many relationships, the beginning was full of faith and romance. But by the start of the COVID-19 lockdown in 2020, as they were living together in his apartment in Denver, Colorado (a new city where she had no relatives and a few loose acquaintances), Mercii said her boyfriend began to try to control her every move. She felt that he became emotionally, financially, and physically abusive. She had little to no access to her own money. He'd convinced her to quit her job because he said he could financially provide for both of them. She said she watched him shred her bank cards and cancel her Uber rides when she tried to leave the house on her own. "He tried to make it so I would have absolutely no means to get out," Mercii told me.[9]

She, of course, contemplated leaving many times over the course of the few months they were together in that apartment. But her fear of uncertainty, of not knowing what would be on the other side of her escape, that he might chase her down, cautioned her to wait until she'd created a true safety net, a secure route to leave—and never need to come back.

Calling the police, she felt, was not an option. As a Black woman, she feared that if she called the authorities on her partner, a successful Black man, she'd be seen as a villain rather than a victim. She was scared that the police—and the larger community—might not take her side. "Here I am, this Black woman that so easily can be discarded," she said. "I'm constantly confronted with this idea that I must endure. I must make exceptions . . . at the cost of my own safety and well-being," she told me.

As with so many survivors of abuse, her fear of uncertainty necessitated that she identify and reach out to only those who were certain to be helpful to her in a time of crisis. Believe it or not, social media became her most valuable resource and her channel to safety. She luckily still had access to her phone, and through Instagram, she began following the National Domestic Violence Hotline. She also connected with the Allstate Foundation's program for relationship abuse. She was able to safely connect with social workers and, ultimately, a friend with whom she would text using simple, innocuous emojis signaling if she was okay or if she was in real danger. "Having that community investment, having that external support . . . tangible resources, or just someone to say, 'I believe you.' That made a huge difference not just in my ability to leave, but to just completely separate myself from such an unhealthy situation," she said.

While Mercii's fear cautioned her to be strategic about her exit because it could mean life or death, she did not drag her feet—another important lesson. She acted with a sense of urgency and immediacy that was exclusive to this situation. Every hour, every day mattered, and she used her time effectively. Even on those days where she remained still and obedient to a ruthless man, she was working toward her goal of finding a solid landing strip where she could be safe. She told me it was frustrating because people still wondered why she didn't leave sooner. "You must trust . . . that survivors know what's best for them at the moment," she said. "Because even in our lived experience, we are doing what we can to survive."

We often have a solid instinct of how to form a plan that will help us regain balance and safety in uncertain situations. The trick is to learn what this fear is trying to tell you. Your fear is protecting you, keeping you on high alert, contemplating the what-ifs, and creating an escape plan. This is all part of the foundational work needed to make your next best move. Whether you're experiencing a dead-end relationship, tumult at work, or deep uncertainty in your personal life— trying to make a decision like going to college or not, getting married or not, having kids or not—**your fear is helping you lay the important groundwork for getting out of an uncertain mess.**

As your fear of uncertainty pushes you toward more certainty, it is not always requiring action from you. And although we may think throwing money at the problem can help, you can't always pay your way out of an uncertain time, either. Sometimes the fear is wanting you to be still and concoct a plan with your existing resources, which are often vaster and far richer than any amount of money. Our community, skills, patience, network, education, and past experiences can all prove useful when deciding how to move toward a more secure life. This fear keeps our head above water until we are ready to swim fast. It is telling us to pause and take inventory so we can identify to whom and what we can turn when trying to restore the serenity and empowerment we seek in life. You'll know it's time to make your big move when you start to feel what you've been missing—confidence and trust.

Once Mercii identified the right people who would have her back, and once she had a viable plan in place, she was ready to go. *Where* she immediately landed was not important. It just needed to be safer. Once there, she knew she could think more clearly, seek more help, and make a plan with staying power.

Bottom line: Your plan doesn't need to be perfect. It just needs to take you to a better place where you can begin to firmly rebuild.

CREATING CALM IN THE CHAOS

From a very young age, my mom taught me to clean up after myself. I was not yet in kindergarten when she demonstrated how to load the dishwasher. She thought she was equipping me with the sort of life skills that come in handy when you're living on your own—or I guess living with a partner who doesn't believe in sharing household responsibilities. Luckily Tim has never been *that* guy.

What she gave me was far richer. To me, tidying and organizing has become a coping mechanism, an emotional exercise that I can count on to provide some instant gratification and validation when there's chaos—physical and mental—all around me. Maybe it's silly, but to know that I can create a welcoming and harmonious space for myself—even as the world is anything but—helps me feel more focused, confident, and certain that things will be okay.

When the fear of uncertainty arrives and we're not going in the direction we want to, look for what you can control. Find the things in your life that are rock-solid and can't be derailed.

When her Montclair, New Jersey, bakery was deemed not "essential" during the first months of the 2020 lockdown, Rachel Wyman was forced to furlough 75 percent of her staff. She was familiar with this fear—of financial uncertainty—and it was telling her to lean on her past to help her ride out her current challenges. "When I started the bakery, I didn't have two pennies to rub together," she said.[10] "I had to make it work, or I wouldn't be able to pay my rent . . . to keep my family fed and safe."

What was rock-solid for Rachel was her experience as a resilient business owner and her tireless work ethic. "I got my hands dirty and worked side by side with my team." When they were unable to produce their normal volume of baked goods, Rachel shifted to selling grocery staples and other basics that, as a single mom of three kids, she guessed others were also in dire need of. "I started listening to my friends, and I knew what my family needed. Since food was scarce at grocery stores, and I didn't have any problem sourcing anything from my vendors for the bakery, I just started offering it to the customers here."

She and her team also created a new DIY donut kit and offered frozen raw cinnamon buns on the menu, since most customers were looking for ways to bake from home. "I don't know why it never occurred to me to make them before, but that was something that came from the quarantine that has endured," she said.

Back in 2009 when I got laid off, I disconnected from the outside world (read: stayed in bed) for a little while (I was in denial and embarrassed), but my fear of uncertainty kept me awake and the wheels in my head turning: *Farnoosh, what are you going to do?* The fear taught me what I know today: remember who you are, your ambitions, your gifts, and what you're capable of. These are the unshakeable truths that will propel you to greatness in uncertain times.

This fear gave me the kick in the pajamas I needed to take inventory of all of that: I was a woman who could demystify the world of money. That wasn't a small thing. I had many sources and relationships in the media. I wasn't afraid of hard work. I knew how to write. I knew how to talk in quippy soundbites on TV. I knew how to operate a camera. I was also very good at things like facing rejection and being alone. So, that summer, I started my own media business out of my studio apartment. I leveraged what I could. I created my own order in the disorder, as opposed to waiting for someone to hire me and provide me with the stability I craved. Really, that pink slip, while it took away my title and salary, also highlighted all the things it couldn't take from me. And those certainties were my ticket to venture out on my own.

The Fear of Uncertainty Self-Inquiry

- What is the uncertainty I'm actually afraid of?
- What's something I can do to healthily regain empowerment?
- Am I running too fast with this fear? Maybe I need to slow it down or find a temporary solace to hatch a long-term plan with certainty.
- Who can I trust to help lift me out of this uncertain time?
- Am I paying enough attention to my instincts?
- I can't control everything, but what is within my ability, network, and know-how to do, create, and provide for myself?

6

THE FEAR OF MONEY

and how it encourages landing on your (true) money story and pursuing financial independence

SUSPECT WHAT YOU MIGHT be thinking. "*I thought this book was about money. Why is she only now getting deep into it?*"

The truth is that the fear of money is super complex and, in many instances, rooted in the fears we just explored. As I wrote in the introduction, when we're talking about money, we're talking about life. At its core, the fear of money is intimately tied to all of our other dreads. But don't be mistaken. This fear has its own look, feel, and even sound.

For me, that sound is either dead silence or fists banging on a laminate kitchen countertop. Unsurprisingly, the money fears we carry into our adult life emerge from our earliest experiences with it—namely how our parents, caregivers, or loved ones dealt with money when we were growing up. I first learned about money by watching Sheida and Farrokh. Their challenges usually orbited around it—Mom lacking it and Dad controlling it—which they seldom addressed without explosive arguments followed by an awkward silent treatment that stretched for weeks.

I remember being home during spring break in college, peeling an orange at our dining table and watching my mom clean off some dishes, when she turned to me in tears, explaining that she was having a hard time with my dad—again.

By now, after more than two decades of marriage, there had been some reckoning, mainly driven by my mother's insistence on becoming more financially independent. After completing her college degree and working salaried jobs here and there, she had managed to gain some economic power in their relationship. She had her own savings account and a retirement fund. She was contributing to a few household expenses. Most dignifying of all, she didn't have to ask my dad for money to get her roots done.

But my father still managed the bulk of their finances and didn't involve Mom in matters related to their shared investments, the mortgage, or his own expenses. She wanted password access to review their accounts and get a sense of where their finances stood, but he pushed back, saying it wasn't necessary. They were doing "fine," and that's all she needed to know. He said if she had questions, she could ask him, and he would provide answers. Giving her the log-ins, to my dad, seemed like an overstep. Was it tied to gender role expectations and protecting his Iranian male ego? One can only guess.

My mother had a scarier sense of what might be going on; she suspected his need to assume more financial power in the relationship meant that he must be hiding something from her. Was he making wild investments? Were we in more debt than she knew? Why else would he be so resistant to showing her their accounts? This tension around their finances left her feeling anxious and afraid of being financially vulnerable. Rightfully so. "What if something happens to him?" she asked me. "Farnoosh, can you get him to understand?"

Serving as a conduit between my parents over a deeply personal matter was nothing new for me. My mother was smart to assign me as the chief communication officer in the house when she was fearfully at odds with my dad. He had a much harder time saying no to me, especially over a topic like financial independence. To me, my father always stressed the importance of being thoughtful with money. He'd helped me open my first bank account in high school. He insisted I save half of my paycheck when I got my first serving job at sixteen, and he refused to allow me to take out loans for college, for fear that I'd enter adulthood in financial ruin. (What a blessing that was.) He was the man who taught me about credit scores, 401(k)s, and the importance of asking for a raise. Why then did he act so differently toward his wife?

My fear over their lack of financial transparency and how it might compromise my mother's life sprang me to action. When I spoke to my father later that same afternoon, I laid out his contradictions with how he treated me versus Mom.

He stayed mostly silent, nodding once or twice. Was I a little afraid of how my dad would react? Of course. Was my fear initially telling me to dodge my mom and pretend I had to go, uhh, meet up with a friend? Start pleading with her to just leave me out of it? I considered all of those things. But the image of my mother being left in the dark shook me to the core. The fear of her scrambling to learn about their household finances in a crisis was far more haunting than facing my dad's furrowed brows when asking him why he was acting so strange. The visceral nature of that financial fear compelled me to protect my mom and take a hard but important step right then and there.

That night, following dinner, Dad printed out all the passwords to their accounts and handed them to my mom. I'd like to think it was simply because he saw the hypocrisy. But it probably didn't hurt that he was outnumbered by the Iranian women in the house. Either way, this was a real victory—for all of us.

My mother's financial fears had enveloped me that day—in a healthy way. It's because I took the fear to the edge and saw the ugly, messy disaster that could unfold in a marriage where only one person knows where the money is—and how to access it. I saw the fear in *her* eyes, and it prompted me to wedge my way into my parents' money life. This is one of the most awkward, hardest things a kid may have to do, no matter how mature they've become. But the fear became a clear signal of what I needed to protect: my mother's security. And I wasn't just aiding my mom. My dad, whether he trusted it or not, would benefit from more openness. If he fell sick, my mom (and I) could help manage the money and protect the assets. In his absence, our family wouldn't be overtaken by financial confusion and stress. And, maybe most important of all, he'd forge a deeper connection with his wife.

The experience that day, while somewhat excruciating, also taught me that fear can push you to express love in courageous ways. And in the end, love is *greater* than fear. When a family member was grasping for their financial livelihood, as my mom was, I faced my fears and saw that they were motioning me to help. When she asked with tears in her eyes if I could intervene, I did. My own trepidations diminished. *I got this*, I realized. And in that moment, I no longer felt fear. I felt purpose-driven, brave.

Witnessing my parents' financial fears had another upside: lessons on how to be a financial advocate—for myself and others. For one, I learned that money can elicit a tug-of-war in marriage and any relationship, and early on I decided I would never lose my financial power in a partnership. I'd rather stay single than be dependent on another person to support my financial needs or feel it necessary to hide my (copious) shopping bags from them after a Target run.

Watching my mom navigate corporate America, I saw how unfair the system can be toward women and minority workers. When she asked for a raise in the early 1990s, the response wasn't just "no," it was "goodbye." She was promptly fired.

The fear of job fragility came from watching my father, too. At our family dinners, many of the conversations were about belt-tightening due to possible layoffs at his tech company. With so much consolidation in the sector, the threat of losing his engineering role was an almost annual affair. As a little girl, I remember hearing Dad talk about the option to take the "package" at work. I hoped he would, because it sounded like a present. And maybe there'd be a gift in it for me.

After all this, it's no accident I built my career in personal finance. For good and bad, money was never a taboo topic in my household. Being open about money and its related fears was a homegrown lesson I took with me into adulthood.

Whoever preaches that money can't buy happiness probably has a lot of it. Or doesn't know what it's like to suffer through life paycheck to paycheck or below the poverty line. I believe that more money affords us more control and choices in life. And isn't that a nice feeling? But you don't need to take it from me. Scientists say it's conclusive that having at least a certain level of money is inextricably linked to happiness. And a recent study out of the University of Pennsylvania finds that there is no dollar value at which money stops affecting our well-being.[1]

At first, we may think that the right response to financial fear is avoidance, to look away from our numbers. But when this fear emerges, and whether it's tied to the threat of a recession, job loss, or disagreements over money with a loved one, it may well be there to help us protect our livelihood, our independence, and, I'll say it, our happiness. The fear of money can be a surprising ally.

But what is money . . . *really?*

IT'S JUST MONEY . . . SO WHAT'S YOUR STORY?

Money is not a state of mind like some of the other fears we explore in this book. It is just a *thing*, a soulless, mindless, and unmotivated thing. It is motionless and seemingly inconsequential. Before crypto, digital, and even paper currency, we had coins. Before that, it was shells. It's a tool like any other. "Money is a hammer," said Christina Blacken, founder of The New Quo, a leadership and equity consultancy.[2] "You can use it to murder someone," she continued, "or use it to build a birdhouse."

It's only when we engage with money that it becomes this activated tool and takes form, shape, and influence. And so, to say we are afraid of *money*, I've come to learn from Christina and through my many years in this field, is to say that **we are afraid of what our relationship with this tool represents**. There may well be a frightful story there. But is it true?

Christina joined me on my podcast to talk about narrative intelligence, a method she teaches clients who want to rewrite their limiting beliefs and biases blocking their full potential. Her work reinforces so much of what I've learned in my time in this field. Similar to our fear of loneliness, when we're afraid of *money*, we're often afraid of the stories we tell ourselves about money, and what those stories expose about us.

Many of us hold on to conflicting ideas of what money represents, and whether you have it or don't, this can feel like a lose-lose situation. We're afraid that if we don't "have enough," we'll be lonely. But then, if we're "rich," we fear we will become less likeable, and that can also lead to loneliness. Being in debt means you're behind in life. And, wait, we can't possibly be better off than our parents because that would make them feel uncomfortable. It's a vicious cycle of stories. We don't like them, but we've stuck with them because they've been ingrained in us over the years. So many of our theories about money are based on our upbringing and the influences we've had. If we fear money, it may also be because of cultural stereotypes that we've bought into that say money equals greed or is the "root of all evil."

Then there's the idea that net worth equals self-worth, which, according to Christina, is a massive story (or myth) that has snuck its way into the subconscious. We associate having more money with having more success and admiration. "There's a lot of assumption that if you're wealthy, you're inherently smarter, harder working, and more trustworthy. And if you don't have a lot of income, you're lazy. You're not smart, you're a degenerate. And that's just factually untrue. We have data to prove that that is not true at all," she told me.

Christina's interest in narrative intelligence stems from overcoming cultural fallacies and biases, including her own money story. She is a Black, liberal woman and descendant of enslavement ancestry. She was raised in a working-class family in Utah, in a largely Mormon community where she didn't see many people who looked like her, let alone shared the same values. When she thought of money, she thought of its limitations and the struggle to live paycheck to paycheck, given her family's struggle, real-world barriers, and assumptions about money. Her story did little to inspire her to think and act more expansively. The thought of investing, for example, was frightful because it was foreign.

"My family had a lot of stories around survival and community, and depending on each other, and a bit of distrust through the communities that we were part of because there was a lot of racism, there was a lot of turmoil that they experienced and I personally experienced, but because of that, my family was always sort of working poor. So, they worked very hard," she said. Her parents had stable jobs, but they weren't wealthy, and Christina remembers her first money narratives centered around the importance of just keeping your financial head above water, paying your bills, and keeping debt to a minimum. "It had really nothing to do with understanding the financial system or understanding how wealth is built or even understanding how to not live paycheck to paycheck," she said.[3]

Like all tales, our money stories can be rewritten. The first step toward taking control of this fear is to understand the inaccuracies you may be carrying around, which Christina says we often don't realize are embedded in our conscience. If we break these down, we can see how they may be tied to something much deeper and possibly bigger than money. Jot down your money beliefs on a piece of paper and then probe at each one with research and your life experiences. Begin by asking why. Why do you believe this? How did you learn this? Do you think this is true? "You'd be surprised by the number of things that you can challenge," said Christina.

In her own life, Christina revised her money narrative when she moved to New York City and started building her own company. She began to see money as a tool for the change she wanted to see personally and for her community. She wanted to use money to right some of the wrongs in the systems that breed racism and sexism. Her "why" in her story became wanting to use money as a leveraging tool for shifting power, she told me. To that end, she strives to earn more so that she can pay her employees as much as possible and invest in strategies and ideas that change systemic issues.

"I do care about using my money," she said, "to expand my message, to invest in other people's labor . . . to think about the policies and practices around me and how I can bolster their messages."

For me, if there's one scary financial story I wish I'd crumpled into a ball earlier in life, it is that becoming a wealthy woman will come at a great cost. I was that person who thought it would mean losing out on love and meaningful relationships. When you're busy making money, who has time for anything else? This was the story I told myself. For the longest time I equated making more money and being extremely ambitious—particularly as a woman who also wanted to have a family—as a zero-sum game. You can't have both at the same time.

What you gain as a financially powerful woman you will lose in your life as a wife, a mother, and a friend. This is what I believed because I didn't have any role models growing up to disprove this. I believed it even after writing my book *When She Makes More*, which is all about how to thrive as a breadwinner in your relationship. I still had limiting beliefs about how much wealth is *too* much wealth (for me). This mindset left me afraid to pursue bigger paydays. Instead, I wish I had thought, *Farnoosh, there is no shame and no penalty in wanting to be richer than you are.*

My story is funny: while I was raised with a narrative that the key to success was to study hard and rise up in my career—my father provided scripts for how to declare my worth in job interviews, and I was encouraged to ask for raises—cultural and family tradition also dictated that I "settle down" at some point, dutifully deprioritizing my career and dedicating more time and effort to raising a family.

Even a close relative, who had arguably the highest expectations for me and was considered the "rebel" in our Iranian family because she married a man for "love" and not status, power, or money (can you imagine?), once pulled me aside at a Thanksgiving dinner in the early 2000s, when I was in grad school, to give me what she probably thought was the ultimate compliment: "You're going to do big things, Farnoosh. I can see you one day marrying a senator."

Being a wife who was powerful and held in high regard merely by association was, in her view, as good as it could get for a woman. Despite being pushed to "succeed," the money message I received was clear: If you *can* somehow get to the top of your career and make a lot of money and raise a family . . . good luck! You'll need it.

The day I detached from this fear—and rewrote my story—came not long after having my first kid. I was on my bed one afternoon with the door closed so I wouldn't wake up Evan asleep in the other room. I'd scheduled Barbara Huson, a wealth coach for female entrepreneurs, for a podcast interview. At this point I was the family breadwinner and had written about it. I was adamant about helping more women reach their fullest financial potential. I was proud that I had taken a chance on starting my own business and had managed to grow income every year since. I had afforded a life of many conveniences and privileges. We had a full-time caregiver, owned our own apartment in Brooklyn, my podcast was taking off—I felt like I'd reached "enough" in so far as I could pay for our household needs and more, including donating to causes and nice vacations. I was grateful for the fact that I had managed—of course, with some real luck—to do the thing that many had doubted: be a high-earning woman with a business *and* a thriving family. But I was also afraid of pushing that luck, afraid of wanting more, thinking bigger, and earning, dare I say, double or triple what I currently made. No way. I could almost hear a Persian auntie in the background saying, "*Beesheen sar-eh jawt!*" That's Farsi for "Sit back down and in your place!" I was afraid of being too ambitious for my own good.

That afternoon, Barbara said something to me that really challenged my story, and to this day, I credit her for convincing me that I could (and should) strive for more.

First, some background on the singular Barbara: She is a leading authority on women, wealth, and power. She has written several books. My favorite is *Prince Charming Isn't Coming*. And interesting fact: She is the daughter of the "R" in H&R Block. Despite a wealthy upbringing, she admittedly made several financial errors throughout her life, and her fear of again being financially reckless led her to allow her husband— who she thought was a compulsive gambler—to manage her inheritance. Despite believing he had an addiction, she continued to give him the financial reins in their marriage. This arrangement became a major problem for her. In the wake of their divorce, she said she received surprising tax bills for over $1 million. Her dad refused to bail her out. She was a single mom to three daughters at the time—and flat broke.

"I signed whatever he told me to sign because that's . . . how ignorant, how terrified I was by anything to do with money," Barbara told me.[4]

All this to say that Barbara is now a pro at detecting financial fears in other women. And in our conversation, when the topic turned to my career and my belief that I'd reached the pinnacle of "enoughness," she shot back with that simple question: "Why?" I gave her all my previously stated reasons. She challenged them one after the other. My money fears, she concluded, were rooted in the antiquated, patriarchal way I'd been raised.

The first step to reversing the script on this fear was to disinherit that narrative. Barbara's own falsehoods around money stemmed from being told as a kid to never talk about money, so she recognized immediately how my upbringing created a mythical fear around money and a limiting ideal around "enoughness." These stories were preventing me from having a healthier relationship with the idea of building wealth. I had assumed that being able to comfortably support my family was as pioneering as I could get. *Or, as I should get.*

Barbara reminded me that more money means more power. Not the sort of gross, morally hazardous power I'd been associating with this word. She didn't mean the power to conquer, take over, or be controlling, but the power to positively influence, support, and make an impact. Ah, right. The other use cases. Had I ever thought about the beautiful connection between money and power and why this might appeal to me? The short answer was: no. I was narrow-minded and, to be honest, hadn't developed a strong enough "why" for setting my sights on more money. This, she said, was another big step in working with this fear.

The truth was, I did want to be more philanthropic. I did want to leave a bigger financial legacy for my kids and community. I did want to create more financial security for myself, so that if I wanted to take a year off work for any reason, I could afford it. Now that I knew my why and the amazing power (yes, power!) more money could create, I was more intent on taking action.

And if I was afraid that making more money would mean sacrificing time with my family—as my culture had alluded to—I needed to challenge that notion, as well. Making more doesn't always mean working harder, Barbara said. "Farnoosh, how can you work smarter?" she asked. I thought about it and came up with a plan that, initially, entailed some investments. The most impactful was hiring a full-time assistant (the one and only Sophia!) who was a whiz at running my day-to-day operations like podcast ads, fact-checking my work, and securing media opportunities, which then freed up my time to be more financially strategic. I was able to create bigger client partnerships and workshops. I also raised my speaking fees (on a hunch that I was underpaid, and it worked—try it!).

This new money story of mine, that I could be richer without the risk of backlash, allowed me to go after bigger paydays with confidence and enthusiasm. In two years' time, I had doubled my income and crossed the million-dollar threshold.

And now I want to tell everyone, especially women who have felt further marginalized by their race or economics, who feel frightened by how making more money might be a costly burden: Be less afraid of money and more afraid of your *attitude* toward it. Be afraid of how you're interpreting your relationship with it and that your story has gone unexamined. **Let me be the evidence that you do deserve to be rich. It is your birthright.**

I wish I could meet the person who wrote this disturbing financial confession in *New York* magazine during the pandemic and tell her just that.[5] It was penned by a twentysomething tech worker who cashed out $6 million in her company's IPO. I'd be smiling all the way to the bank if it were me, but her fear of money was intricately bound with her fear of rejection and loneliness.

She explained in the confession that she was beside herself with stress and worry about her newfound wealth. She was afraid that being seen as "rich" might alienate her. And that maybe she was unworthy or undeserving of having wealth. She was scared about her "place" in the world and whether having more money would mean she would become someone unapproachable or unlikeable. "You don't know how your friends are going to look at you," she wrote. "'So don't talk about it with them,' my dad said. 'Don't talk about it with these relatives or your siblings; you don't want them to feel insecure.' My mom has gotten bitter. She said, 'You're going to have more money than your dad and I combined, and we've worked all our lives.'"

I would like to tell this woman to stop letting this fear spew lies about who she is and force her to feel small. Instead, I would tell her to assume that fear wants her to ask herself, *Why is it fair to think that I'm not worthy of this money? What if I don't allow myself to receive wealth? What is the impact I won't be able to make because I'm denying myself the chance to be more financially well off?* I would tell her that she has somehow adopted this convoluted money fear and has every right to drop it. The fact is, I would assure her, with more money you can make a greater difference in your life, your community, and beyond. Will she lose a few friends and alienate people in the process? Based on her family's reaction, maybe. But I believe that has more to do with *their* money story. Not hers.

ARE YOU AFRAID OF MONEY . . . IN THE *RIGHT* WAYS?

Some financial fears are worthier of our time. The best carry with them an individualized message and a healthy dose of urgency to encourage us to understand the stakes and commit to a plan toward more security for ourselves and loved ones.

For example, fretting over a someday recession, or the "R" word as the media likes to say, doesn't offer much in the way of personal guidance. Neither does fearing the general cost of climate change. Or whether another bank might collapse at some point. These fearful what-ifs do, of course, carry grave risks, but, held in the abstract and with no sense of timing or connection back to our personal reality, they only stress us out. *What if, what if, what if . . .*

A healthier way to process a fear like that is to bring it to your doorstep, introduce it to your personal life with immediacy, and answer this question: What are you afraid will happen to your financial security . . . specifically and now? Whether we're talking about a market collapse, a flash flood, or a failing bank, what would that signify for you and your financial goals, savings, investments, or debt in this moment? In many instances, it's more helpful to focus less on *what if someday* and more on *what if* **now**?

So, back to that recession fear. As we read headlines about layoffs, anxiety brews. To best leverage this fear, though, consider a reframe: What if I lose my job *tomorrow*? (It probably won't happen, but let's imagine.) What would you immediately do? Examining the fear in this way might prompt you to, at the very least, research your state's unemployment benefits and how to secure health insurance so you're prepared if and when the day arrives. It would make you more curious to tally up your savings and calculate how long they'd stretch. It might finally convince you to refresh your LinkedIn page. It will spur you to gather the facts and face your financial reality, armed with a plan.

With climate change, there are many frightful question marks surrounding our warming planet. But if you want this fear to spark action in you, bring it to your neighborhood and home. For me, the fear of a hurricane flooding my basement is legit, as I've seen our town experience the wreckage in recent years. I've been thinking about it more: What if the next season's storm devastates our house? This more specific fear led me to promptly review our area's flood zones, and while it appears we're somewhat "safe" for now, I'm convinced it's wise for us to invest in flood insurance sooner than later (something I didn't even know you could get if you're not in a technical flood zone!).

And although we've seen banks go under, we can't control the timing of the next failure or which bank gets hit. Instead, fear this hypothetical thought: What if *your* bank runs out of money tomorrow? Is your money safe? What's a step you can take now—in lieu of cashing out all your funds from the nearest ATM—to properly address this fear? I'd probably do a quick internet search to see whether my bank is FDIC insured (look for the seal that's usually at the bottom of a bank's website). Let this fear prompt you to read the fine print, understand the consumer protections in place, and, if need be, transfer some or all of your money to a safer institution today.

I had an early lesson in how certain money fears are more instrumental in fortifying your financial life than others. It was one morning, sophomore year in college, when my credit union balance read *negative* $130 (and 33 cents) on my computer screen. How could this be? A possible cyberattack? A delay in my checks being processed? Whose account *was* this?

At the time I was holding down three jobs and, by all accounts, as a twenty-year-old student, I was raking in the dough.

My commissions as an advertising account rep at our college newspaper were upward of $200 to $300 per week. As a part-time server at the downtown Italian joint I earned another $100 to $200 in weekly tips, and as a professional notetaker I banked $40 for each set of typed-up notes from my accounting class. (Never mind that I almost failed the final.)

I was afraid that if I didn't make enough money, at least a couple thousand dollars by the end of the semester, I'd fail to convince my parents I could afford studying abroad the following year. Earning more, I thought, meant having more independence, a license to do what I pleased.

But for some reason, all my hustle and determination had equated to nothing more than a barren, broken bank account.

The fear of realizing I had absolutely no money could've drowned me. It might have inspired more financial self-sabotage. I was already in the hole. What's so bad about spending another $500 that I didn't have?

Instead, because I'm so well groomed in the art of panicking, I used the adrenaline to make a plea for help. I picked up the phone to call (and beg) my bank. (You thought I was going to say Sheida? Please, the fear of money is enough. I didn't want the fear of God, too.)

My negative balance, as it turns out, was the result of multiple $30 overdraft fees all in a forty-eight-hour period. This was before the days of being able to opt out of overdraft protection, so each time I'd gone to swipe in recent days—at the general store, at dinner, at the shoe store—the transaction would clear, even though I didn't have enough (or any) money to cover the cost. The bank was doing me a "favor" by not declining my card at the point of purchase, avoiding a possible embarrassment after spending thirty minutes trying on sneakers and getting the saleslady's hopes up about a commission. My fear led me to confess my error to the bank and insist this was an honest mistake. After reviewing my account, they said they'd only charge one overdraft fee—not five—and that instantly brought my balance back into the black.

I felt triumphant, but the fear of this happening once more stuck around. Would I be so lucky the next time? How to prevent another shortfall? I recognized that I'd been so exclusively afraid of not earning enough that I'd lost sight of something more cautionary: living beyond my means. It was a loud call to create a plan for my money, track my spending, and save automatically.

The fear to make more money is a recurrent one, especially as the cost of living escalates at a rate well beyond our annual raises. While this fear can spark some creativity and encourage us to find new ways to earn, it might only get us so far. Ultimately, it can, like it did for me, lead us into the throes of "hustle" culture where we spin our wheels to accumulate cash. And all the while we forget to be as insistent upon protecting our money by saving, investing, and spending carefully.

That fearful moment in the summer of 2000 taught me this. We sometimes think that once we make more money, all our problems will go away. Except we know what happens to lottery winners, right? And young athletes who come into great wealth? Many times, despite the windfall, they end up squandering their earnings.

I'm all for getting more money into all our hands. We should all be millionaires, as my friend and entrepreneur Rachel Rodgers preaches. But let's not downplay the serious threat that comes with failing to assign a viable and deeply personal plan to our money so that every spend feels like it's going in the right direction. That fear, in my opinion, often produces a higher yield.

THE GIFT IN FEARING THE FINANCIAL *WORST*

Researchers have found the thought of losing money to be naturally associated in the brain with fear and pain.[6] And this, while it may seem cruel to say, can be powerfully beneficial in real life. Why? Because when we feel pain, we want nothing more than a real, lasting cure.

It's a healthy practice to really let yourself face your very worst money-related fear. Don't just throw out the expression "What's the worst that can happen?" if you don't mean it. Look into it: What Is the Worst That Can Happen? See it. Feel it.

Remember that audience member from the intro who wondered if it was okay to quit his lucrative job in tech to start a hair salon? He was afraid of whether he could make ends meet as an entrepreneur. But when we chatted, I learned that he also suffered from a fear of rejection. He was afraid he'd disappoint his Chinese immigrant parents, who loved telling relatives back in Beijing that he worked for the one and only Google. He felt indebted to his parents, who had sacrificed so much to put him through college and raised him to be financially independent. He feared losing their pride and not living up to their expectations. As I listened, I heard how he was afraid this career pivot would potentially derail not just his bank account, but his most important relationships.

To which I said: "There's a worst-case scenario you're not considering. You can make a smart decision here, but you need to consider: What's more painful? Disappointing your mother or *yourself*? Regret of not taking a chance on a thoughtful plan and pursuing something that brings you more joy?" **This is not a rhetorical question. You matter. Take this fear to heart and understand the risks that come with never trying at all.** Not surprisingly, this was the more painful fear and it led him to move toward opening the salon. And as he did, I wanted to remind him that while his parents may not support him at first, their disappointment speaks more to *their* fears. Who knows? He might be able to inspire them to expand their thinking. I assure you, stranger things have happened.

Across the country, a new mom wrote to me, contemplating quitting her career to become a stay-at-home parent. She was afraid of trusting a part-time caregiver or the daycare down the road and worried how a full-time career might compromise her ability to be present as a mom. Not to mention, she was afraid that the cost of childcare would stretch the family budget too thin. She told me that her partner was happy to take on the role of sole financial provider. This gave her some reassurance to quit. But she was still torn. She explained her fears of giving up her income and profession—after working so hard to arrive where she was—and how it might impact her independence and options down the road. She was full of apprehension and doubt. I assured her that what she was fearing was spot-on. She should give these money fears some real space. She would benefit from letting this fear drive her to have a conversation with her husband and understand what her fears might be communicating about her security and livelihood. What scared her more—not spending as much time as she imagined with her child or not having a career that might provide more financial independence for her and her family?

This particular financial fear of being unable to simultaneously pursue a career or job and parent successfully—especially the terrifying math of how expensive childcare can be—has the tendency to convince moms they should abandon the workforce to be the primary and full-time caregiver. The fear can lead us to only see dead ends. Moms don't see a path where they can prioritize their financial well-being and be the actively engaged parents they want to be. But to this listener and all frightened new moms and moms-to-be hoping to use their fears in a constructive way, I say this: Go to the edge. You're afraid right now of the present day and the beginning weeks and months of being a new parent. But let's examine a far scarier scenario. What if you get divorced and risk becoming a single parent who, because she didn't earn money during the marriage, has no savings to pay for legal fees and her own expenses? What if you become a widow, and there's not enough money in the bank to support your family? What if you simply decide, five years from now, that you want to reclaim your professional life. How will you be able to find a new job as a parent who's been out of the workforce for several years?

Give this fear the depth and respect it deserves. From that vantage point, you can discover a secure strategy forward. Before this new mom took a leave of absence, I suggested that she protect her financial autonomy by securing her own savings, and we developed a plan for her to ramp back into the workforce within a couple of years.

For Katie Gatti, a twenty-eight-year-old financial podcaster and money expert, the fear of not being able to pay for an unexpectedly serious expense was her worst-case scenario. "I think what grounds me is fear, to be honest," she told me on my podcast. "Here in the US, you're one major medical emergency away from potentially bankrupting yourself. That's terrifying. When you're aware of how precarious things can become . . . that is a grounding force for me."[7]

In the beginning, though, this money fear made Katie painfully frugal. She hadn't yet done the groundwork we discussed earlier of finding out why she was afraid and what was at the root of her personal money story. Her unanalyzed fear led her to an "overcorrection," she said, where she avoided restaurants, lived with multiple roommates to reduce her housing expenses, and skimped on groceries. Envisioning a worst-case fear could only be so constructive, because she hadn't reconciled a problematic narrative that said the only way to be financially secure was to hastily save, save, save. She assumed that if she tried to earn more money, she would have to struggle. It was only when she started to step into a more creative field of podcasting and financial content work for her business Money with Katie that the money arrived abundantly and relatively easily. She then began to see how when you enjoy what you do, you have a higher potential for earning. It doesn't have to be grueling. Katie still feared the worst, but now, with a rewritten money story, she was able to live a more financially fulfilling life, one that didn't deprive her of living comfortably.

She and her husband admittedly spend less than 20 percent of what they collectively earn—but the difference is they're earning far more than they need in Colorado. Rather than hoard cash, they're investing a great deal in the stock market and in retirement accounts. Katie admits that her approach is more aggressive than most people's, but it's one that gives her comfort, security, and confidence.

In understanding our worst money fears, we're more willing to see and accept the holes in our financial lives. I saw this time and again when serving as host and money coach on the TV show *Bank of Mom and Dad*. Our guests feared the shame connected to seeing their delinquent credit card bills. The fear drove them to shove statements in junk drawers, all while their financial stresses mounted. Any relief they experienced by avoiding their bills would, at best, be temporary. So my idea was to take a stroll into the future with them, where they'd see how, with no changes, they'd land in a far deeper hole. What's more frightening? Facing your bills today? Or denying your numbers and ultimately denying yourself the goals you hope to reach? You may wonder, *Is it too late to release myself from this abyss and get back on my feet?* It's not, but I hope it doesn't take getting this far down to want to. By predicting it, facing the depth of how rough this can get, the fear can lead to a critical change. You might decide to seek help, negotiate with your creditors, or pare down your expenses.

I once urged a millionaire entrepreneur on my podcast to shift her attention to a more serious financial fear than the one she confessed on the show to having. Her fear, she said, was that she'd blow all her money. She described how the trauma of growing up poor never went away. To manage the fear, she handed the financial reins entirely to her husband and chose to keep her head in the sand. She didn't even know the log-in to her bank account. She didn't *want* to know. This, she thought, would make her relationship with money *easier*. Her words, not mine.

But all I could see was danger ahead. I ought to mention that this woman had figured out how to start a business with virtually no cash and raise seven figures from clients in a single year. How is this the same person who feels incapable of looking at bank statements? My concern was that she was letting a fear that was rooted in her past derail her future. Her reaction to this fear wasn't just unhelpful. It was potentially catastrophic.

I attempted to paint the scarier picture: What if her husband was unable to manage the money for any reason? How would the bills get paid? What if she experienced an emergency and needed money quickly and her husband was unavailable? What if he suddenly passed away? What if he picked up and left? What if he's secretly mismanaging the money?

I pleaded with her, letting her know that she had not just the right but the responsibility to know how her hard-earned money was getting spent. You're not financially free otherwise.

We didn't keep in touch after that podcast, but a few years later, I learned that she and her husband eventually divorced, and she had since started a new business, hopefully carrying with her some lessons from her previous relationship (with him and with money).

Years after that interview, Queen Latifah joined me on *So Money* and confirmed the dangers of turning your back against your finances and entrusting your money entirely to someone else. She shared details of growing up with a single mom in Newark, New Jersey. I learned how she had paved the way for so many women artists and was determined to pursue her passion and carve out a career in music, as well as in film and production. But she hadn't had a healthy fear that her hard-earned money could disappear in the hands of a professional. And in the early days of her career, she experienced the financial worst: an advisor running amuck with her money.

"I went to meet with them . . . there was no money in the bank. . . . All of these checks had been written out to this and that and . . . they were signing these things and I had no money," she recalled.[8]

The experience made her reassess her own relationship with money and delivered that reasonable fear of what could happen if she got too lax again about her finances. It drove her to hire a more trustworthy team through referrals and become more personally involved in her books. The fear would put her in a much more financially secure place.

"I've taken bumps and bruises through the years, trying to manage things and learning [about money]. I had to sign all my own checks and not leave things in other people's hands, because they get away from you. You realize that you're working, but you're not watching where everything is going, and it keeps it away from you. You just got to pay attention to it," she said.

Queen's story reinforces why it's so helpful to map out these terrifying possibilities in advance. At the beginning of the pandemic, when

Tim and I moved our family out of Brooklyn, the home we bought cost us a little more than we'd planned to spend, but in that moment of crisis, we were willing to pay a premium to buy ourselves a swift, clean exit from the tumult of living at the epicenter of COVID-19.

We were privileged to be able to afford the move, but during those first few weeks in the new house, I'll be honest, I was financially stressed. I'd lie awake in bed, worried about our job security, our savings, and our investments. It was the spring of 2020, and with so much uncertainty hovering over every aspect of the global economy, I crafted a worst-case scenario for our finances: What if our investments snapped in half? It was possible. A little more than a decade earlier, during a financial recession, investors had seen their portfolios drop by 40 to 50 percent. Back then I wasn't afraid of those red arrows in my retirement plan. With thirty-five or more years until retirement, I was confident my portfolio would bounce back and land where I could comfortably retire. But now, what if I woke up one day and realized that with just twenty or so years left until retirement, I could lose ten or fifteen years' worth of compounding growth? Would I ever be able to retire in my sixties? Would we be forced to sell our house? The thoughts kept me awake for hours in bed.

I carried around that fear for weeks, stuck over what to do. But when I expanded on all the terrible, awful things that could happen, I got clearer on what it was I wanted to protect—my long-term financial security and mental well-being—and the fear left me with no other choice than to do something about it. It drove me to a decision that I'm extremely proud of in hindsight, though at the time I was a little embarrassed to admit: I scaled back my exposure in the stock market. I wrote about it for *Bloomberg* in a piece called "Why I Caved and Altered My Investment Portfolio."[9] I explained my rationale, driven largely by my fear of worst-case what-ifs: "I'm concerned about the fundamentals of our economy," I wrote. "I'm worried about if and how the job market can rebound anytime soon, and I'm not as bullish on long-term stock returns. Continuously exposing my nest egg to all this risk now feels overzealous. Although the stock market appears to suggest we're headed for a robust recovery (cocktails in hand, no masks required), I'm not buying it. Literally."

To be clear, this was not me impulsively ditching stocks. But after some key considerations, I ultimately decided to risk less in the stock market. I turned forty that year and was aiming to tap the portfolio starting at sixty. With another twenty solid years before needing to draw down on those savings, I knew I had enough time to ride out the downturns. But my appetite for financial adventure was lower because I was my family's breadwinner and our house in the suburbs was a giant addition to an already full plate of financial responsibilities. Plus, I'd opened up this investment account in my late twenties, when I was in a much different place in life with more years ahead to "ride the wave," and hadn't adjusted it for risk since. "I don't have as much room now for a highly unpredictable, volatile investment portfolio," I concluded.

But I was nervous. I felt like I was abandoning the standard professional advice to "stay the course" and "do nothing." Still, I knew it was the right move for me because my sleep returned. And to reconcile the need to feel "safe" with my desire to still have as robust a retirement nest egg as before, I committed to investing more each month into my new, scaled-back portfolio. This way, even though my smaller position in stocks would potentially mean slower growth, I would be able to work toward building a similarly sized balance by retirement. While I couldn't control the stock market, I could control how much to contribute.

When it comes to investing, there's plenty to be afraid of. The threat of losing money in a market where you have absolutely no control is enough to prevent some of us from ever contributing to a 401(k). Or we feel the immediate need to sell when stocks drop. The key to using fear more constructively in these moments is to first reflect on the *intent* of your fear. What goal is your fear asking you to protect? And in a worst-case scenario, how might your goal become compromised . . . or not? Would it mean retiring comfortably or waking up in our older age needing to ask our children for money? Are you okay to roll with the punches or do you want to make some adjustments to your finances now to address the worry and strengthen your position?

For some of us, fearing the financial worst due to uncertainty may lead us to save more in an emergency account, earn more, pay off debt faster, or cut expenses—moves that are more within our control. At the end of the day, this fear wants you to take inventory of what you value and from there, determine the most practical ways to preserve it. It wants you to investigate the facts, like when I looked under my portfolio's hood to discover that my stock exposure was, indeed, greater than what felt aligned with my risk tolerance and goals. I felt compelled to act. For others, the conclusion may be to change nothing. And that's okay, too, as long as we've given ourselves the benefit of exploring the truth.

And if you're still struggling to decide the healthiest next move, connecting with a certified financial professional to understand the real risks you may face can help. Because sometimes, our financial fears stem from a lack of context or knowledge and they're nudging us to explore and learn more so we can gain the certainty and confidence we seek.

WHEN YOUR FINANCIAL FEARS COME TRUE: A PRACTICE IN GRATITUDE

For *New York Times* bestselling author Geneen Roth, the worst-case money scenario surfaced when she least expected it . . . and it gave her a new lease on life.

When Geneen learned, along with thousands of other investors during a cold month in 2008, that she'd lost her life's savings to Bernie Madoff, her fear of "losing everything" was no longer a hypothetical. The criminal financier who'd been managing her wealth had wiped out thirty years' worth of personal investments. "I felt as if I had died and for some odd reason was still breathing," she wrote for the *Huffington Post*.[10]

Years later, when Geneen joined me on my podcast, I discovered how she had managed to pick herself up and rebuild after living through what is, for many of us, an absolute nightmare. "We had enough to make it through the month but not any more than that," she told me.[11] After spending some time grieving and getting "hysterical," she realized very soon that her survival hinged on something basic, though easily overshadowed by the devastation and loss. "If I was going to survive . . . I was going to have to learn how to focus on what I *hadn't* lost," she said. "That was the only way I could get through—on the fact that I still had a roof over my head at that moment, the fact that I had enough to eat at that moment, the fact that I still had friends at that moment. . . . Nothing of any value had been lost."

It was the adage "be grateful for what you have" that lifted her out of her despair and gave Roth a renewed sense of purpose and drive. She started writing again and turned her story of tragedy into a cautionary tale for others. An article she wrote for Salon.com chronicling her experience with Madoff, called "I Was Fleeced by Madoff," soared to the top of the site's most-read articles.[12] It led to a book. "I realized that even before we had lost our money, I still lived in this low level of anxiety. I was afraid of losing it, I was afraid of so many different things really . . . . There was a vigilance about bringing myself, my mind back from the cliffs of terror and shame. An urgency, a necessity to do that."

Roth's story reminded me of the wisdom Seth Godin had shared on my podcast just a couple of years earlier. Seth, a multi-bestselling author and thought leader, and I were in a deep conversation about the meaning of money and what it means to be rich. He said that it has less to do with the accumulation of money than we think. Rich, he said, is far more accessible than we believe. "If you have resources, if you have the freedom to choose, if you have the ability to not just spend money but spend time and to create things that touch other people, you are rich," he stated.[13] "And you ought to make some intentional decisions about what to do with that wealth."

So the next time you're afraid of going broke, rather than feel helpless over something so vague, imagine something even more specifically frightful that may provide a better sense of how you can start to remedy the pain—failing to recognize and leverage the bounty and richness that comes with the company of friends and family; a sense of belonging to a community; your wisdom, network, experiences, and skills; the ability to love and feel and do. **When you see what you possess, you recognize you have more to work with than you thought.** To feel gratitude, we sometimes need to work backward. The first step is to find the things in your life that are worth fighting for. The next step is to use the fear of losing those things to help you level up. Finally, determine how you can reconnect with what matters when everything is lost.

My grandmother, Mamani, made sure to deliver a similar message to me when I was a child. "There's always a lower level," she liked to say while shuffling her cards ahead of a fresh game of solitaire (her favorite pastime). "Appreciate what you have, Farnoosh. Complaints about lack of time, resources, or money can keep us in a zone of scarcity. See what you do have, see the richness in the love that is in your home, the warm food on your dining table each night. And remember that it is not guaranteed. You have been dealt a lucky hand." Later, before bed, we'd play *pasoor*, the two-person Persian card game. We would wager an ice cream. It would be the biggest risk either one of us would take all day.

The Fear of Money Self-Inquiry

- Why are you afraid of money in the first place?
- What is the story you're telling yourself about money?
- Is that narrative really true? How can you rewrite it to develop a healthier relationship with money?
- Is your financial fear constructive? Or is there a scarier scenario you haven't thought of—but that could nudge you toward the right move?
- Are you going for the jugular and confronting your fear of the worst?
- What are the riches you possess beyond dollars and cents?

7

THE FEAR OF FAILURE

and how it helps us to find the wins, honor red flags, and do the next right thing

THE RED LIGHT INDICATED I had a voicemail, which was strange. I'd left work around 7 p.m. the night before and now it was 8:15 in the morning. How was my job as a junior financial reporter at *Money* magazine researching reverse mortgages and 529 plans so *urgent* as to prompt someone to call me overnight and leave a message?

I hit play.

"Hey, Farnoosh, when you get a minute, can we talk? It's about your article."

The recording was from one of our top editors. The time stamp on the call: 9:45 p.m. the previous evening.

As I made my way over to his office, I needed to pass "Editor Row," the string of rooms reserved for senior staff with inflated salaries. It was evident from the death stares directed at me through their glass doors that I was about to be the last in the office to learn something very disappointing about myself.

I knocked on my editor's door and he invited me to take a seat. He handed me a copy of the new issue of the magazine that had just arrived from the printing press. He opened it to the article I'd written about the popular dollar store trend.

Now, I'd like to say that, back then, it was rare for a newbie on staff to have her pitches taken at *Money*. Much of my work consisted of assisting the staff, researching the news, and fact-checking other people's work. On occasion, I'd have the chance to share some of my own ideas, and even then only one or two might win the approval to appear in print.

My pitch about dollar stores had stemmed from the growth I'd seen in companies like Dollar Tree and Family Dollar. Their stocks were trading at near all-time highs, and one Paris Hilton had been photographed leaving the bargain-basement store in Los Angeles with bags full of goodies. Could dollar stores be the new sexy place to shop? My four-hundred-word piece ran in the front section, one of my first bylines in a national magazine. My father framed the page.

But now this editor, who'd helped me write the article, was no longer impressed.

"Do you see the mistake?" he asked, as I held the magazine on my lap.

I hadn't a clue.

"Here's the sentence." He began to recite my work, " 'Dollar stores— where all items cost one dollar—are rising in popularity.' "

Me: *Stares blankly. Hopes he can't hear my stomach churning.*

My editor: "But is *everything* at a dollar store just a dollar? Some things cost more, right?"

"Oh, sure," I said. "But *most* things *are* one dollar."

"But you didn't write 'most,' " he corrected me. "You wrote 'all.' "

Ah.

He was right. And now my error was languishing in dental office waiting rooms around the country. It was a miniscule mistake in the grand scheme of the magazine's reputation. It was not the sort of gaffe that was harmful or offensive. But to me, this felt decimating. I feared what this failure might say about me, that I didn't have what it took to survive the pressure cooker of working in national media. I couldn't even be trusted to write a simple article.

Before I'd completed the full walk of shame back to my desk, Mike, our associate editor, poked his head out of his lair and motioned me to join him inside. He was the kind soul who'd advocated for me to get this job and brought me on board. His normally upbeat and jovial tone was suddenly serious and solemn. He'd been briefed on my mistake and explained that if I screwed up again, I'd have to turn in my badge.

This was the ultimate fear, the ultimate failure—getting fired and the humiliation that would inevitably follow. I was afraid of being seen as someone who'd lost her grip on her career. I'd come to New York to make something of myself, to prove I could rise through the ranks of the big, competitive news world, one byline at a time. Maybe someday I'd become an editor in chief, and this time in my life would be where I could say it had all begun. But that morning, this narrative promptly ran out of ink.

I could tell Mike was sad for me. I promised I'd do better and proceeded to head back to my desk. But first, I made a turn for the restroom. I went inside the stall farthest from the door, sat down, and soaked up my tears using the ends of my sleeves. The damn dispenser was out of toilet paper.

YOUR FEAR OF FAILURE PAVES THE WAY TO THE FINISH LINE

The fear of failure runs rampant. We are a society oriented toward success. Triumph over loss. This goes all the way back to our sandbox days. Whoever has the most toys, wins.

And, honestly, losing stinks. It's full of embarrassment. Failure is a signal, maybe a slap in the face, telling you that you're unworthy. You don't measure up. And now everyone knows it.

As you are probably aware by now, I source my sense of self-worth from achieving things. It's a rush like no other to feel accomplished, even in the smallest of ways. Those three to four mornings every year when I manage to wake up early and work out, I feel fantastic. So you can only imagine the adrenaline rush when I learn a business deal has gone through or I beat out the competition and secure a TV gig. **Anticipating success is a fruity antidote to the fear of failure, which goes down like poison.**

As humans, we're not conditioned to manage this fear of failure with any great sophistication. In the world of money, there's a scientific study around this. Behavioral economists discovered a strange but true phenomenon called "loss aversion" where a real or probable loss is psychologically *more* painful than a gain of that same amount.[1] So the happiness associated with winning $1,000 is less than the anguish of losing $1,000. As the saying goes, *losses loom larger than gains.*

Our fear of failure can also be blamed on coddlers. I remember my high school teacher Mrs. Pertschuk was interrupted on more than one occasion because another insistent parent had called to inquire about their son's B that quarter. Why hadn't it been a glowing A? Forget that this person thought it was okay to call a teacher in the middle of the school day. This parent, misguided by the fear of failure (and having no shame), was overstepping to ensure their child received a 4.0, because anything short of that would mean doom. It would mean not getting into an Ivy League school—and we all know that the rest is downhill from there. So what will happen when that teen later discovers he failed his bar exam? Good luck to Mom if she plans to dial the American Bar Association on his behalf.

As Arthur C. Brooks wrote for the *Atlantic*, in his piece called "Go

Ahead and Fail," a generation of helicopter parents made it so their millennial and Gen Z kids wouldn't suffer even the faintest failures.[2] Mom and Dad thought they were doing us favors, perhaps. Instead, Brooks wrote, our generation grew up lacking "the emotional fortitude required to withstand the inevitable, larger failures of adulthood." And the fear of failure, he said, "can steer us away from life's joyful, fulfilling adventures, by discouraging us from taking risks and trying new things."

As grown-ups, when we *do* anticipate failure, we imagine things falling apart to the point of no turning back. We imagine our parents getting very worked up. We envision all the subsequent, inevitable failures because the cranky voice in our head tells us failure is all we are capable of. And we let this voice play on repeat to the point where we become transfixed by our own made-up thoughts. We become terribly stuck, doubting ourselves and our capabilities. If we allow it, the fear of failure can be self-sabotaging.

But throughout life, I've seen in myself and others how this fear has important advice to share about what to do next. We can get confused by its presence and feel the need to make a quick turn. In our haste we might try to run for the woods but end up going in the totally wrong direction.

After a string of dates (that you thought went well, but then they ghosted), you conclude it's better to be alone than face all that disappointment. You take down your dating profile.

Fearing your startup idea will fail and you won't have enough financial runway to keep hacking away, you scrap the business plan.

Or, fearing that you'll get fired at work, like I was years ago, you might immediately want to quit so that you can at least say you left *voluntarily*. You can save face.

But your fear of failure is here to show you a much better path to success. And if you're willing and patient, it will help you get there . . . with your dignity intact.

WATCH OUT FOR BAD DRIVERS

Back at *Money*, I decided I needed air. I left the bathroom, grabbed my tote bag, and left the building to shed more tears safely among the anonymous New York crowd. I dialed my mother because I needed to tell someone, anyone, about my morning, even if it meant another scolding. As I paced 49th Street, I held the flip phone close to my cheek, cupping the mic to block the city's sirens.

"*Ah-magh!*" my mom shouted over the phone. This is Farsi for "idiot."

Bafflingly, my mom wasn't referring to me. According to her, the *ah-magh* in this scenario was my boss. I explained that he wasn't wrong for being upset, that it was my job to proof my work, but then she said, "Didn't your editor read your article ahead of time, too? Why didn't *he* notice the mistake, either?"

Leave it to my mom to point out how your fear of failure sometimes has much to do with other people's errors backfiring on you. Mamani would say that, in life, no matter how good a driver you are, you must watch for "the drunks on the road." There may be a domino effect or a failed system at play; it's important to recognize it's not all in your control. In the personal finance world, it's common for folks to talk about how they single-handedly went from rags to riches. It's a misleading narrative that makes others assume that this person's successes and failures were solely within their realm. So it tracks that had they *not* been able to achieve financial success, they'd have had only themselves to blame. This couldn't be further from the truth.

When I was six years old, I was invited to a younger neighbor's birthday party at McDonald's, and every kid—except me!—received a Happy Meal. For some reason, that day there were too few kids' boxes to go around, and so I, being the slightly older child present and perceived as less likely to throw a tantrum, was told to select off the regular menu. Even though this meant more food for me, it lacked the most important part of going to McDonald's as a kid: securing the free miniature plastic toy in the Happy Meal.

My parents had always insisted I follow orders, so I did. As I took a bite out of my too-big burger, I watched the other kids play with their new, colorful cars without me.

After the party, I went over to the birthday boy's house for a play-date. Kiran lived next door to me. No longer seduced by his Happy Meal car, he was now playing with all his new gifts. That's when I went in for the steal. I knew it was wrong, but I couldn't help it. When nobody was looking, I slipped his toy car into the front chest pocket of my OshKosh B'Gosh overalls. I just wanted to experience the same thrill the other kids had at the party, to absorb a little bit of the joy they'd experienced earlier.

But within minutes, things took a scary turn. My friend was suddenly looking for his car again. A search party ensued throughout the finished basement where we'd been playing. "Farnoosh, have you seen Kiran's car?" his mother sternly asked me. "No," I said quietly, as my chest screamed with the bulge of the tiny toy.

The next thing I remember, his mom pulled me aside upstairs, propped me up on a wooden stool in the kitchen, and stared me dead in the eyes, not unlike those eyes following me down the hallway years later at *Money*. The room suddenly became very warm, the boil of the *saag paneer* on the stove behind her intensifying by the second. "I know you have the car," she told me point-blank.

Slowly I removed the car and placed it in her hand, with tears streaming down my face. "What you did is *stealing!*" she protested. "Do you know how wrong that is? I can't believe you watched us all search while you had the car the *entire* time. What would your mom say?"

Kiran's mom walked me back to our side of the townhouse development. After she had explained my misdemeanor to my mother, Sheida Joon replied, "Thank you for letting me know. I'm so sorry," before letting me in and shutting the door.

Later that night I got a lecture on stealing and lying, but rather than send me to my room, Mom let it go. I overheard her tell my dad a different version of the story during their evening chai break. "The nerve of that woman! She should know better than to be so unfair to a child and make Farnoosh be the only one to not receive a Happy Meal. *Chee FEK khard?*" she said in Farsi, which means "What was she thinking?" My father nodded in agreement.

It was hardly the reaction I was expecting, and in that moment, I felt seen and validated. My impulse to steal had been spurred by neglect. My mother understood how a child might naturally feel when the other kids got shiny new objects, and she was the only one left out. The next day, Mom took me to McDonald's for lunch and bought me my own glorious Happy Meal.

One of the biggest reasons we fear failure is because we fear that it says something about us, personally. But decades later in Midtown Manhattan, as I sobbed over my dollar store mishap, my mother reminded me again how failure doesn't always occur in a bubble. Accidents don't just happen. They are usually part of a chain reaction. I, of course, believe in taking accountability for one's actions. I'm not saying individuals are *never* to blame for their mistakes, but there's often more behind it that may be out of their control. It may be because the facts were not clear, the other people on the individual's team (or in their relationship) didn't live up to expectations or do their jobs, or there was a pandemic and, without an extra-large savings cushion (that few ever have, because life is egregiously expensive), they had to shutter their business.

And let's not forget, there may have been some serious biases involved. I've reported on racism and ableism contributing to the wealth gap. I know that sometimes no matter how hard you work, no matter how prepared and ready you are to achieve a goal, you are systematically set up for failure—by design.

When you fear failure, recognize this as an opportunity to discover what's missing—and how to address that void. Are you set up for success? Are you doing the most fulfilling tasks you could be at work? Are you effective? Or is it time for a change?

REDEFINE SUCCESS AND CLAIM THOSE WINS

The threat of getting fired at *Money* and having to face up to that failure was too much to bear. This was supposed to be a key pillar in my media career. I looked around. Some of the top editors had been with the magazine for over ten years, making comfortable salaries that afforded them at least two floors of a Park Slope brownstone and private school tuition for their kids. The journalism prestige and platinum corporate AmEx were nice perks, too. That could be me one day. But wait. *Was that really what I wanted?* Or had I assumed this recipe for success was befitting because, well, it's objectively great? Had I even stopped to ask myself what *I* wanted?

While I enjoyed writing articles, I wanted to tell stories across many platforms. I wanted to work in television. I wanted to write books. I wanted to give speeches in front of large audiences. My fear of failure in that moment, as I questioned what the hell I was doing there and why this all was happening to me, led me to self-explore, and when I came to, I saw that I'd been trying too hard to fit into a place that wasn't right for me. **I was afraid I would fail at my job, but what I *really* should have been afraid of was neglecting to define success on my own terms.** It was quite a breakthrough.

It was important to rethink success in such a way that I could immediately earn some victories. Because I needed them desperately after the day I'd had. I needed some wins—even small ones—to regain confidence. Like all those times in college, when I was anticipating days and weeks where things just were not going to go my way because I hadn't slept and midterms were killing me, and I would put on my to-do list very easy, low-hanging-fruit tasks that were sure to make me feel accomplished and progressing. Things like: wash hair and make a to-do list.

At *Money*, my fear of failure encouraged me to ensure I would not go down in flames (i.e., not get fired). I flipped my fear of failure and found a new definition of success by remembering what I'd initially come for—an investment of my time in a worthwhile experience. I wanted to be recognized as a dedicated journalist who was able to learn from her mistakes. I wanted the job to provide me with a good reference for the next post. And so, I insisted on improving. I proactively sought out mentors to teach me the ropes (win!). I arrived at 7 a.m. to gain the attention and respect of the top brass who were also early risers (win!).

When the next fact-checking assignment crossed my desk, a thrilling story about home maintenance costs, I knew this was my make-or-break moment. I sat and dismantled it word by word.

And, my friends, do you know how many errors I caught? Eighteen. From misspellings to incorrect statistics to misquoted sources, the piece seemed almost purposely riddled with mistakes. Were they . . . testing me? It sure felt like it.

Days after I turned in the draft, the deputy managing editor (second in command at the magazine) called me into her dimly lit office. There she was, sitting with the writer of said article that was so grossly erroneous. They held up the papers, bloodied with my red-ink notes.

The editor turned to me and just when I thought she'd say, "You missed a spot," she said, "Great job."

The writer chimed in, "Yes, thank you."

It felt . . . amazing. Vindicating.

A month later, I resigned. Just as I'd promised myself, I was leaving on a strong note.

On my final day, the same editor who'd burned me for my dollar store mistake stopped by my desk to bid me adieu. "Were you not happy here?" he asked. "So happy," I replied. "Just feeling ready for the next thing." My fear of failure had spoken, and it was urging me to course correct. I realized that *Money* might be a dead end for me. I felt I hadn't been properly mentored there. I feared being in a role where I was on the hook for correcting everyone else's factual errors, with no one there to catch my own falls. I left after seven months, which some may have thought was not long enough for the optics on a résumé . . . but I was done.

The fear of failure sometimes shows up when you have been trying too hard to pursue a goal that isn't aligned with who you are and what you want out of life. It can be a sign you may need to reconsider your definition of victory. Are you using other people's terms instead of your own? To reboot your self-esteem, look for how you can achieve some quick, immediate triumphs. Use your fear of failure as fuel to seek a new destination.

Shortly after I gave my two weeks' notice, I started my TV producer role at NY1 News. My fear of failure had led me to this buzzing newsroom where I felt ready and prepared to make my next big leap. Also helpful: I arrived understanding past mistakes, no bridges burned.

GET UNSTUCK BY BEING IMPERFECT

We often know the fear of failure has arrived because we feel really stuck. This feeling is akin to how we feel when the fear of uncertainty strikes, but this sense of immobility is caused more by a deep worry that you'll make an imperfect move. My college friend Diana used to stand inside the downtown Ben & Jerry's for fifteen minutes, hesitant to pick any one flavor of ice cream for fear she would make the wrong choice and, unable to request a refund, would immediately face remorse. By the time she would land on Phish Food (if she'd even decided), I'd already collected my change and was halfway through my Chunky Monkey.

As a kid in front of the rows of candy at Duffy's Discount, I had once been Diana. I was afraid of failing to make the *best* choice. But every time, I left the store crying and empty-handed. Failing to select the right candy isn't the worst that can happen. The worst is letting your indecision run you over and choosing nothing. At least if I'd lamented grabbing the box of Whoppers, I'd have been *that* much closer to deciding on a winning candy during the next visit. And while I didn't care for the malted milk interior, the chocolate coating was pretty good. At least, better than the salt of my tears.

After college, Diana's fear of failure would manifest as a refusal to compromise. She was a star student and insisted on landing the "dream job" at a fancy, name-brand firm. But her relentless pursuit of perfection took a toll, stretching over two years. Meanwhile, she continued to live in her childhood home, serving tables at a local diner where she'd worked in high school. To her, this seemed far better than "settling" for a less-than-ideal full-time role, even if it cost her the chance to live independently. She stuck to what was familiar, mistakenly thinking this would reduce the chance for failure. But the truth is, intentionally refusing to venture out and avoiding new experiences *is* a form of failure. It hinders progress. As you wait for something extraordinary to arrive, valuable time slips away, time you could have spent learning so many wonderful things about your potential.

Women, and in particular women of color, I've had the opportunity to interview over the years often share these moments of "stuckness." As with Diana, there's often some perfectionism at play. Their fear of failing stems from a childhood full of adversity and seeing how the world was not necessarily going to be as patient with their differences. An obsession with achievement and being "the best" was their way out of this fear, but it could dangerously push them to a point of paralysis.

Candice Cook Simmons, one of the country's top female attorneys, joined me on my podcast and reflected on her upbringing in Atlanta in the 1990s and that of her friends who were Black, like her.[3] She said it was typical to be told, "You must be *better* to be considered *as good*." By the time she was in her mid-twenties, her fear of not being able to afford mistakes had led her to a feeling of resentment, and later, as a top attorney, it brought her to a realization that she was far from fulfilled. "I called my parents, my dad, to vent and essentially projected all of this anger on him. 'You all are making me work every night and Saturday night at 11 p.m. I'm here with my assistant working on a brief. You all did this.'

"My dad let me do my entire rant. He said, 'Candice, nobody asked you to be at work at 11 p.m. on a Saturday night working on a brief. You chose this job. You've chosen your life . . . . If you have decided that these choices do not bring you joy, do not assume and project that you need to do something to make us proud. We've been proud. There's nothing more you can do that will change this barometer of pride with us.'"

At a certain point, if your fear of failure is driving you to misery and stuckness, Candice said, you must stop and ask yourself, "Whose dream is this?"

When you are a child of immigrants, or anyone born with the pressures of carrying the torch of the generation before you, striving for perfection can feel like a full-time occupation.

My parents arrived on American soil with nothing more than the proverbial two suitcases and a relentless hope that things would pan out better than if they'd let the doors close on them in Iran. I knew that I had been immediately granted freedom just by the nature of being born here. I never had to cross an ocean for that privilege, so what would my excuse have been for not being ambitious or not giving something my all? What would my parents think of me if I wasn't buttoned up *all the time*? I was embarrassed to ever admit my struggles.

In my mid-twenties, my fear of failure and letting down my family consumed me. One night as I sat in the darkness of my neighborhood theater at the corner of Broadway and 67th Street watching *Big Fish*, I began to feel a medium-grade panic attack building in my chest. When I'd left *Money* to pursue my *next* dream job as the business producer for NY1 News, these recurring episodes of sheer and utter overwhelm had first presented as wrenching stomachaches. "It's just par for the course," the first gastroenterologist told me. "Welcome to working a high-pressure job in the big city."

I should have been thrilled to be where I was. At twenty-three years old, I'd already become a producer in the country's largest media market. The day a former classmate had forwarded me the NY1 job posting with the subject line *Thought you might be interested*, she'd had no idea how much I needed it. I'd regained my dignity at *Money* magazine and was no longer known as *the dollar store dummy*, but I was more eager than ever to pursue financial journalism on television. My hope was that I'd start behind the scenes as a producer and later become an on-camera reporter. NY1 was fertile ground for that trajectory, evidenced by the scores of writers, producers, and editors who'd gone on to rule the anchor desk on national news networks and cable TV.

After reading the job description that day, I moved everything aside and quickly shot off my résumé with an 870-word cover letter to one of the newsroom managers. I vividly remembered him speaking to our journalism class at Columbia the year prior and mentioning how he had attended Holy Cross, a small college in Worcester. And so, when I wrote to him, in addition to sharing that I was a NY1 devotee and an ambitious financial reporter, I referenced his talk and our Worcester connection. "Your story made me smile," I wrote. "It was the first time in a long time I'd heard someone properly pronounce my hometown."

A couple days later I received an email from the news director (his boss) to come in for an interview the following week. The wheels were in motion!

Ahead of the interview, I studied their news shows and became familiar with the roster of talent. I arrived fifteen minutes early, wearing my one black suit, from Marshalls. My secret weapon? A spiral-bound PowerPoint deck fresh off the Kinko's printer. The nine-page color presentation cost $22, an investment that I hoped would prove me a standout as I walked the interviewers through my ideas and plans for making their programming more engaging for viewers.

The snazzy presentation was the reason I got the job! Or maybe it wasn't?

Shortly after joining the company, my boss noted that my deck was "impressive," but also that one candidate had rudely taken a non-urgent phone call during his interview. Another had repeated how important and successful her father was, thinking it would score her points. To be honest, I probably could have left the glossy presentation at home and just sat there with my hands folded, nodding, and landed the gig. **Pro tip: Sometimes your "competition" in life is nothing to fear. Sometimes rivals are just teeing you up for success**.

So while it's not certain that my deck had anything to do with my hiring, one thing became very clear within weeks of arriving on the job: I was sorely under-delivering all the promises from that proposal. I may have gotten over the imagined threat of Serena trying to sabotage my job and no longer felt the fear of exposure and imposter syndrome, but I continued to make all sorts of errors at work. I was now a certifiable screwup.

Here's the thing: The learning curve from magazine writing to television production is steep and brutal. ENPS, the godforsaken newsroom production software system that I told you about earlier, was completely unintuitive and buggy. It took me a while to get the hang of it and to troubleshoot, while also trying to meet my deadlines. It didn't help that each day I prepped multiple live and pretaped segments that relied on that screwy ENPS around the clock. And every day felt like a sprint to a finish line where I collapsed on cue.

This was far from the leisurely pace at *Money*, where we met monthly deadlines and some employees wouldn't come into the office until 10:30 a.m., followed by a two-hour lunch.

My NY1 anchor, the person I was assigned to support by writing and uploading scripts into the prompter and sending her cues from the control room while she was live on the air, was showing me a lot of patience. She was a pro, but I could sense her frustrations. My failures were fast becoming the thing I was known for. "Farnoosh didn't update the script in the prompter . . . again," the operator in the control room would say teasingly.

Many evenings, I came home to my apartment, the one I shared at the time with a married couple (and their sixteen-year-old cat), utterly defeated. How I managed to get up every morning and start all over . . . I have no good answers.

If this wasn't failing with a capital, cursive "F," then what was? The fear grew as I imagined getting the other "F" word—fired.

I was afraid of failure largely because I was afraid of how it might bring dishonor to my family. I was afraid they'd say, *We told you so!* It had been difficult convincing them that I should take this career path. In Persian families, children are typically expected to become doctors, lawyers, engineers, or PhD holders. The notion of working in the news industry was a radical concept to my parents, and I was afraid that their doubts may have been right. I was scared that my recurring challenges were pointing to real and unfixable shortcomings. Maybe I should switch careers. Maybe I should use that finance degree and become an Excel spreadsheet monkey. It sure would pay better.

Now, after months of carrying this stress with no solution in sight, I had full-blown anxiety. The panic attacks always arrived in the most inconvenient places and times: while watching the bodega worker spread jelly on my toast, or while wedged in between two construction workers on the crosstown bus.

And then, the Torabis came to visit. On one of those nights, sitting in a movie theater with my thirteen-year-old brother, Todd, every breath, once again, became a labored chore. I thought about excusing myself and running to the restroom to calm down. But something inside told me to grab his attention, that somehow seeing his older sister hyperventilating wouldn't traumatize him. As he sat staring at the screen, holding an overpriced box of buttered popcorn, I brushed his arm and whispered, "I can't breathe."

Todd was barely a teen, but he could immediately tell I was broken. His achievement-obsessed sister had lost her way. The tragic look on my face petrified him, suggesting he had no time to squander. "Let's get Mom and Dad," he said. As we dashed out of that theater and began searching for our parents in the adjacent one, Todd never let go of my hand. Things were not okay, but his grip assured me that better days were ahead.

Before that night at the movie theater, I'd miscalculated my little brother. I mistook our more than ten-year age difference as meaning that I was always the one who needed to have her you-know-what together. I was the one chiefly responsible for paving the way and providing care, not the other way around.

Todd immediately found one of the ushers and asked if he could help locate our parents in the adjacent theater. I was concerned they'd suffer heart attacks when faced with the man's flashlight and his whisper, "Your kids need you." But, like true Persian warriors, they sprang up immediately and walked toward the back to collect their mess of a daughter. Truth be told, they'd been in the midst of watching *House of Sand and Fog*, a depressing story of the downfall of an Iranian immigrant family, and probably didn't mind being interrupted.

The four of us were now standing in the drizzling rain outside the Lincoln Square on the Upper West Side, waiting for me to confess what in God's name was going on.

"I'm miserable at work. I'm failing every day. I don't know what to do."

It wasn't the first time my family had heard about the pressures of my new job as a television producer, but they didn't know the extent to which it was crippling my health. I felt glued to my problems. But my parents believed I had some clear options.

"You have two choices here," my father said. "The first is that you can quit."

Really? Option one had never crossed my mind. But to hear my super practical, play-it-safe dad tell me that it would be okay to quit, that it wouldn't be a step backward, was liberating. I wouldn't have been as shocked to hear that from my mom, a woman who once upon a time threw a bottle of Windex at her boss at Service Merchandise before quitting.

"The second option is to find a way to manage this job because right now, this job is managing you," Dad continued.

He was right. Rather than leverage my fear of failure to work up the courage to fight for my wins, I had allowed it to turn me into a victim.

We spent the rest of the night playing out hypothetical scenarios at work and how to best handle them. The repeated advice from my parents was to just shrug the negativity off. "Pretend you're listening to the criticism, but then have it go out the other ear," they said. Essentially: get laser focused on your work and ignore people.

The next day I went in early, kept my headphones on for most of the day, tuned out the chaos around me, and dove into work. I knew I needed to step up my game, but not stressing as much about my imperfections, mess-ups, and what others thought of me gave me more mental room to focus on becoming a faster writer, a more creative producer, and someone who could ingest video in her sleep.

Weeks went by. I gently laid down my fear of failure. My stomachaches went away. I slept better.

Outside the movie theater that night, on that cold corner of West 67th Street, my father had given me the gift of seeing my work as something that I could control—not the other way around. And in this instance, I saw how my fear of failure had been signaling to me all along what I needed to do—take the reins at my job. I loved it too much to leave. But knowing that I *could* quit, walk away, essentially fail gave me the strength and the wherewithal to do what I really wanted to do . . . which was to stay and improve.

When you fear failure and are not sure what to do next, a good question to ask yourself is: *What is behind my unhealthy need for perfection?* **How can I reframe my thinking or loosen up in order to focus on what matters most so that I can achieve what I'm really after?**

We may be good at practicing this in small ways, day to day. If we're afraid of failing an exam, which may then mean failing the class, we hit the books harder or apply for extra credit. If we're afraid of failing to remember to pick up our kids at the bus stop on early release day, we set an alarm on our phone (and preferably a backup alarm). If we're afraid of losing our way and failing to show up at a job interview on time, we map out our route, check traffic, and head out early. We can do this for bigger wins in life, too. If we want to avoid failing in our relationships, we can seek help from a counselor and make efforts to communicate more effectively with our partner. If we want to avoid making a financial blunder, we can ask questions, save, and read the fine print.

At NY1 News, I was afraid of losing my job (a recurring theme in those early career days), so I decided to use the energy I was spending on the day's embarrassments and disappointments to instead fight harder to protect my role. That is, until I quit two years later. Turns out Option A that my father had laid out wasn't a bad one. I'd just needed more time to learn and grow before moving on. That job had taught me important lessons and skills, mostly about how to navigate a stressful work environment, collaborate with people, and multitask on deadline. But it wasn't where I was going to work for the rest of my life. It was just one of many bountiful stops.

LOVE ME SOME RED FLAGS

Years ago, we were considering a major home renovation. Just five days before we were scheduled to break through the walls and combine our Brooklyn apartment with the studio next door, our usually reserved and easygoing contractor was suddenly being rude and off-putting. As he sat at our kitchen table for the final budget meeting before kicking off our complex, four-month-long project that would earn his company more than six figures, I sensed he was not all there.

As our architect's right-hand contractor for years, he had come to us with glowing reviews, so Tim and I felt we were in capable hands. In previous meetings and conversations, he was buttoned-up, collaborative, and a good listener. But on this day, he had walked into our home a tad sideways—literally. He was chattier than usual, a bit snarky, and terribly unprepared for our budget meeting. As in, he forgot to bring the budget. When I questioned the price estimate he'd given us on the new flooring, he got aggressive and snapped at me, "I thought you liked fancy things!"

His moodiness had us all shook up; we decided to end the meeting early and reconvene the next day. Later that night, our architect checked in with this contractor to find out what in the hell had been going on with him. He acted innocent at first, but then he confessed that he'd taken some prescription back pain medicine, followed by some beers at lunch. Our architect insisted she'd never known him to show up under the influence of alcohol or drugs at work. She said she'd completely understand if we no longer wanted to work with him, but at the same time, didn't reject the idea of staying the course.

Honestly, I think we all wanted to look away because firing the contractor would mean that the project failed from the onset. It would take weeks, maybe months, to find another contractor who had the availability and skill to do a job of this scale. We'd lose thousands of dollars on a storage rental and a sublease that we had already paid for.

Still, the fear of what might happen if we didn't fire him was greater. What if he got into a drunken fight with a worker and someone got injured? What if in a medicated state, he tore down the wrong wall? What if the city decided to do an impromptu job inspection while he was under the influence? If we hired him, we couldn't trust that the next time he made a mistake, there wouldn't be sharp objects or heavy machinery involved. I could see failure approaching from a mile away. And I was scared.

I had prepared for the project to be stressful, but I hadn't prepared for the whole thing to blow up in my face. And on this fateful afternoon with just days to go before demolition, I was convinced it *would* go sideways—unless I immediately made a change. I saw some deep red flags, and I didn't hesitate to react. The red flags told me to cut my losses and find a new contractor. **If you recognize that there's the potential for things to really go astray, do what you need to course correct—and fast.**

The next morning, we fired our contractor.

When your fear of failure cautions you to do something to protect yourself or your loved ones—listen to it. Anytime you find yourself unsettled or frightened by a person's demeanor, words, or actions, listen to that fear. Even if it means failing in the short term. Be thankful for those red flags. Walk away.

Taking red flags seriously and acting on them, while possibly difficult, costly, and stressful in the beginning, is the wisest thing to do in the long run. Red flags are part of the wisdom of the fear of failure and one of my favorite things to look out for. Ask yourself: *When failure arrives, will I look back at this moment and see how I could have done something—but didn't? And will I think that this is where the fail-*

ure started? If the answer is yes, it's a blazing red flag. While we think ending a deal or a relationship because of a single red flag will require some damage control, imagine the much scarier circumstance of ignoring the warning signs.

There's always the possibility that someone will turn out to be the opposite of who you hoped they'd be, that despite a glowing résumé and referrals, they don't do what they originally said they would. In my experience, that's a decent percentage of the population and they are very good at hiding red flags, at least at first. Accept that some people overpromise and underdeliver. Some will be overconfident to a fault. They'll assume it's okay to attend a business meeting after washing down painkillers with a Guinness. We all make mistakes. But be frightened when someone is so bold as to not take ownership right away for their actions and thinks you're too weak to call out their b.s. That's failure staring you right in the face, and you want to be terrified of it.

Same goes for those of us determined to land on true love. Don't be frightened to break up because you fear that it will mean you are failing at your pursuit of love. If you make the wrong assumption that this relationship is the end all, be all, you may even internalize and think there is something wrong with you for the fact that *it's just not working out*. In that scenario, your fear of failure is telling you that it's time to move on, take what you've learned from this relationship and apply it to the next, where you may find more fulfillment. Remember your goal and let that focus you. Your motivation is to ultimately succeed at finding a partner, and in the meantime, you must not fear short-term "failure." Staying in such a relationship means risking your happiness and delaying your pursuit of a real, deep, and meaningful union. Breaking up ensures that your pursuit of love can, in fact, endure.

KNOWING THE NEXT RIGHT THING

"Farnoosh, Richard is on line one."

I was an account executive at the *Daily Collegian*, our giant campus newspaper at Penn State, a training ground for how to sell, market, and think on your feet in front of intimidating people like the six-foot-four Richard, who, at the time, was the general manager of the biggest food and nightclub operator in State College. As an ad rep, I oversaw managing client accounts and placing the $2 pizzeria coupons for pizza or promos featuring the night's lineup of bands downtown. I worked off commission, and Richard was my most lucrative—albeit prickliest—client. So, as fate would have it, when I forgot to place a very important half-page ad for a big musical act at one of Richard's clubs—*on the day of the concert*—he called me at the office, shouting so loud that my colleagues could hear every word over the phone.

My knees buckled. It was too late to place the ad, and I was afraid that this failure would breed more failure. I feared it would ruin my relationship with my client, that he'd bad-mouth me to other prospective clients, that I'd lose my reputation at work, and that every time I saw Richard around town, he'd be sure to remind me of this royal error. A long list of potential failures loomed. How would I prevent this from becoming a dark cloud until my final days of college?

I could have lazily given into this fear of failure, said I was sorry and crossed my fingers that our business manager would give me another big account and that Richard would just chalk it up to "mistakes happen" when you're working with a bunch of college kids. Instead, the adrenaline kicked me into action. My fear of failure was asking me: *What is the next right thing?* Whatever you do, aim for excellence.

With that question in mind, I took inventory of my resources: my time, a copy machine, and humility. Maybe *I* could become the ad? I cleared my schedule for the rest of the day, printed hundreds of promotions on eight-by-eleven paper, and became a walking solicitation for the band, handing out over five hundred fliers that afternoon. I even ran into the band members on the sidewalk, who'd just arrived off their tour bus. They were blown away by my fandom. (I didn't, of course, tell them the real reason driving my zeal.)

The fear of failure tends to stop us in our tracks. But in those moments when you sense defeat, even if you're already down, look around and examine your immediate next options. Act on the one that feels like a win and get back in the game. Also, wear sunscreen. It was scorching hot that day.

We should not fear the fact (yes, fact!) that mistakes big and small may happen under our watch. We'll forget to complete assignments, we'll commit to the wrong person, we'll screw up at work. **Fear less the mistakes (they happen to the best of us) and fear more not using the fear of failure as a motivator.** Admit you made a wrong turn and then find a way to still accomplish what you had set out to achieve.

Years later, in my mid-twenties, this blueprint came in handy again in my role as a financial correspondent for TheStreet.com, when I'd landed a major interview in D.C. with one of the country's leading CEOs. Except, I forgot to hit record on my camera. (Details.)

Toward the end of my twenty-minute interview with the CEO of DuPont, I noticed that the red light that usually blinked to indicate my camera was recording . . . was gray, dark, dead. I could feel my heart pounding at the bottom of my throat. Here I was about to conclude one of the most sophisticated financial conversations I'd conducted, with no filmed evidence of said conversation. The camera had basically been a dull prop. Fear started to mess with me. *Maybe I was a dull prop?*

This was an interview that I'd traveled over two hundred miles to land. I'd convinced my executive producer that it would be worth the travel and expenses. DuPont wasn't as sexy a company as Apple or

Google, but at the time it was a blue-chip company and a bellwether of the economy.

They teach you in journalism school to prepare for a lot of failures, often tied to things that are out of your control. But, knowing myself, I also had to be cautious of my own forgetfulness. On past work trips, I'd left a business suit at home. I'd neglected to bring extra batteries or the right recording equipment. I've been known to hit traffic and risk being late for an interview. With every near failure in the past, I'd had a contingency plan. I located the nearest department store and Radio Shack to resolve wardrobe and technical issues. I always left for interviews early, with my MapQuest printout. By this point in my career, my fear of failure was a well-flexed muscle. During my days of being a New York City television producer and reporter (and usually a one-woman band who did both the on- and off-camera work), part of excelling on the job was fearing all the bad things that might happen on the shoot—and using that fear to prepare myself to clean up the mess before the boss found out.

Case in point: One time on the way to a local interview, just as I'd exited the subway, my left sandal fell through an opening on a metal grate. I'd always feared falling in one of these black holes in the street, but never just losing a single shoe in it. I tried balancing on one foot as I stared at my lonesome shoe resting in the dark next to dirt and candy wrappers twenty feet belowground. My first thought was to call and postpone the meeting by an hour. In the meantime, I'd wait outside Ann Taylor around the corner until it opened, to grab a new pair of heels. But I lamented the idea of probably needing to pay full price for some random shoes. Was there another option? I scoped my surroundings and fancied myself as MacGyver, the unconventional problem-solver we all loved to watch on TV in the mid-1980s. I spotted a utility worker a few feet away, and implored him to review the tools in his truck and help rescue my sandal. He was so kind. He immediately secured a rope with a hook on the end, and within seconds, I was back in business. My meeting went on without disruption. My bank account didn't suffer a blow. The day was saved. Just another classic New York City moment.

But forgetting to record a dang interview? In D.C., I'd reached a whole new level of sloppiness for me.

And let's not forget: Reporters aren't allowed to return from the field without the story, particularly if there were travel expenses involved. That moment in our nation's capital, numbed by the failure, I imagined the look on my boss's face back in New York. I dreaded being torn apart before never being trusted again or possibly getting fired. I imagined the phone call to my parents over said debacle. I envisioned that I would become the ultimate failure and what it would say about me, or rather what it would, without a doubt, confirm: I was in way over my head, trying to become a TV reporter and thinking I had the talent to interview high-level executives. Perhaps I should settle for less demanding assignments like dog shows and the annual Coney Island hot dog eating contest.

But the idea of interviewing uppity Chihuahua parents felt like a more horrifying fail. I desperately wanted to keep my dignity intact and avoid consequences at work. I contemplated saying the tape got lost on the trip. Or that the CEO never showed up. But I feared that if I got caught lying, it would only sink me into further trouble. I had to use my fear to save myself with the next right move: leaning on others for help. Also, begging.

Before the interview began, the CEO's media team had said he was pressed for time, so they wanted to see if there was a way to multitask and have one journalist conduct the interview while everyone filmed his answers. Because I was the early bird, and thus positioned in the front row, I offered to conduct the Q&A while everyone else recorded it alongside me. No good deed . . .

Desperate in the aftermath, I turned to the five camera operators behind me who'd all been piggybacking on my interview. I scoped out the friendliest face, the sole guy who'd thanked me for doing the Q&A, and confessed my problem. I asked if he'd be willing to share his recording with me. He paused to think about it and kindly agreed to help with one condition—he would need to take his tape back to his station first and upload the interview. After that, he said he'd promptly send me a copy in the mail, and we shook on it. Had it been a year in the future, newly invented cloud services like Dropbox would have let us instantly upload and share files. But this was before any of that. This was basically the technological Stone Age. When I returned to work, I was nervous as hell that the tape wouldn't arrive. I had no tracking number for the postage and followed up with that camera operator no fewer than six times in the following forty-eight hours. If I'd had to rent a car and drive down to D.C. myself to wrest the tape copy from his claws, I would have. I am comfortable being *that* person if need be. But when it finally popped up in my mailbox three days later (and before my boss came asking for the footage), my faith in humanity was restored. My trust in my ability to ask for help when I really needed it was also reinforced.

When you fear failure, sometimes your assignment is to look around. Sometimes a solution is outside of your domain. Before you succumb to this fear, let it guide you to a creative solution, which may just mean getting humble and resting your trust in others.

WHEN FAILING IS THE POINT!

My friend and author Karen Rinaldi wrote the book *It's Great to Suck at Something: The Unexpected Joy of Wiping Out and What It Can Teach Us About Patience, Resilience, and the Stuff That Really Matters.* When she came on *So Money*, she talked about her experience with learning how to surf in her forties, a pastime she continuously "sucks" at but insists on pursuing.[4] Surfing has equipped her with the emotional strength to accept failure and be open to criticism. "By sucking at surfing, I was able to get over my fear of public humiliation. Because when you surf, you are surfing where everyone can see you wipe out and miss waves. I got really used to being okay with that. Then I realized I could apply that to my writing. I started sharing my writing more as I got accustomed to that and thinking, 'Well, the worst thing that happens is somebody sees my writing and they don't like it,' right? I mean, I'll be okay with that." Sucking at the small things doesn't prevent you from sucking at the big things—it just provides training in self-acceptance and self-compassion—especially when the stakes are higher. Because we will fail at things that matter. That's a guarantee.

Personally, I think I, at times, suck at parenting, which is far from a "recreation." It's a full-time, all-consuming job and, in my opinion, the stakes are even higher there than at work, let alone surfing. Still in all my nine-plus years of being a mom, I've learned that sometimes your parenting "mistakes," especially the ones that are harmless, are just acts of pure genius. It's okay to (sometimes) suck at parenting. Your fear of failure may make the long days of raising a human feel impossible to navigate, and you begin to doubt your instincts and size up your skills against other moms and dads on the playground. But instead, when this fear arrives, see it as a calling to give yourself more credit. After all, being a little messy and carefree is what parenting often begs for.

For instance: I once sent my then five-year-old son Evan and little sister Colette to the wrong birthday party at an indoor soccer field in Brooklyn. My first thought upon realizing my royal mess-up was *Is this for real? How could I be so scatter-brained?*, followed by *You know, I should really do this more often.*

That day I'd asked their babysitter to accompany the kids to what I *thought* was a birthday party for Evan's friend Blake. I already knew that Evan wouldn't know some of the kids at this party since Blake was in a different kindergarten classroom, so when he told me after the event that he didn't "know *anyone* there!" I didn't think too much of it. I figured he was exaggerating.

Our babysitter even said they'd had a "good time," despite Evan being a little grumpy. Colette had a blast kicking the soccer balls and chasing the older kids down the field. They ate chocolate cake and left with treat bags full of sugar and choking devices disguised as toys.

But Evan wouldn't stop complaining about how he knew absolutely no one. "What do you mean you didn't know *anybody*? Blake was there and you know *him*," I reminded him.

"No, he wasn't! Blake wasn't there, Mommy!" he pressed.

My heart began to race. I checked the Google calendar on my phone and saw what I had feared at that moment—Blake's party was, for crying out loud, the *following* Saturday. Same place, same hour of the day. But *next* weekend. I'd let my kids crash an innocent child's party, and chill for hours in the presence of complete strangers.

Was I the sloppiest excuse for a parent ever? Who in their sane mind sends not one, but *two* children to the wrong birthday party? I wanted to blame Tim because why wasn't *he* more involved in the children's social calendars, you know? But then, I hadn't added him to this appointment on our shared calendar, so he wasn't even aware there was a party. Nope, this was all on me.

What is the appropriate reaction to such a colossal parenting fail? Hell if I know, but after realizing my pure act of negligence *and how there was nothing to do about it*, I burst out laughing . . . as did Evan. Even at his age, my sweet son knew to smile and shake his head at me, all to say, *Mom, you silly goose*. We filmed a quick video and confessed our crime to Instagram. Parent friends sent back a bunch of skull faces, I guess to say that the story had downright killed them (in the best way, of course).

I kept replaying the mental images of my kids crashing a party where they knew absolutely no one, my son perplexed, yet agreeing to sing happy birthday and stress-eating cake, and all the while the parents of this innocent birthday boy possibly (or possibly not) wondering who in the world Evan and his sister were, and not questioning it because, well, they hadn't previously met all the parents or the kids, so who even knows? I have most definitely hosted events for my kids and not been familiar with all the faces ahead of time. Had random kids joined in on my kids' parties? Were parents doing this all the time?

While I laughed my pants off, my husband was a tad mortified. He called the soccer venue the next day and shared what had happened and offered to pay in case the family had been charged for two unexpected guests. The venue manager just laughed and said not to worry about it. Nobody had noticed.

The fact that this failure had zero consequences for anyone—except maybe little Evan, who was bummed, but *please*, he ate Doritos and snagged free toys, he was fine—was unbelievable. It was the most magical part of the whole story.

And then, I wondered . . .

This indoor soccer venue ran multiple events round the clock, every weekend. Could I have been releasing my children to random birthday parties for years while I had the afternoons to myself? Why hadn't I strategized this before? This was February in New York City, after all, when it's too frigid to play outdoors and particularly hard to find indoor activities for kids. If this mishap truly wouldn't raise any concerns, well then by golly, I should have been pulling this fail on purpose on the reg. And if you, dear reader, have yet to attempt this, feel free to hatch a similar plan. You're very welcome.

Rather than letting your fear of failure make you doubt your capabilities . . . sometimes the better move is a big old belly laugh, because as long as the kids are okay, not much else matters.

The Fear of Failure Self-Inquiry

- Are you afraid to fail because your definition of success is borrowed and not really yours?
- Who or what may be setting you up for failure?
- How can you use your fear of failure to pivot and drive home some wins on your terms?
- Is your insistence on being perfect contributing to your fear of failure?
- Are you spotting red flags? How can you course correct right now, even if it means cutting your losses in the immediate future?
- What's the next right move that harnesses what's already within your reach?
- Could failure lead to a fun (or funny) twist and thus be so worth it?

8

THE FEAR OF ENDINGS

and how it sparks action,
deepens an appreciation for
what endures, and showcases
the beauty in regret

WHEN DESCRIBING A MISCARRIAGE in Farsi, we say, "*BAH-cheh of-TAWD.*"

Translation: "The baby fell."

And *how* did it fall, precisely? My understanding was that it was often the mother's fault. When a relative retells the story of her first pregnancy, a baby girl that she lost in her second trimester, she says it happened after installing heavy curtains in her house in Shiraz. "The doctors told me that I should not have extended my arms up high for so long," she says regretfully.

Generations of women in our family have been led to believe that a failed pregnancy—the sudden death of an unborn child—was due to their own misdeeds. "She would have been a girl," my relative will say, her heart still broken decades later.

And so, when I suffered my own miscarriage years ago, I naturally assumed the same.

Was it because I'd had a few drinks that one night before realizing I was pregnant? Did I overextend myself while attempting a standing split at Physique 57? Is drinking New York's tap water making me infertile?

It's devastating enough to experience an ultrasound that shows absolutely nothing, all while a few weeks prior your doctor had, from that same screen, pointed to the poppy seed–sized embryo for whom you'd already begun drafting a list of names.

"I don't see anything," Dr. Bradley said as she stared at the computer nine weeks into our pregnancy. "I'm very sorry."

This was our first try at conceiving, and honestly, we were surprised to have a positive test so quickly. But we were not prepared for being told that something we really wanted, that we had thought we'd secured . . . was now gone, and there wasn't anything we could do about it. The miscarriage made me afraid of trying to get pregnant again, for fear of another, too-sad ending, one that would leave me heavy with more guilt and shame. Another miscarriage would reinforce just how little control we had over our "plans" to become parents. I feared I would not be able to endure the grief. The fear made me want to just give up.

DEMYSTIFYING THE FEAR OF ENDINGS

The fear of endings is a biggie, an amalgamation of many of our other fears and concerns, from loneliness to rejection, failure to uncertainty. And because endings are inevitable and affect us all, this fear is one of our greatest common denominators. As we ponder the end of a relationship, a friendship, a job, a dream, or a life, we become afraid. Never is this fear more present than when we reflect on our own inevitable passing, which "haunts the human animal like nothing else," writes Ernest Becker in his Pulitzer Prize–winning book *The Denial of Death*.[1]

This fear exists partly because our brains are programmed for wanting happily ever after. We want pregnancies to end with healthy babies in our arms. We want graduating from high school or college to mean that we're on our way to true adulthood and supporting ourselves. We want to know that the departure from one job means a more satisfying role with better benefits awaits us. We want the end of a relationship to be mutual, marked by two individuals parting with kindness, respect, and an appreciation for what they shared. We want to die peacefully, surrounded by family and friends, moving into some kind of afterlife. We don't want to feel regret, grief, or doubt. We love the thought of ample closure, which often means that something new is in the wings. When we sense an ending on the horizon that fails to meet some or all of the above criteria, the fear is all-consuming. We are afraid of the emotional upheaval, doubting we'll ever recover. In short, we are afraid of getting stuck in the ending.

In our efforts to fight off this fear, we can become hyper-irrational. There's a tendency known as the "banker's fallacy," which says that our preference for happy endings makes us eager to make desirable short-term decisions even if it means risking bad long-term outcomes. (It's called "banker's fallacy" because the stereotypical banker prefers the "quick gains" in the market and not so much the slow, stable growth over time.) Our draw toward short-term benefits can lead us to continue a toxic relationship, job, or project because it may mean earning a paycheck and claiming a certain status—for now.[2] Even when we see the handwriting on the wall, we're afraid and, thus, reluctant to make an exit.

But goodbyes are integral to how we achieve happiness, gratitude, and our goals. If we want the good things in life, we need to prepare for the fact that bad days are part of the journey. And the only way to venture to the sunnier side is to commit to working our way through the darkness. One step at a time.

When we fear endings that we feel are within our power—moving, selling a home, or ending a partnership—it's because we don't want to feel like failures for the rest of our days. We try to fight the fear or ignore its presence because we don't want to face uncertainty. We stick with the status quo. But if we invite this fear in and engage, it can help inspire us to live with deeper meaning, impact, and growth. Even for endings we can't control, like a layoff, a miscarriage, or losing a loved one, there are ways to use this fear to find the next doorway and walk through it. You may still experience loss. You may still grieve. But the fear of endings can be the ultimate motivator to prepare you emotionally, mentally, and even sometimes financially for what's next.

As a forty-something woman who's survived many heartbreaking goodbyes, I am intimately aware that nothing is forever. And in the aftermath of a tough ending, you may be afraid of ever putting yourself out there again, of trusting yourself. It's profoundly hard.

But let's, instead, appreciate this fear as an urging to protect your desire to live a life where you have many good—possibly better—days. This fear is ultimately leading you toward healing. As Becker wrote, to live fully is to live with an awareness of the terror that underlies everything. "Whatever man does on this planet," he says, "has to be done in the lived truth of the terror of creation, of the grotesque, of the rumble of panic underneath everything. Otherwise, it is false."[3] A large part of your success in managing this fear is to stay aware of what is *not* ending, and holding the two in balance.

A podcast listener once asked me, "Farnoosh, how do we prepare for the *world* ending?" I am reminded of this existential fear every time I watch *The Handmaid's Tale*. I appreciated that this person thought I had a clue. Build a bunker? Or better yet, say to yourself: *I know there's a chance for a cataclysmic ending someday. Tomorrow is never guaran-*

teed. But what is real right now? What do I still possess? How can I lever-
age this to make today matter?

A PROMPT TO RISE TO THE OCCASION

Let's begin with the jugular: the fear of death. As evolved humans, we have no real, concrete evidence of a rainbow-filled afterlife, and while many have faith in this prophecy, we can't help but grow anxious over the very real concept of death. Biologically, we're conditioned to focus on living. Studies say the brain rejects and compartmentalizes fears related to death *on purpose*.[4] But thinking about death, scientists at the University of Kentucky concluded—specifically, our own death—can trigger a greater appreciation for life.[5] It can make us happier. So this is a fear worth inviting into your life, but only by invitation. I don't recommend an open-door policy.

The fear of death can guide you to appreciate and respect what you have—including your mortality. It can be there, quite literally, to save your life.

My brain freaks out at the thought of skydiving. Are we 100 percent sure the parachute will open? While others might think it's fine to take the leap, there were thirty-five skydiving-related deaths between 2010 and 2019.[6] Of course, there were also 6.2 million jumps. And sure, you are more likely to die in a car crash, but skydiving is not a need. It's not how you get to work or the grocery store. It's a voluntary pastime that is designed to flirt with death and thus the Persian daughter in me cannot engage. As my dad likes to point out—*things only have to happen once*. This is an immigrant-dad risk calculus that, while statistically improbable, leads to a gargantuan *"Aslan!"* Appreciating and respecting our own mortality is how we can connect wisely with this fear. With feet planted on the ground.

As she led a new life in America, my mother was always terrified of losing her parents and not being with them in their aging years, especially when she lived so many miles apart. When I was eight or nine years old, and we'd bid farewell to my grandparents after one of their infrequent visits to the States, I watched my mother head to her bed, lie on her stomach, bury her face in her arms, and cry. I walked over and stood by her side, unsure of how to react, but knowing I didn't want to be anyplace else.

Decades later, in the summer of 2010, my then fifty-year-old mother would travel to Iran with her older sister to visit their parents. With both Todd and me finally out of the nest, she had more time to make these longer trips overseas and was committed to making them happen out of a fear of the ultimate ending: her parents passing.

The month-long voyage that year began as any typical return trip to Shiraz: family gatherings, gift-giving, and stocking up on saffron. But near the end of this stay, my grandmother would catch pneumonia. The infection spread quickly to her chest and lungs. The night they called the ambulance to rush Mamani to the hospital, my mom remembers holding her frail mother as she struggled to breathe. As the sirens neared, the sisters knew this was the end. Mamani passed away hours later.

My mother is a spiritual person who takes comfort in knowing that she was by her mother's side in those difficult, final days. The thought of receiving a phone call in the middle of the night, the one where she heard nothing at first when she picked up because the operator was trying to forge the overseas connection, terrified her because it would mean just one thing. The fear of being absent at the end of a parent's life prompted my mother to be with hers as much as possible. To have been with Mamani before she left this world, when she could easily have been several thousand miles away, is not something she takes for granted or believes was just luck. It was her intention.

When my friend Cameron Huddleston learned her mother had

been diagnosed with Alzheimer's disease, the fear of her mother's death stayed with her each day for the next twelve years, until she finally passed. It triggered an important conversation with her mom to craft a contingency plan and understand what she could do to help manage her health.

Cameron's fear of her mom's life ending drove her to restructure her own life as a wife, mom, and author so that she could become her mom's primary caretaker—from being her health advocate to attending doctor visits, managing her finances, and settling her mom into a memory care facility. Then her mom got struck by cancer. After that, a COVID infection. Her mom passed away in January of 2021 in a hospital bed relocated to the inside of Cameron's sunroom. "I told her it was okay to let go . . . and she did. She is finally at peace," Cameron shared with friends online.

Reflecting on those last few weeks of her mother's life, Cameron talks about anticipating the worst amid the pandemic. When her mom tested positive for COVID, she was no longer able to remain at her memory care facility. Rather than being overwhelmed by the ending, Cameron used her fear of it to prepare. When the time came, she was ready.

"When it comes to worst-case scenarios," she shared, "it's easy to tell yourself, 'We'll cross that bridge when we come to it.' From my experience, if you plan, you can actually cross the bridge rather than get swept away by a river of emotions that will cloud your judgment when emergencies strike."[7]

Cameron's story is another beautiful example of how the fear of an ending can inspire us to rise to an occasion, to serve the people we love most when we know our time with them is limited. Cameron wanted her mom's legacy to be preserved and remembered fondly, something her mom could no longer ensure on her own. It would be Cameron's opportunity, the role she was destined to play in those final months of her mother's life.

My own death is a serious worst-case scenario I revisit from time to time. I fear how that ending might impact my family's financial well-being, and that fear has been good for me.

One evening in 2020 . . . or was it 2021? (it was hard to keep track of time back then), lying in my daughter's bed as she fell asleep (our ritual), my instinct was to start panicking. She was fine. Everything was fine. But my mind started to imagine all the dreadful possibilities of me or my husband getting sick, getting hit by a car. I had a scare a few summers ago when I located a small lump in my left breast. A scan revealed it was just a benign cyst, but the thought of leaving the earth too soon, before my kids were on their own, lingered.

I sent a casual text to Tim from the bed beginning with the words: "If I die . . ."

What followed were very specific instructions for how to dole out my life insurance and social security benefits. I even offered him two options, one that involved selling our house and moving to Pennsylvania to be closer to his parents. The other scenario involved keeping the house and staying put until the kids were in college. You know, just in case I didn't make it until the end of the week, or the next morning? And as anyone who suffered with their kids through Zoom school during the pandemic knows, this was not a far-fetched prediction. Tim didn't reply. Instead, he ran into Colette's room, where I'd been texting in the dark. "Do you need to tell me something?" he asked nervously.

"No." I laughed. "But please don't delete what I wrote."

FEARING THE END, TREASURING WHAT ENDURES

When life moves on, our biggest fear is that we won't have the ability to travel along. But let that fear allow you to head toward the next chapter. While this truth might be hard to acknowledge when you're grieving, it's important to remember it. After all, we don't want our sadness to suffocate us; we want it to propel us to walk into this next phase of life with a deeper appreciation of what remains. And what is still possible.

My father has shown me how fearing an ending can catalyze you to not only embrace—but leverage—what endures. Because he's a Torabi, his sense of self-worth is deeply bound to his professional achievements. And when his forty-year career became threatened later in life, he feared a shattering of his identity. For much of his profession, he'd worked as an engineer in the semiconductor field (aka microchips). Over the decades, with so many mergers, acquisitions, and consolidations happening around him, he was routinely worried that his job might come to an end. We were all concerned for him, not sure how he'd manage the loss, having done something he loved so much for most of his life.

But then it happened. Well into his sixties, my dad got laid off. Some in his age group would have taken this as a cue to retire a little early, but for my father the fear of waking up and not feeling motivated to work on problems and equations was like losing the ability to walk. This fear of his work life being interrupted, possibly forever, convinced him to get proactive and creative. He realized that while the end of his old job meant the loss of his daily interactions with colleagues, a title, and salary, it didn't mean the loss of his stamina, work ethic, ambitions, and connections. And it certainly didn't kill his lifelong appetite for learning. This all helped him strategize a new career path and explore how he might reemerge. Maybe it wouldn't be the same type of work. Maybe the job wouldn't pay as much or have the same prestige as his last position, but the fear and grief of being disconnected from his passion and professional life (and his fear of sitting bored next to my very active mother, let's be honest) was greater than the worry of putting himself out there again to rejuvenate a career in an ageist market.

So, after registering for state unemployment, my dad began researching his next steps. He decided to channel his skills and his love for math into a new field involving machine learning and artificial intelligence. He registered for free online courses through both Coursera and Stanford University. He woke up each morning to read, test, and update his LinkedIn profile. He knew this process would take time and that rejection might happen, but the fear of an ending made him unstoppable. Within eighteen months, he had a full-time role. He was doing something quite new and different, but he was back at it again. The ending of his previous job was now just a moment from the past.

In my own career, I've had many pinch-me moments, but presenting on television tops them all. Nothing makes the little girl inside of me, who loved to perform in solo acts in her bedroom, happier than being on television to share advice or host programs. Whether it's sitting across from Kelly Ripa (an absolute class act who is as loveable and kind off-camera as she is on. Proof again that being yourself is the key to likeability) or hosting my own series on CNBC, I never feel more in my element than in those instances. I've come a very long way since that first *Today* show blunder.

And in my twenties and thirties, I thought pursuing a steady television career like, say, the one Suze Orman led on CNBC, or the one Barbara Corcoran continues to have on *Shark Tank*, was the ultimate endeavor. It would unlock all my dreams. It would lead to stardom, riches, helping more people than I could ever imagine.

But each time I got the chance to pilot a new show, I never reached that promised land. The programs became what I call "one-hit non-wonders" never to be renewed (or remembered much) after the first season. Reflecting on it now, it's easy for me to be at peace with these endings, to see them for what they were—momentary successes. But the anticipation of waiting to hear from the network powers-that-be about whether they will give you and your hardworking crew *another* go at one of the best jobs you've ever pulled off is, in a word, miserable. The fear of endings during that waiting period, which usually stretches for weeks, possibly months, brews uncertainty and doubt. With so much hope riding on the continuation of a TV project, I feared the end because, well, what would I have to go back to? Would it be any better? Could I ever top this experience? How else would I reach the pinnacle?

The *New York Times* bestselling author of *Eat, Pray, Love*, Elizabeth Gilbert, talks about this dilemma, where you fear whether you will be able to surpass a previous creative accomplishment. When one achievement ends, be it writing a book of poetry, producing a television show, or painting an award-winning piece of art, and you're hoping (and expected) to strike again with that same "genius," how, Gilbert asked in her famous TED Talk, "Your Elusive Creative Genius," do you avoid the fear of not being "doomed," and dying "on a scrap heap of broken dreams"?[8] The advice she shared is what I've most taken to heart and what I clung to when I feared the end of my CNBC show, *Follow the Leader*, in 2016. And it is this: You are not a genius. But you sometimes do *have* a genius. It may not always strike. And that's not your fault. **The results and the reception of your work are not entirely up to you. Especially in the creative field.**

You can give your all to a magnificent TV series, but so many stars need to align for this experience to continue. If the network airs it in a bad time slot and does little to promote it, if the production company rushes to film and cuts corners, and if the audience is underwhelmed because the episodes lack the table-flipping drama as seen on Bravo TV, then you're not going to get a second season. That's not your failure. That's not an ending that you caused. *That's just facts, Farnoosh.*

And you know what? Maybe the point is that not all jobs and projects need to go on forever. Had that TV show lasted many more seasons and become a constant in my career, I wouldn't have complained. But rather than allow the fear of an ending to freeze me or make me feel like a failure, I used the moment to find opportunity.

Months after the last episode of *Follow the Leader* aired, it was confirmed that the show would not return. The decision had been made and there was nothing I could do to reverse it. Instead of letting the ending feel like a dead end, I let it swing open a door by asking this question: *Was there something I'd been pushing to the side but still very much longed to do? And could that perhaps bring me much more happiness?*

I was sad, of course, and all those normal fears came up, but in the aftermath of this finale, the fear helped me to gradually identify what my next act would be. This departure would be an invitation to something very exciting in my life, something I'd always wanted but may have been too nervous to pursue because of our production demands: expanding our little family. Now, with time and space opening up, a new, more beautiful beginning was possible. The following year, our daughter, Colette, was born.

The fear of an ending is often crippling because we dread losing the ideals we've assigned to a project, job, or relationship—more than the thing itself. When he got laid off, it's not like my dad feared the farewell to pointless meetings and an insufferable boss. When the network yanked *Follow the Leader*, I was not afraid of missing out on the endless travel and being away from my family for weeks at a time. But because my father and I were so attached to what our jobs said about us, our merits, and our capabilities, we assumed that if and when they ended, so would our sense of accomplishment and the chances of achieving at a high level again. It was that aspect of the ending that gave us anxiety for a bit of time. But because the fear of endings is so intent on having us reclaim our purpose, it ultimately steered our focus toward all the good that remained and how, even with the passing of these jobs, we still had much to experience and enjoy.

Outside of our professional lives, too, we may be hesitant about ending a romantic partnership and moving on because we're more attached to the image of what it represents from the outside looking in (commitment, love, security) than the person we are with. You're less afraid of not coming home to your partner again and more the elimination of "us" and all that your union symbolizes to the outside world. Part of the fear of finalizing a divorce is that being linked to a "long-lasting" marriage will no longer be yours. The ending may also lead to a sense of failure, loss, rejection, and loneliness. But that happy couple you sketched in your mind was a rough drawing, an ideal that no longer really existed (if it ever did). What is true—and what was true all along—is that you deserve better. Your fear wants you to re-member this and use it as a catalyst to map your exit.

So when fearing an ending and unsure of the direction to take, I find it's helpful to ask yourself: *Is what I'm scared to give up . . . a real thing? How will my truth inform my next move?*

This dynamic plays out in parenthood, as well. On the blog *Just Plain Beth*, which coaches moms of transgender teens and young adults, its founder Beth Richardson writes: "It took me years of therapy and a lot of self-reflection to recognize that what I was grieving was the loss of the idea of having a daughter."[9] As the eldest sister of four brothers, Beth had longed to have a sister. When her daughter was born, her dream of having a lifelong bond with a girl was realized. But when her daughter came out as transgender, this mother writes, that dream died again. At first, she thought her grief was related to her child's transition. But it was about herself and coming to terms with an ideal she'd tried to pursue all her life. "My body re-lived all the disappointment of learning my youngest brother was a boy and the pain of never having a sister. I grieved more than just the loss of my daughter. I mourned the sister I never had and the childhood I always wanted." Beth's fear over this end-ing was tied to a loss of hopes and dreams imagined. What remained— and what was true—was that she was still a mother to a wonderful child whose main difference now was being much happier. And that perspective was immensely helpful. It provided her the understanding that her child's journey was separate from her own.

As a mom, I, too, have certain hopes for my children as they grow older. But what I've learned from more experienced parents is that your children will be—and must be—who they are. A job well done as a parent is to equip your kid with a sense of independence and autonomy, a desire to choose for themselves. If we fear an ending to the *thought* of who our children will become and resist and reject who our kids *really* want to be, it may mean the end of something much more significant and final: our bond and connection to our most important people. Be more afraid of that—and let it lead you.

Endings are never a small thing. We may need to give our grief more time. Life may feel uncomfortable and unfamiliar for a while. At first I go for the box of tissues, a dirty martini, and doomscrolling. Eventually and often slowly, I venture for, and find, a new beginning. My fear propels me to what is waiting for me on the other side of the sadness. Though moving on can be hard and require a lot of work, and we'll be forced to start over, find new meaning and purpose, our fear motivates us to keep dancing, working. **Feeling capable and strong in a world full of finales and last stops means appreciating what remains. And starting fresh.**

Following her mom's funeral, my own mom's fear of staying permanently in an ending led her to find some unexpected hope and a renewed faith on the other side of *her* sadness: a little bird. This wasn't Tooty from my days in kindergarten, but a robin that decided to build a nest outside her kitchen window. This bird, she told us, would visit each day for months and peck at the glass. It was, at first, a curious distraction as she struggled to come to terms with losing her mom, but then, as the bird tried harder to earn my mother's attention, she saw how it symbolized something more. Because it was chatty and insistent like Mamani had been, Mom was convinced the bird was a sign from above. Her mom, she believed, was watching over her. That allowed her to trust that her relationship with her mom was not stuck in an interminable ending. The belief comforted her, and gave her the hope and resilience to move on with a little more resolve that her mom's life was in a continuum. It allowed her, in a way, to think less about her untimely death and more about the bond they had shared for all the years Mamani lived—and even still.

IT'S OKAY TO CRY

The grieving that follows learning you've miscarried is insurmountable. And I was afraid to be open about it, afraid of being judged for overreacting, as we all know it could have been worse. *At least I was able to get pregnant in the first place. At least Tim and I are healthy and we can keep trying again. At least, at least, at least.*

So, I grieved in silence. First came denial (*are you sure?*) followed by anger (*how can this be?*) and rationalizing (*well, I mean, a lot of women don't even know they're pregnant and miscarry this early on*), and then, soon after, came depression. The sorrow hit hard after we arrived back at our apartment and in the long weeks and months after. When I called my mom following our devastating appointment, I broke into tears. So did Tim.

"It's okay," my mom responded. "It's very normal." I could tell even she was struggling to remain strong for us. But my mom never likes it when her children grieve. She doesn't want us to get stuck in the ineffable mourning of an ending, she wants us to move on—and quickly. Except that in order to use your fear of ending to find that open door, you also have to feel all the feelings. In order to move on, I knew I had to do that. And not be ashamed or embarrassed by it.

It wasn't just my mom. I listened to many friends dole out well-intentioned but unhelpful advice following my miscarriage. They told me that I shouldn't be upset. *You don't want an unhealthy baby*, they said. *Your body is doing what it's supposed to do*, they reassured me. *This baby, Farnoosh, was not meant to be.*

Stuck in my grief, I was afraid and reluctant to try to get pregnant again and risk experiencing more despair. And every morning, the pain of this miscarriage and the fear of it happening again would be waiting for me as soon as I opened my eyes. A miscarriage is, of course, far more brutal and heartbreaking the farther along you are. But however and whenever it happens, allow yourself to go through the hurt. Maybe nobody will ever tell you that what you need is a big, long cry. But I am telling you, it's okay. Sob and sob and sob. Why? Because when we give ourselves the space and patience to grieve without limitations and be with our thoughts and reflections, we have a better chance of accepting our loss. "For many people, they need more exposure to those memories to really understand what happened and how they understand the experience," said Dr. Mary-Frances O'Connor, an associate professor of psychology at the University of Arizona, in a conversation about grieving on the podcast *Speaking of Psychology*.[10] By allowing yourself the right to feel and act upon what you're feeling, whether that means crying, curling up in a ball, or furiously organizing your sweaters, you're building strength and resilience, and finding your way through, opening the pathways. When you let yourself grieve, you won't be lost in your ending anymore. You'll be able to look up and out for your new beginning.

One time a female entrepreneur who was clearly in a dark place joined me on my podcast. I'd ask her softball questions about her company or her greatest money memory as a kid (typical for the show), and she'd pause and throw the questions back at me. "I don't know. What's *your* greatest money memory?" she'd say snarkily. Trust me when I say it took everything in me not to politely end the interview quickly, but I played along. I knew her hostility wasn't about me. She was dealing with something, and so I let her throw her daggers. And eventually, on the podcast, she revealed the underlying pain in her life. She confessed she'd suffered a miscarriage earlier that year. My heart went out to her. And while I wanted to dive in and discuss her grief on the show, I didn't want to hijack her suffering if that wasn't what she was prepared to do.

But when I stopped recording, I told her how sorry I was, how I knew this pain well, and that the one thing I wished someone, anyone, had told me in that moment was this: "It's okay to be sad. Be sad for as long as you need."

Dr. Ellen Vora, author of *The Anatomy of Anxiety*, shared with me on my podcast that crying is "absolutely necessary."[11] "We really betray ourselves and get ourselves blocked and stuck when we are fair-weather friends with our emotions. I think that in our society, which can be a bit emotion-phobic, we're underdeveloped in our relationship to grief. Crying . . . that's one of my favorite things that I think we need to rebrand. When we cry, we try to suck it back in, make it as small as possible and apologize, like it's a burden to the people around us. I think we all need to normalize it. Let the crying be big. Don't apologize for it. It's the wisdom of the body giving us an opportunity for a release," she said.

And we can learn from our years spent crying as children, Dr. Vora continued. "[Kids] have a built-in release system. They have meltdowns, and it's not pretty. We don't like it. But that's how they get their release. I think adults really have a lot to learn from that. We need some built-in release, and tears are a wonderful opportunity for that release. But we pinch it back, like the way someone pinches in a sneeze. What we really need to do instead is dive into it. Let it be big and complete."

I, for one, am a big snot-nosed crier. I cry watching Instagram reels of dogs reuniting with their soldier mommies and daddies; I tear up when my daughter tells me she loves me while sitting on the potty (it's where we all have our deepest thoughts, isn't it?); and I am bawling, needing to pull over, as I drive listening to journalists' harrowing dispatches from wars and natural disasters during the BBC World News radio hour.

The world is full of triggers that make you want to weep. And only now in my forties can I say with certainty that if you are sad about an ending, you have all the permission in the world to have a deep, beautiful (or even ugly!) cry. Be sad. Don't try to move on too fast or look away. Instead, when a chapter in your life is coming to an end, feel it in your bones. Feel it travel from your head to your heart to your gut. **Mourning can be a way to pay tribute.** Allow the sadness to run its course and recognize how meaningful those days were. Sadness can be your path to dignify the love and attachment you had to a dream, an experience, a person, this life.

My miscarriage coincided with my thirty-third birthday. Tim gave me a beautiful ring that I have kept on my finger ever since, a reminder that grieving is a sign of love and that your sadness does not take from your strength.

FEAR NOT THE REGRET IN AN ENDING

I had a best friend once. I loved her like a sister. But when our parents had a falling out, our relationship, something I had never thought would expire, became collateral damage. Our phone calls and texts ceased in 2006. We never discussed it. It was just understood, sort of like in a divorce, some friends will side with one spouse over the other. Sometimes we make the choice based on survival—*who will give me more of what I seek in life?* My friend and I chose our parents.

When I rebooted my Facebook page following my marriage, I had to re-request all my friend connections on the platform. I never reached out to this particular friend, too afraid my request would sit pending for a lifetime. Today, if I search for her on social media, my limited access only shows her profile picture from over fifteen years ago, just as I remember her. And I grieve.

We didn't know it at the time, but we'd share our final meal at her apartment in Philadelphia during her first year in law school and after my big break working on-camera as a financial reporter. We sat across from each other over her glass coffee table, sipping chilled Chardonnay, feeling very grown-up and on our way. We retold stories from our days spent in high school, attached at the hip. Those many weekend sleepovers, trips to the shops at Suburban Square, and that time I joined her at her private school when my public school was closed for teacher meetings. I loved spending time with her so much, I elected to sit alongside her in her AP French class on my day off.

We were both Iranian. Both big sisters. Both fans of foreign language films, musical theater, and all the scented soaps from the Body Shop. We spent much of our teen years imagining our futures—the careers we would build, the people we might marry, and even the smallest details, like how we'd dress our babies based on our own personalities. Hers would be in preppy, seersucker overalls. Mine in bomber jackets and lace-up boots.

It continues to be one of my deepest regrets in life that we never followed through on sharing the moments we pledged we would as adults.

Regret is a sibling of grief. And it can be all tied into our fear of endings. But do we need to fear regret?

No. Regret is one of the best teachers in our lives, says Daniel Pink, pop-science writer and author of the bestseller *The Power of Regret*. In his book he synthesizes research in psychology, neuroscience, economics, and biology to dispel the widely held philosophy: "no regrets." Instead, Pink calls regret "an essential component of the human experience" that is ubiquitous. "It doesn't just make us human. It also makes us better," he says.[12]

The trick to using regret as a source of power, he writes, is looking back at these challenging times in our lives when we made a deliberate—or not so deliberate—choice to end something by thinking *if only* rather than at least. "At least" thoughts elicit gratitude and encourage us to hold sacred the healthy and happy emotions tied to that past relationship or experience, but they don't necessarily propel us toward better decisions in the future. On the other end, examining regret through the lens of "if only" gives us more grief—but that is the point, Pink concludes. "By making us feel worse today, regret helps us do better tomorrow."

The exercise for all of us: Think through your "at leasts," so that you can provide yourself with gratitude, and then focus on the "if onlys," so that you enhance your decisions, improve your results, and make more meaning in your life. For example: *If only I had told her I loved her. If only I'd been a bigger advocate for myself. If only I'd looked for the signs sooner.*

This exercise is not meant to make us feel like victims of our decisions or like we should have known better. The point is that we know better now, thanks to examining our regrets.

Two years after our miscarriage, Tim and I welcomed our first baby. We named him Evan. The name popped into Tim's mind when he woke up one morning close to the due date. He suggested it over breakfast, and I immediately loved it. We later learned the name means "God is gracious," and although neither one of us is particularly religious, it felt fitting given how much our faith had been tested in recent years.

Evan's birth announcement was featured on my social pages, accessible to, say, a long-ago friend who might be as curious about my whereabouts as I was about hers. Though I never heard from her, I had a feeling she had to know that somewhere in Brooklyn my son was dressed like a rock star.

Two years later, through the grapevine, I learned that my once-upon-a-time friend had given birth to a boy, too. It was bittersweet to discover this only through word of mouth, far from how she and I had ever envisioned sharing milestones. But then, through the grapevine, when I learned her son's name, my heart skipped a beat. Her chosen name for her little guy? Evan. Funny coincidence? Most likely yes. We had parallel tastes in so much—books, fashion, movies. Why not also in baby names? But if I'm being honest, part of me wants very much to believe that this was her not-so-subtle way of saying, *I see you, Far-*

noosh. I remember us. If only we had stayed connected. Now through the gift of a name, through our children, we can be.

The Fear of Endings Self-Inquiry

- Is what is on the other side of the ending going to help you?
- Will you look back on this moment and feel as though you did what was best for yourself?
- Will this move provide you with more of what you are seeking in life, like balance or more stability or money?
- Would you benefit from reframing the notion of regret?
- Are you allowing yourself to grieve and find strength in your sadness?
- How can you reflect upon the regret of this ending with thoughts of "*if only?*"

9

THE FEAR OF LOSING YOUR FREEDOM

and how it fuels self-advocacy
and inspires a legacy

M Y PERSIAN DAD LIVES and breathes numbers. He eats them, too, if you count his on-again, off-again obsession in the mid-nineties with the Points Program from Weight Watchers. Back then if you told him what you ate in a day, he'd calculate your consumed points in his head, along with the odds of you being disgusted with yourself at the next weigh-in. He was never wrong. There is rarely a winning rebuttal to my father's risk calculations. This is particularly true if what you are risking is your freedom.

So it should not have surprised me when, in the summer of 2003, my father raised deep concerns over my plans to move to Iran, the country he and my mother had purposely left in pursuit of more access and opportunities. At the time, the US-led "Global War on Terror" was playing out in bordering Iraq. All eyes were on the Middle East, and the world begged for more uncensored, raw narratives of what was transpiring in the region. As I finished my journalism degree at Columbia, I felt a calling to embed there as a freelance reporter and unearth these stories. I had been inspired throughout the school year when international reporters visited to express how rewarding it had been to travel the world and shed light on civilian life amid wars and political conflicts. Was it dangerous? Very. But these brave journalists were fulfilling their life's mission to give a voice to the voiceless.

I remember one evening during grad school sitting tall in the back row of our packed auditorium to catch a glimpse of Christiane Amanpour sharing about her on-the-ground coverage of the Persian Gulf War and the Siege of Sarajevo, as well as her challenging interviews with Iran's president and other global players. She had blazed the trail I thought for sure I wanted to follow.

That summer, as US forces were attempting to zero in on Saddam Hussein, I heard of a few male classmates heading to the Middle East to report on the global event. Of course, I knew they had a leg up and could go more freely because of their gender. But it didn't deter me or make me feel less capable of setting similar goals. I was used to being the odd one out. And I loved the fact that I was doing something a little daring for once. Like we all do in our twenties when we are finally on our own, I was craving a sense of purpose. If this endeavor lived up to expectations, it could be the start of something big. I trusted that the investment would pay off.

I got the ball rolling. As our graduate program was ending that May, I secured my media credentials and began contacting newsroom editors to let them know I'd be in Iran—and soon. They eagerly awaited my articles. My plan was to use my fluency in Farsi and my family connections in Shiraz and Tehran to help me navigate and identify reputable stories. I would eventually call my aunt and uncle to ask if I could stay in their guest bedroom. I mean, why not?

My professors praised my fearlessness. "How intrepid of you, Farnoosh!" They openly shared resources and insights on how to make inroads abroad and get those front-page scoops.

My dad began to see that my flirtation with venturing to Iran was fast becoming an obsession. He and my mom listened closely as I laid out my final plans over breakfast a few blocks from my apartment later that summer. My father hadn't touched his egg white omelet. He waited patiently for me to finish before leaning in to tell me the thing I needed to hear, voicing a haunting fear that I'd been avoiding deeply. "If you go there, Farnoosh, you will die," he said. "They will kill you."

He proceeded to remind me of who I was: a US media reporter, a woman, and the daughter of parents who seemingly betrayed their country during the revolution and left to live in enemy territory. I was a triple threat and not the good kind. If I dared go, it was best to wake up to the fear of losing my freedom to a tyrannical regime, he said.

Since the 1979 revolution, Iran's oppressive government has imprisoned and tortured women and journalists many times over. Earlier that same summer, Zahra "Ziba" Kazemi-Ahmadabadi, an Iranian Canadian freelance photographer, had been raped and killed by Iranian officials following her arrest as she was photographing families of detainees outside a prison in Tehran.[1] My parents' fear was that the police there would target me, capture me, and do what they wanted with me.

Next to my dad, my mother sat with a look of horror on her face. When she was still and allowed my father to talk, it usually meant that she couldn't believe how *fearless* her children were being. She needed my dad to step in, bring the terror to the forefront, and save us.

I knew this overseas assignment would require guts and grit and being bolder than I'd ever been. But giving up the freedom to pursue my livelihood? I couldn't have that. I wanted to do what I wanted to do.

At that moment, though, the nervousness in my father's shaky voice made it difficult for me to ignore the grave reality of embedding in Iran. His words reminded me that pursuing freedom, even as an American-born citizen, is not always straightforward. In theory, I had the free will to travel independently and follow this desired career path. But not without accepting what was at stake. The question for me then became: Did I want the privilege to be a journalist, or did I want to stay alive? Because in Iran, for me, those two things were mutually exclusive. I couldn't have both. I'd need to choose.

THE FRAGILITY OF OUR FREEDOMS

These days, despite living in a democratic nation, we are growing fearful of not being able to reach various freedoms and practicing them as we want and should. A 2022 report found that a majority of Americans—on both sides of the political aisle—believe that over the next ten years they will lose more freedom than they have right now.[2]

The topic is fragile these days. Even if you feel confident to openly speak your mind, there are probably other moments when you fear being boxed into a corner and left powerless. At critical junctures in your personal, professional, and financial life, you may feel dread over not being able to fully pursue life as you want to because you don't have enough money, access, education, or political influence.

This fear shows up when needing to answer to an unsympathetic authority at work who could fire you on the spot. It's there as we contemplate major commitments like getting married, having kids, or buying a home. We worry that this serious life move may prohibit our ability to use our time, energy, and money freely. We're afraid we won't be able to choose what we want, or use our voice to protect ourselves. This fear is especially real if you have been underestimated, marginalized, or labeled as different. **With this fear, we're afraid of losing ourselves.**

Sometimes this fear rises when we've lost some control. In the harrowing months and years of the pandemic, for example, we saw a disproportionate number of women forced out of the employment market, as they grappled with holding down a career and caring for loved ones at home. The two occupations that they had somehow once juggled simultaneously became competing full-time jobs, seemingly overnight, because the already-shaky societal support system for childcare and eldercare—daycare, schools, neighbors, or loved ones—fell away, leaving them with nothing to fall back on. When it comes to looking after others, women are expected to be at the forefront of this duty. Upward of 75 percent of all caregivers are women, according to the National Institute of Aging. And compared to men, female caregivers may offer as much as 50 percent more of their time in support.[3]

Thus, during the pandemic, millions of women exited the workforce, some without wanting to. This wasn't their hope and dream. They just didn't have good choices to continue being both ambitious caregivers *and* paid workers, while also keeping their families safe and healthy, freedoms they may have had a better time managing in the *before* times.

What happened to women in 2020 and 2021 is yet another example of how freedom carries a cost. When two freedoms butt heads, as they did for women in the pandemic, we may need to choose. In other cases, affording one can be far too expensive in and of itself. For me, going to Iran all those years ago would have meant exercising my freedom to be the person I wanted to be: a truth-seeking journalist. And while my father never said I *couldn't* go (he wasn't about to stop the plane), he made clear that once I landed on Iranian soil, I could spend my remaining days in an Iranian prison. It might mean risking my life. Would I be able and willing to afford it? Would it even be worth it . . . for me?

This tension of not being able to rely on absolutes in terms of freedom hits home for all of us in our own ways. I'd learned how, in pursuit of the American Dream, my parents had to practice above-average courage and put aside comforts like the closeness and support of relatives, as well as the ability to express themselves freely and be *Irooni* in public. In those early years, my father was afraid of speaking up to horrible bosses at work, afraid it might mean retaliation and losing his visa. That was part of the price they paid to inherit certain allowances here. All the while, their new life in America required them to say goodbye to a way of life back home that, while imperfect, was, at least, predictable.

I reserved exploring the fear of losing our freedom for the end of our journey here because this fear is most vital to our existence. What could be more important, as we venture out into this world—that honestly does feel as though it's *out to get us* some days—than our fear of losing our freedom? If you ask someone who's in the later stages of life, whose wisdom is unmatched, they're likely to say that what they fear most—more than approaching death—is losing their independence.[4] They are willing to put their lives on the line to insist on freedom. For without it, then what is left?

This final chapter is not about how to use your fear of losing your freedom to cure pandemics, save democracy, or become a revolutionary, although I have all those articles bookmarked on my laptop. What I *am* here to share is how to leverage our fear to design or possibly remap the liberties we seek in our personal lives. When we feel as though we're stuck along our journey toward independence, we'll discover how the fear of losing that grip can spring us into action and carry us to a better place. It's also telling us that to make our own decisions, have more agency in our lives, and pursue the world as we want, it helps to get loud, sound the alarm, and self-advocate. Finally, the fear of losing your freedom sometimes wants you to lay some important groundwork for the next generation. This fear can be a gift that keeps on giving.

WHICH FREEDOM WILL YOU FIGHT HARDEST FOR?

Before we dig deeper, let's huddle for a moment to talk about how we can't have all the freedoms. And believe me, I struggled coming to terms with this. But the dumpster fires are real, my friend. Do you ever get the feeling that no matter how far you progress in life, no matter how many hills you climb, battles you win, frogs you kiss, and all the other metaphors, that you're still a ways away from ever feeling and being truly independent? That you're oh-so-close to creating the harmony and richness you crave and deserve, to walk through life needing to answer to nobody, to know you can use your voice and, in doing so, not only achieve what you desire, but lift others along the way?

And then, something blows up in your face. Your life starts to unravel. The Supreme Court overturns a critical law. You're told you can't have what you want. Something—or someone—is blocking your pursuit of living life on your own chosen terms.

In America we have many rights that people in other countries would die for. As I write, women in Iran are marching in the streets and into the line of fire, knowing they could be killed as they fight to earn back fundamental human rights that vanished more than forty years ago. What started in early September 2022 as a protest in the wake of the police killing of twenty-two-year-old Mahsa Amini for not wearing her headscarf properly in public, turned into a mass revolt by Iran's citizens, with rallies around the globe demanding a regime overhaul.[5] Freedoms can be seized at any moment. For this reason, we must value the ones we have, identify which we care for most and why, and save our energy for defending them like the brazen *tarsoos* we are.

For as long as I can remember, I have wanted the ultimate freedom of being a woman who could stand on her own two feet financially so that when the love of her life arrived, she could fall head over heels and not be concerned with the figures on his W-2. Even as a kid, I remember thinking that as long as I had money in the bank and a driver's license, I was bulletproof. That was the freedom I was willing to fall on my sword for. And it was a bit of a climb to reach this personal pinnacle, as society and culture weren't totally supportive.

As we know, I finally found this big love in Tim. It was—and remains—a relationship that didn't threaten my desires to be career-focused and financially ambitious. But in the beginning and until we were engaged, my parents were on the fence about the fact that I had a more advanced degree and earned more than Tim. We laugh about the time, a couple years into dating, when my dad tried to convince Tim to earn a PhD *and* an MBA.

At first, my mom wasn't sure that, despite insisting I grow up to be an independent woman, it was "right" or even sustainable for a woman to be the higher earner in a marriage. What happens when you have kids and, as the mom, you want to leave your job to raise them as a stay-at-home parent? Oh, the irony! If only she could see that I desired my financial independence in marriage because I'd watched *her* struggle to possess it.

We reconciled for the most part on this issue, but Sheida Joon loved to keep me on my toes. When Tim pulled my parents aside to share his plans to propose in 2010, she got weird again.

"Farnoosh, do you know Tim just asked us for your hand in marriage?" she said with her arms crossed, leaning up against the bedroom door.

I raised my MacBook off my lap, moved it to the side of the bed, and took a beat before locking eyes with my mother. My heart was racing.

I had known full well that Tim was going in for "The Big Ask" that weekend while visiting my parents. The plan was that I'd hide out in their downstairs guest bedroom while he gathered them in the kitchen to have the talk.

Asking for my hand may be antiquated, but Iranians are obsessed with formalities. Whenever a relative calls from Shiraz, the first twelve minutes are spent exchanging prim and proper pleasantries before mentioning that a great aunt passed away in her sleep. It's like a *Downton Abbey* scene but at a higher volume.

And although my parents had never explicitly told me and Tim that receiving their blessing was a prerequisite to getting married, I knew it would make them feel good.

"Well," Sheida Joon said, "we told him no."

As my mom and I moved out of the bedroom and approached the men to "have a discussion," I saw Tim staring down at his feet. I felt so bad for him.

Persian Dad, however, was in a different spirit. He was grinning from ear to ear.

What in the world?

"What are *you* so happy about, Dad?" I snapped.

And that's when the room erupted in laughter. I looked at Tim for an explanation. He glanced at my parents and then turned to me and said, "They actually said *yes*."

"I tricked you!" my mom said.

Unimpressed, I reached for some wine.

Wanting my parents' approval raises the complexity of being an independence-seeking woman today. We have been sold a myth of being able to "have it all," which, in practice, is damn exhausting. We can't have *all the freedoms*, and while we know this to be true and have come to terms with it, it still hurts. We hear: Become the CEO! Run for office! Start a business! But also, be sure to pack their bento lunch boxes with equal parts protein and grains or else what kind of a batty mom are you? Society loves to raise us up and then knock us down. It glorifies female entrepreneurship, but then warns such an entrepreneur that she won't find a suitable partner if he's intimidated by her success. A woman may choose to be a full-time uncompensated caregiver at home, but behind the scenes she loses financial autonomy because her partner makes and controls all the money.

I was in the seventh grade when I first reflected on the many layers of freedom. Our civics teacher, Mr. Pinsky, a recent college grad who, with his cargo pants and brown boots, resembled the sort of adventurous male you'd spot in a Patagonia catalog, went around the room and asked each student to define the word in their own way. "What . . . is . . . freeee-dom?" he asked as melodramatically as possible.

We were seated alphabetically, and by the time Mr. Pinsky reached me, I'd had the benefit of time to reflect on my answer and hear the other kids provide theirs. Their replies began to echo one another: "Freedom is doing whatever you want to do." "Freedom is having control." "Freedom is power." "Freedom is not needing to ask your mom."

I chimed in with a different take: "Freedom is not free."

I thought it was profound, unaware that it was an already well-established viewpoint among grown-up society.

Mr. Pinsky stroked his goatee. He squinted his green eyes, nodding slowly. "Riiiight," he said. The poor guy was probably unprepared for things to get so dark.

I wasn't trying to be a contrarian or depressing. I was merely taking a step back and examining freedom for what I had learned it to be as a child of immigrants from a war-torn country.

Had my parents *not* been joking that afternoon when they said they wouldn't give me and Tim their blessing, I was ready to fight for the freedom I desired more than most: the opportunity to marry the guy I wanted. In my eyes, freedom shouldn't be defined as upholding antiquated values. Wharton professor and author Adam Grant once said, "Too many people spend their lives being dutiful descendants instead of good ancestors. . . . It's more important to make your children proud of you than your parents."[6] My parents had made me proud of them. And now I wanted to try to re-create that sense of honor in my own family by exercising my choice to marry the person who valued me, even if he wasn't who my parents had imagined.

As we piled into the car and headed out for a celebratory lunch, I realized there is no price too high for certain personal freedoms that I see as nonnegotiables—to pick my own partner, have sovereignty over my body, and work and earn a living as I desire (and safely). The list continues, but these must-haves are at the top. And this is fundamental to what this fear is urging us to clarify and claim.

Having your personal freedom—the ability to make choices for yourself, live life freely, and show up as yourself without damaging consequences—is what you and all of us unequivocally deserve and need. Scientists have explored the relationship between autonomy and human psychology, and they basically confirm what we already know: possessing free will is fundamental to our ability to achieve goals, have healthy relationships, and be happy.[7] There's often no better feeling. And yet.

THE SPARK FOR A NEW, AUTONOMOUS BLUEPRINT

I don't expect things to always go my way, but when they haven't, and it threatens my ability to practice an important freedom, I've been quick to find a back door, a hidden staircase, or create my own space-flying contraption to land safely.

This determination has been a theme in one of my recurring night terrors—the one of me flying solo through the skies. I've Googled it and apparently it means that I have a deep-rooted desire for doing what I want, when and how I want. *Oh, hail the omniscient Google.*

This dream sequence usually begins with hearing a burglar roam through our Worcester apartment. I'm four or five years old and alone and in my twin bed. As I tiptoe to my window, I'm scared but decide I must be brave. I shall leap out of the third floor and make a peaceful landing on the patch of grass below. I close my eyes, and just as I'm about to descend, a lightness takes over my body. I'm being carried up to the clouds. I recall a sense of relief, floating above the neighborhood, our white Camry resembling a fleck of snow in the driveway. Moments go by, and just as I begin to enjoy myself, fear sinks in. How will I land? How will I find my way back home? What if my mother is searching for me? I'm faced with a myriad of fears: insecurity, loneliness, feeling lost, getting in trouble. And then, just as my body loses altitude, I wake up. I am brought back to reality and left wondering what to make of it all. Luckily this is just a bad dream. But in real life, there are moments when I've felt a loss of control over my own freedoms. Like that recurring nightmare, they were wake-up calls. And they've prompted me to rise up.

When the fear of losing your freedom arrives, it's tempting to start the blame game and focus on the externalities that pose threats to living your best life. What's wrong with them? What gives? Why me? But the healthier question this fear is urging us to answer is: *What's an option that I, myself, can create?* Maybe it's not a change you can design today, but you can start plotting now to arrive at a place where experiencing this freedom is possible. You can reverse engineer a preferable outcome for yourself. Look for better examples of how you'd like to live your life and draft them as part of your new blueprint.

I'm reminded of what can inspire a new design or approach to exercising our personal freedoms when reading Brit Marling's essay in the *Atlantic*, written during the height of the #metoo movement, called "Harvey Weinstein and the Economics of Consent."[8] She openly shares how, after arriving in Los Angeles in the early 2000s to excitedly pursue acting, she experienced how awfully threatening the industry was to women. "I quickly realized that a large portion of the town functioned inside a soft and sometimes literal trafficking or prostitution of young women (a commodity with an endless supply and an endless demand)," she writes. She recalls the time she read for a role plainly entitled "Nurse," and how most of the women in the waiting room, including her, were planning not to show off their artistry but their bodies because that was the expectation. "I was dressed like a sex object," she says.

Power dynamics in Hollywood, she concludes, are economic dynamics. To have the freedom to pursue acting feeling confident you can refuse predators like Harvey Weinstein without consequence is partly a matter of financial security, Marling writes, because these men could and would punish women by making sure they'd never work again. "That's not just artistic or emotional exile—that's also economic exile," she says. Fearing her security and safety while attempting to practice this profession, something that should have been her right, led her to develop a new persona, one that still gave her the opportunities to practice her craft but with far more agency: a storyteller and creator. So she stopped going to auditions. She landed a day job and spent her off hours devouring screenwriting literature. She spent years constructing a new blueprint. By 2011, she had cowritten and acted in two films, both featured at the Sundance Film Festival.

A few years later, she *would* meet Weinstein for a "meeting." He would attempt to coerce her into having sex with him. Terrified and shaken, she hurried out of the room and began crying. "I wept because I had gone up the elevator when I knew better. I wept because I had let him touch my shoulders. I wept because at other times in my life, under other circumstances, I had not been able to leave."

On the other side of the country, entrepreneur Sunny Israni knows well what it feels like to have your professional freedom threatened by awful, external factors. He joined me on *So Money* to talk about the backlash he received working on Wall Street as an openly gay South Asian man.[9] His ambitions to become a stock trader and climb through the ranks of the investing industry at his company were quashed when a straight, white, male colleague told him that he didn't have the right "mannerisms" for the job. "To get far in finance, it really is about building those connections and networks, and it was difficult for me," Sunny said. He knew he wouldn't be free to grow at this firm, so he left shortly after and eventually started his own business. He listened to what his fears told him about continuing to work in a hostile workplace: save a little money, raid the supply closet, and then resign.

In our personal money world, I've also seen the fear of being trapped in a system be a catalyst for forging a new, autonomous plan. For example, if you're drowning in debt and living paycheck to paycheck, the long-term solution is not to wait to earn a small raise or hope that the federal minimum wage increases soon. Let the fear of losing your freedom to the inequities in our economic system push you beyond these boundaries. This may mean living with family to save, or maybe even declaring bankruptcy to earn a clean slate. But at least then, you are freer. You won't be shackled to a life that was calling the shots for you.

Later, as I navigated my way around various newsrooms, I began to examine how women in the media struggled to build their careers while raising kids. I watched pregnant colleagues, looking to take time off work after giving birth, review their "options" and learn how paltry their benefits were. I learned that you could legally take twelve weeks off, thanks to the Family Medical Leave Act, but those weeks would be unpaid. Maternity leave policies varied between workplaces. At one company, you could take a leave of absence for family matters by using your vacation days (a maximum of two paid weeks), but if you wanted to continue earning your money beyond that, you needed to go on short-term disability, which paid just a small weekly stipend. I watched a colleague, due to deliver her baby in a few months, return from human resources in tears. She'd been told she had far less paid time off than she'd thought. I saw women go on leave after having children and then never return.

I was starting to become afraid for my future and my ability to maintain a thriving career *and* be a mom. How was I going to manage that by working for these companies that seemed to offer little infrastructure or support for parents? At the rate I was going, I feared running out of options myself.

I'm grateful to have learned early on and ahead of time just how limited I was in trying to afford myself the freedom to comfortably and securely work and parent, in the absence of proper systems and social nets. My options were few, but they became very clear once I saw how little I could depend on others. The blueprint would be to either make and save a lot more money, or to have my own business where I could call the parental-leave shots. I would literally have to buy my way off this treacherous road and afford my own ticket to the promised land, where I could attempt to create a sustainable system for practicing my freedoms as a working parent.

By my mid-twenties I had begun reverse engineering a better path to help myself when (hopefully) children arrived in my life. That first meant addressing my income. My $44,000-a-year job at NY1 News, earning an annual raise at the pace of inflation, was not going to cut it. I began by taking on side hustles, including babysitting and pet sitting. But I needed more. I had been asking for a raise at work to no avail. Finally, out of curiosity, I asked the human resources manager for my salary band or range. This is the amount a company will set aside for a role. Not all employers have salary bands, but if they do, it's something you're privy to. And do you know what I discovered? My position had a salary range of $42,000 to $90,000. I was basically at the bottom of the barrel. As frustrating as it was to learn this, I used it to my advantage when I started searching for new jobs.

Months later when I interviewed for a video correspondent role at TheStreet.com, I had a sense this place could pay me far more. When I scanned their quarterly statements (which are accessible to the public), I saw that they were profitable and had a nice cash position. I knew that the role I was up for was a big priority for them, too, and I was pretty sure I was the only one they had interviewed. All this to say, when they asked me how much I wanted to earn, I didn't hesitate to ask for $100,000. Knowing that NY1 could have paid up to $90,000 and that TheStreet was financially healthy and eager to hire, I felt confident throwing out that figure. In the end we settled on $90,000. A year later, I got a raise, and started making $100,000, crossing six figures for the first time. But, alas, my friends, that still wouldn't be enough—not for this woman who needed to manage one day to take care of herself and a family in the most expensive city in the country. For my next attempt at leveling up my earnings, I would need to develop my own projects and create multiple revenue streams. I needed to have *ownership*. That epiphany led to doing what I always do when I'm scared: writing.

Evenings after work, I'd sit at the Panera on the Upper West Side from 6:30 p.m. until closing, using their high-speed internet to develop a book proposal for *You're So Money*. Through fellow author friends I connected with a literary agent who took a chance on this newbie, landed a publisher for the book, and with my advance I immediately paid off the remainder of my student loans and banked the rest. These lump sum payments were key to accelerating my financial independence. The book launched during my time at TheStreet.com, and a year later, when I got laid off, it became my parachute and the inspiration for starting my own business. Because authoring a self-help book immediately positions you as an expert and thought leader, you find yourself eligible for several new revenue streams: speaking on stages, column writing, lending your authority to brand campaigns, and consulting. My savings account was growing, but so was my time bank—the true definition of wealth. I was fully in control of my hours. That is, until my babies were born. But at least by then I never had to get "permission" from work to take time off to be with them.

Throughout the entire process of working overtime in my young adult life what anchored me was the fear of not having the agency to live life on my own terms. That drive and determination endured well after becoming a mom, thanks to all those years of practice and the continued motivation from the brilliant women and mothers who'd graced my podcast offering financial wisdom. In fact, once Evan and Colette arrived, I realized my income had grown steadily during both pregnancies. I wrote a piece for *Money* magazine entitled "Being a Mom Has Made Me Rich." The first sentence: "A funny thing happened after I had my first kid—my income doubled."[10]

Creating a new blueprint can happen in any arena of your life. Some people covet their individual freedom more than their desire to be in a partnership. They're not commitment-phobes. They have plenty of close friends but choose to go about relationships differently. Melissa Banigan wrote about this for an op-ed in the *Washington Post* entitled "I'm

Not Afraid of Commitment—I Just Love My Independence."[11] In it, she says she would not be willing to sacrifice any aspect of her packed, developed life in exchange for being swept off her feet. "As a self-sufficient writer, single mother, and founder and managing editor of a feminist nonprofit group, I felt not romance but frustration when a recent boyfriend gushed: 'I need you, and I feel complete with you,'" she wrote.

For Banigan and others who fear that in a relationship they will have to give up who they are, the solution may not be to avoid partnership altogether. Instead, the new blueprint may be to embrace a partner who shares or respects this fear and together create conscious boundaries to preserve and uplift each other's need for autonomy. Maybe that means exchanging vows but not getting legally married. Maybe that means seeing each other frequently but living separately. Maybe that means splitting expenses but not combining your finances. It's about learning how to "better balance the independent self with the togetherness of being in a couple," writes Banigan.

When it comes to our desire to pursue certain daring freedoms—you're not always going to be protected. Especially as women, people of color, and members of any marginalized group, there are very real and possibly terminal consequences to defying patriarchy, racism, and other systemic oppressions. And the fear is not always telling you to go rogue. Sometimes it's nudging you toward the route that will benefit you the most.

That morning, seated in the diner in New York, listening to my dad tell me I shouldn't go to Iran, I didn't want to believe his fears. Not at first. I wanted to prove him wrong and to be met by his pride and respect upon returning safely from Iran. But I couldn't unhear his words, "They will kill you." Later that week, when I shared to an American friend how "radical" my dad was being, she uttered the words that made me realize this wasn't an irrational fear: "Your dad is right. Please don't go," she pleaded.

I decided to stay in New York for another year, telling myself that

I could always revisit this plan another day. Going to Iran was not the only way to be an influential journalist, I convinced myself. I didn't have to risk my life to tell important stories if I didn't want to. I felt cowardly at the time. I'd let down myself, my professors, and an entire audience of people who were invested in learning about Iran. I told myself that another journalist, even after knowing the cost of this freedom, would have still ventured there. Was this person more determined? It bothered me to think about it. The whole thing felt unfair. Hard truths often feel like that. To move on and feel empowered once more, I needed to find a way to purposefully pursue my career and feel not only justified, but victorious, too. Doing this free of life-threatening danger was key.

As summer turned to fall, I had to quickly find a way to create a new blueprint for freedom (and pay rent). I went for the lowest hanging (and, okay, the *only* available) fruit at the time: an entry-level role at *Money* magazine (where I'd almost get fired). I'd had a summer internship there a few years previously and the folks there remembered me. They came calling when they heard I'd graduated from journalism school. The job paid $18 an hour, free meals if you continued working past 7 p.m. at your desk, and dental insurance, a hard offer to pass up, as I was trying to keep boots on the ground in New York City.

I placed my international press documents in a manila folder, vowing to revisit them when "the timing was better," which is to say, not for the foreseeable future. And while I was the sad-faced girl eating bagels in the Time Inc. cafeteria for the first few weeks at *Money*, I'd be lying if I said I didn't begin to appreciate and enjoy this alternative career trajectory. I had much to learn, as we know, but thanks to my encounters with many more flavors of fear in those months and years ahead, I began to develop more agency and control in my profession. As for my parents? They slept much better at night knowing I was not in the custody of Iranian armed forces.

So, thank you, my Persian Dad. I'm grateful I listened to your concerns for my safety, security, and most of all, freedom. With your help,

I did the risk calculus and realized that running around unguarded in Iran, as the American-born daughter of Iranian natives who'd left the country decades ago to provide their skills and hard work to a rival nation, I was not setting myself up for success. Without the full force and protection of a broadcast network, media company, or government, I was setting myself up for a hostile arrest.

What I learned from staying here was that life is full of freedom-defining moments. There is no shortage of thrill. **If your need for freedom is making you afraid because it comes at an unbearable cost or a risk you're not comfortable with, trust that you have the ability to forge a different path for yourself.**

For my parents, their updated road map, as they absorbed what was happening in Iran in the late 1970s during the revolution, was moving to a country that granted many more privileges and opportunities. Rebuilding their life would take time and sacrifice, but it would be worth the effort because in the end they and their children would have a much freer life. And if they were hesitant to come to America, they had the fear of their own parents providing a tailwind. Mamani, equally afraid of her three children losing *their* chance for liberty, would insist that my mom and her two siblings leave Iran for more hopeful lives in the United States and Europe. Although she feared the loneliness and the endings that came with saying goodbye to her children, the fear of seeing them lose the chance to live in a country that didn't strip them of their basic human rights was far graver. That panic trumped everything else. And would spring her to buy them and their spouses one-way tickets out of Shiraz.

ON BECOMING A RAGING SELF-ADVOCATE

Just like with money, outside of maybe your family, nobody cares more about your personal freedoms than *you*. It's not because people are intentionally out to get you. It's not because your elected leaders are plotting your demise (well, maybe they are). It's because your understanding of what a free life means is deeply rooted in your identity, your history, your life experiences. You are the only one who has walked in your shoes, and you know what values are dearest to you. This means, when we fear losing our freedom, we should listen to this cue. It's telling us that we have a responsibility to define what living a life free of restrictions means to us individually—to stand up for it and protect it the best we can. And possibly get louder to convince others that we matter. Because . . . who else will?

In March 2017, the morning following our daughter Colette's birth, I feared something was very wrong with me, but none of the medical staff believed me, a sadly typical experience for women who find themselves at the mercy of our country's fraught healthcare system. Multiple studies have confirmed that the medical industry has a widespread gender bias that often leads to misdiagnosing women or total neglect. In her 2021 book *Unwell Women*, Elinor Cleghorn chronicles the long history of how medicine has systematically failed women.[12]

Here's my story: I awoke in my hospital bed with the most excruciating headache of my life. It was odd. I didn't feel the throbbing when lying flat on my back, but whenever I sat up or climbed out of bed to pee, I experienced this intense and painful pulsing that made it feel like I was spinning on an unhinged carnival ride. When the nurse came in, I explained my strange condition. Without asking any follow-up questions, she gave me two Tylenols and said to ring her if it got worse. Minutes later, when it did, she sent in my doctor, who chalked up my pain to possible congestion. "You were a little stuffed up during labor, as I recall." It was only when she stopped to survey my face and noted how my expression was the equivalent of a ten on the hospital room emoji pain scale (that's the yellow face with fire coming out of the nose), that she realized there might actually be something hellish going on.

She called in the anesthesiologist who'd performed my epidural, the injection commonly given in a mother's back to numb the pain of childbirth. This doctor didn't want to admit that maybe she'd done something procedurally wrong in removing my catheter, but even she could not deny that something epically awful was happening. In short, the doctors concluded that I was suffering from an intense spinal headache, a potential risk from an epidural, triggered when residual fluid leaks from your spine and screws up the fluid pressure surrounding your brain. It happens in a minority of cases, but studies show (and believe me I read *all* the studies lying flat in the hospital bed that day) that it can lead to seizures and brain damage.[13] I should have known when I signed the thirty-page waiver prior to the procedure that something could go wrong.

Public service announcement: childbirth is downright scary, and while doctors and nurses want the best for you, they may not always serve as your best advocates. Sure, you can go in with all your "plans" and your John Legend playlist to relax as your baby attempts its way through the birth canal. But the reality is, you're totally out of control. Your mind wants one thing, while your body decides on another. You may not get the best medical attention. Doctors might not believe you.

This fear is healthy, normal, and important. It will insist that nobody—not even the "professionals"—will be allowed to screw you over.

That day following Colette's delivery, while Tim ran back and forth between our apartment and the hospital, checking in on Evan at home and tending to Colette in the newborn nursery, my fears of not getting the attention I needed led to an unshakeable determination to understand what the hell was going on with my body and not leave the maternity ward until I'd learned all my options. I opted to go in for a recommended operation to block the leak, which only provided temporary relief.

When I arrived home later the next day, the pain eventually resumed. I exerted myself too much, but in hindsight, the hospital should have kept me for at least twenty-four more hours. That evening at home, after Colette fell asleep in my arms following one of her feedings, I attempted to place her back in her bassinet. But when I got up off the couch with her in my arms, my back gave out. The seal put in place to cover the leak came undone (it wasn't secure to begin with; a slight sneeze could have messed it up) and the headache instantly resumed. In total agony, I gripped Colette and somehow managed to rest her on a couch cushion before collapsing on the rug underneath her, shouting for Tim to help secure us.

Terrified to return to the hospital, I called a friend, an anesthesiologist, for his honest advice. He even agreed that driving back to the hospital would not be best. He recommended prescription painkillers (the really hard stuff), and loads of caffeine to help restrict blood flow around the brain and alleviate the pain. Caffeine is actually an active ingredient in a lot of migraine medications. He also said I should lie straight on my back as much as possible for at least one week. He was sure it would work. I was lucky to have this friend in my life. But also, to my credit, I was my "aggressive" self (the thing people say when they think you're being unfeminine, but they're just threatened by your prowess). And it had been my nagging fear, that this illness could get worse, that had prompted me to push through and understand on my own the help I needed.

In all, I was bedridden for eight days after coming home from the hospital. Evan, who was almost three years old at the time, would visit my side to show me his artwork from school and for snuggles. Tim administered my medicine and routinely brought bars of dark chocolate, soda, and coffee, all while propping up my iPad so I could watch *Catastrophe* on Amazon Prime (an underrated show) without needing to raise my neck. He'd bring me Colette wrapped in her cocoon swaddle and lay her on my chest, so we could at least be close and hear each other's voice.

When I finally recovered, I made it my mission to share my story with others in the hopes that just knowing what could possibly happen might mean the next mother won't be left wasting as much time as I had in the hospital, trying to convince those who were medically smarter than I was that *things weren't right*. My body was screaming for help. Nobody was taking me seriously.

In some instances, you aren't as free as you like because *others* have the knowledge, intel, and resources to decide your fate. But if your fear raises its fiery head, that's often your inner knowing knocking on your door. It's urging you to advocate for yourself as best you can.

A stroke of fear drove Ellie Diop, a mom of four, to use the federal stimulus payments to turn her life around and become a financial advocate for herself and her family. Specifically, she was afraid of losing her ability to support herself and her kids and live freely once again. Ellie and I connected one afternoon in 2022 for a podcast interview.

Two years prior, around the time of divorcing her husband, Ellie got laid off. After the split and losing her income, she moved into her mom's one-bedroom home in Inglewood, California, along with her young children—including twin babies. They were all crammed in, sleeping in the living room. Ellie used government food assistance to buy groceries. In the meantime, she applied for over fifty jobs but never heard back from a single employer. This was despite having a college degree and years of experience in marketing, sales, and business leadership. Was it the gap on her résumé from caring full-time for her kids? Just bad luck? She'd never know, but in that time she began contemplating starting her own business. But she was afraid of the unknown. She was afraid of failure, which we know can be unrelenting.

She remembers putting her kids to bed one night in 2021 and being overtaken with tears. And in that moment, this deep fear of never regaining her freedom to live on her own terms and care for her family trumped all her other fears. She wanted the opportunity to support her kids without being dependent on her ex-husband, the government, or her mother's support. This helped her make a critical move toward reclamation. "We all have this fear . . . to do something we've never done, and I was so afraid. But at that moment I became more afraid of being in that situation for another year, another two years. That was more scary to me," she said.[14]

That night, as her babies dreamt, she began writing down a list of career and money goals. She spent hours researching the most common questions people have around starting a business, which then inspired the content she planned to create to attract clients. When her $1,200 stimulus check arrived, she used it to invest in a website designer and a ring light, to begin posting on social media. Her videos on how to start and fund a business went viral, and within months she began making money from coaching and speaking. In a year, she'd amassed over $1 million in revenue—well above her initial goal of making $10,000 per month. And it all started with listening to her fear.

When you want to reclaim your freedom through self-advocacy, but you're rattled by the potential risks, the questions to ask yourself are: *What if I don't make a move? Where will that leave me? How will I feel about that? Who's going to advocate for me, otherwise? Will I still feel stuck and without options?*

Maybe those answers will carry you over the fence and to a new side. But, as with Ellie, it's critical to get there carefully and methodically. So it's not a shot in the dark. Think: Are there ways to pursue this objective without taking on as much risk? Ellie wasn't about to take out a bunch of credit cards and leverage her way to starting a business. She had four mouths to feed and didn't want to sink into debt. Instead, she recognized how fortunate she was to have a roof over her head and a supportive mother. And with that security in place, she knew she could afford to use her government aid during the pandemic to invest responsibly in her business plan. It took considerable effort, but she was committed to growing her online audience with multiple posts and engagements per day, which we know is how many content creators ultimately rise to become stars. She exceeded her own expectations of what was possible in her newfound liberation.

What's more, she's making sure to lock in this achievement for her kids. She's decided to employ her older children to do simple tasks like organizing her office and helping with her social media uploads. This way, she can add them to her payroll and invest their earnings in a custodial investment account. Her fear of losing her freedom extends to that of her children. It inspired her to begin creating generational wealth. Ellie went on to say, "If there's anyone I'm going to show up for, it's these kids, so they can see me and see what is possible."

THE FEAR OF LOSING YOUR FREEDOM, A WORTHWHILE LEGACY

Months after the "skit" my parents played pretending to disapprove of our desire to wed, Tim finally proposed. That day, I'd begun to get quite antsy. Ironically, I woke up in the morning wondering if he was ever going to pop the question. I flat out asked him as much before either one of us had brushed our teeth: "Are we ever getting married?" I was anxious—not because I thought he was going to get cold feet, but that we were now wasting precious time to begin the next phase of our relationship. He smiled. "Yes. Patience."

As we returned from dinner and approached our front door, I noticed Tim was walking a few steps ahead of me, quite eager to get inside. I caught a whiff of a burning candle, specifically the ocean breeze–scented one that I kept on the small entrance table. I began to panic, believing I'd left it flaming during our meal and that our home was now predictably on fire. As we entered, I saw that my senses were correct. In front of me, I spotted the candle, along with dozens more, illuminating our entire apartment. I took a few steps into our living room, heart racing in disbelief, then turned to Tim, who was down on one knee. He gently reached for his pocket. And only then, it finally clicked. This was the moment I'd been waiting for. But before Tim could proceed, my anxiety had to know the answer to a most critical question. I took a deep breath in and looked straight into my future husband's eyes. "Tim, did you have these candles burning the entire time we were at dinner?" I had to know: Was he secretly a man who liked to play with fire? "No." Tim laughed. "I had some help." Later I'd learn that he had enlisted Kate to sneak into our apartment to set up the candles while we were out. He texted her when we were less than a minute away and that's when she slid out our door and hid around the bend as we entered. Phew.

Tim had also arranged a surprise trip for us to New Orleans the next day, which, by the way, if you are looking to completely blow away your significant other after getting engaged, look no further. As I sat in a jazz bar on Bourbon Street, sipping an umbrella'd cocktail at 11 a.m., I decided I had just the right amount of alcohol in my system to call my mother and elaborate on the events of the last twelve hours. I caught her just as she was piling some groceries into her trunk in a Trader Joe's parking lot.

"It finally happened!" I yelled over the phone. I could hear her throw the remaining bags into the car and hustle to the driver's seat, obviously eager to learn every detail of the proposal and our trip. She was thrilled for us and the celebratory *mehmooni* was already in the works. The more she spoke, the more emotional she became. At one point, her voice broke up. And then she fell silent. "Are you still there, Mom?" I was now standing outside the bar in the middle of the sun-drenched road. "Yes," she replied. "I just wish . . . I could tell Mamani the news."

Hearing my mother's desire to tell *her* mother about the joy and freedom that she and I had both earned, even as we journeyed through life scared, even as we did things that were new, different, and unproven, that Mamani may not have approved of, was the confirmation and confidence I hadn't known I needed to travel through to this next stage in life that was full of unknowns.

Honoring Mamani, our matriarch of fear, in that moment was a reminder of just how far my mom and I had both come in the pursuit of our freedoms. We started out as two *tarsoos* in the trenches of Worcester, but we didn't allow our fears to imprison us. Not then, not ever. Our fears gave us the ammunition to create a life where we could ultimately choose, fend, and care for ourselves. Our freedoms manifested differently, but the fear that fueled our individual desire to push through and succeed was the gift of inheritance.

And for you, as you approach your next big, wild, and scary adventure, know that your fears can be your friends. **Maybe even best friends, who inspire you to look inward, define your values, spot what is certain and within your control, and have the tenacity and determination to claim your freedoms to the fullest.** Even more, you will have a legacy, a powerful signal to fellow *tarsoos* around you that you can be afraid and still be extraordinary. And perhaps you are extraordinary *because* you are afraid. You can be both, together, all at once.

The Fear of Losing Your Freedom Self-Inquiry

- When you think of your personal freedoms, what are your non-negotiables?
- Knowing personal freedom is at risk, what is a new blueprint you can design to regain control and make your ambitions more within reach?
- What is your fear of losing freedom telling you about your need to self-advocate?
- How is your fear paving the way for a beautiful legacy?

EPILOGUE

ONE EVENING DURING THE summer of 2018, I walked onto a comedy club stage in Chelsea in front of about a hundred people who'd paid $30 for a two-drink minimum and amateur stand-up, and I grabbed the mic.

I decided to just *do the thing* that I'd been both fascinated by and deathly afraid of for my entire life. And as with most of my self-motivated dares, I didn't dip a toe in the shallow waters first. I cannonballed into the deep end, knowing that I'd eventually float to the surface. Maybe with chlorine coming out of my nose. But I'd make it out alive. *Probably?*

As a kid, I remember watching comedy greats like Rita Rudner crack poignant jokes about marriage and relationships in front of a stadium full of fans, all while wearing a dashing ball gown and embracing her feminine. "If you like easygoing, monogamous men," she once said, gliding across the stage, "stay away from billionaires."

This was my kind of funny lady. And I hoped that I'd grow up to captivate crowds and make people think and laugh just as Rita had.

Life has since led me in many different directions and stages, but I never forgot my promise to come back for that little girl and give her the chance to entertain a crowd, if only for one night. But I had my work cut out for me first. I'd need to experience the ups and downs of becoming an adult. I'd need to have some wins but also make a mess of things. I'd need to fall on my face and pick myself up. I'd need to harness my fears, learn to live life with conviction, but mostly, I'd need to find the humor in my life and be the first to poke fun at it.

That young girl . . . she waited so patiently for me.

In my late thirties, I finally brought my years of learning and unlearning to the spotlight (or whatever I could squeeze into a six-minute set). I joked about the politics of telling someone you're Persian versus Iranian, my childhood desire to be named Ashley, the irony of how immigrants like my parents can be so daring and yet so risk-averse, and how to pronounce George Clooney like only a Persian mom will. I also shared the weird-but-true behind-the-scenes of being a female breadwinner and working mom, jokes I knew Rita would appreciate.

After that show, I did a Hail Mary and uploaded my set to Facebook. I was slightly afraid of exposing my jokes to the world and refreshing my page only to find a slew of unkind comments. But I wanted friends and my parents, who were living in California, to watch . . . and, who knows, maybe it would earn me a Netflix special? That little girl was still dreaming.

As it turned out, that risk did lead to a reward, but not one that I'd ever imagined. A literary agent who watched the video messaged to ask if I had more material. Right away, I got an overwhelming feeling that has only happened a few times in my life. I felt it once when applying to graduate programs to study journalism and another time when my former college crush Tim reached out via AOL Instant Messenger (I know, may as well have been a telegraph) to "catch up." His message flashed across my computer screen while I was sitting, bored, at my new job. The newsroom started to spin, for, as we recall, I'd told the universe in 1999 that I was going to marry him one day, and apparently, those folks upstairs had taken notes. Now, as I read this literary agent's note, I felt that eerie sensation once more. I replied. "Yes, there's more! Does it count if the material is all in my head?"

"No," she said. "Please start writing."

And so, I did.

Completing this book has been terrifying, which is to say, it's been one of the best experiences of my life. There's nothing like waking up every morning tasked with thinking about your fears, turning them around, and discovering their hidden gifts.

I stepped away from this book a number of times.

Eventually, it became the only thing that brought consistency in an upside-down time. I wrote much of it in the thick of the pandemic, working a full-time job and somehow running a business from my bedroom and sometimes a closet. Tim and I tag-teamed helping our small kids learn (and sit still) during Zoom school and raising a growing household.

There were happy moments. Like when I'd capture stories from college and send the pages to my best friend Kate, who'd giggle along. There were times when, after reflecting on a particularly gutting chapter from my past, I went to sleep in tears, worried that my loud sniffling would awaken my husband and that he, concerned for my well-being, would want to *talk about it*. There were other moments when I thought with great worry, *Who will care about my stories? What does it matter? Also, what day is it?*

Many of the stories I've chosen to reveal, I've never shared publicly. And that's been scary. I've been afraid of how my parents may interpret some of my childhood experiences that perhaps only I know and feel to be true. As I would often say to my writing coach, the phenomenal Suzanne Kingsbury, "Please, Suzanne, I just want to be sure that I'm not throwing my mother under the bus." She assured me I was not.

What helped me carry on through the days and not give up (despite really wanting to) was repeating to myself the advice that I like to tell my littles while they're strapped in their car seats with no choice but to listen to Mom's unscripted TED Talks, a move my Sheida Joon was famous for: *Kids, you can do scary things.*

And for you, my friend, I want to offer a little extra, as we part ways from these pages. I want you to know that you can do the scary stuff, too. And more importantly, you really should. Is being afraid a sign that you're perhaps drawn to an idea, a project, a love, a work, so very much that the thought of possibly failing at it, losing it, being disappointed by it, or giving up on it . . . frightens you? I know the feeling. But rather than fearing the possibility of failure or grief or regret or uncertainty or any of it, fear the risk of missing out on an actualized life. Sometimes siding with fear is the way. Because you just might be onto something beautiful. Something more powerful. More you.

ACKNOWLEDGMENTS

First and foremost, thank you to my parents and brother for never wincing when I said, "I'm going to write about our lives." Thank you from the depths of my heart for your constant faith, love, and support.

I am so very grateful to you, Sarah Passick, Mia Vitale, and Celeste Fine, for taking me under your wings, and encouraging me to embrace my past. You made what was just a "someday" plan unbelievably real. I'm still shooketh.

Thank you, Michelle Herrera Mulligan at Atria Books, for your vision and guidance. Everything you say and do and know is gold. Thank you for believing in me. Thank you and Erica Siudzinski for encouraging me each step of the way. And thank you to all at Simon & Schuster who championed this book and me: Libby McGuire, Annette Pagliaro Sweeney, Emma Van Deun, James Iacobelli, Zakiya Jamal, Holly Rice, Richard Willett, Susan Bishansky, Nicole Celli, Steve Csipke, and Jamie Selzer.

Thank you, Richelle Fredson. You brought me light, direction, and joy during the earliest stages of my writing and still. You are a forever friend.

Suzanne Kingsbury, thank you for . . . everything. For your love, mentorship, collaboration, and wisdom. You helped bring the best of me out and onto these pages.

Adam Kirschner, you are a blessing to me, my family, and this dreamy career you've helped me build from day one.

Thank you to dear friends who provided generous and invaluable advice and insights on how to navigate this complex literary journey: Terri Trespicio, Laura Belgray, Ana Homayoun, Ramit Sethi, Tiffany Aliche, Laura Michelle Davis, and Selena Soo.

Thank you to friends who loved me, fed me, laughed with me, and, in many cases, provided much-needed fun during the three years of bringing this book to life: Hannah Alstein, Kate Dailey, Susie Moore, Heath Collins, Adam Auriemma, Margie Cader, Rebecca Jarvis, Annika Pergament, Kathy Braddock, Allison Fishman Task, Margie Fox, Jennifer Norgriff-Bernard, Vanessa Thompson Schreiber, Michael Schreiber, Rea Schreiber, Sheetal Kumar, Mohit Chawla, Reena Mehta, Dash Flynn, Mo Renganathan, and Keri Dole.

To my amazing Lancaster family, the Jaquiths, the Dussingers, and the Knoxes, I love you all.

To my there-are-no-words-to-describe husband and best friend, Tim, who lovingly and so patiently stood by my side (and sometimes urged me out of the house) so that I could complete this massive undertaking with the focus and attention it begged. Thanks to you, I'm the luckiest woman, wife, and mommy. Or should I say, bruh.

This book is for Evan and Colette, my tooties who are my superior gifts. You are wise. You are kind, funny, honest. You are the people I hope to become when I grow up.

Finally, I would be nowhere without the bright, dedicated, and thoughtful individuals in the *So Money* community. This book is, in many ways, the culmination of our time together, our memories and laughs, starting with my very first recording. This book is for you and us.

NOTES

Prologue

1 Adam Davidson, "What Happened to Worcester?" *New York Times Magazine*, April 27, 2016, https://www.nytimes.com/2016/05/01/magazine/what -happened-to-worcester.html.

Introduction

1 Franklin Delano Roosevelt, "Inaugural Address," March 4, 1933, Washington, D.C., https://www.youtube.com/watch?v=nHFTtz3uucY&ab_channel =DonaldPohlmeyer.

2 University of South Australia, "When You're Smiling, the Whole World Really Does Smile with You," *ScienceDaily*, August 13, 2020, www.sciencedaily .com/releases/2020/08/200813123608.htm.

3 E. C. Willroth et al., "Judging Emotions as Good or Bad: Individual Differences and Associations with Psychological Health," *Emotion* (2023), https://psycnet.apa.org/doiLanding?doi=10.1037%2Femo0001220.

4 Malcolm Gladwell, *Outliers: The Story of Success* (New York: Little, Brown and Company, 2008), 35.

5 Ellen Vora, "Anxiety Is the Tone of Modern Western Culture," October 27, 2020, https://ellenvora.com/category/anxiety/.

6 Ellen Vora, *The Anatomy of Anxiety: Understanding and Overcoming the Body's Fear Response* (New York: Harper Wave, 2022), 35.

7 Eileen Gu, "I Admit It. I'm in Love with Fear," *New York Times*, 2022, https: //www.nytimes.com/interactive/2022/sports/olympics/eileen-gu-skiing -fear.html.

8 Caroline Dooner, *Tired as F*ck: Burnout at the Hands of Diet, Self-Help, and Hustle Culture* (New York: HarperCollins, 2022), 1.

9   CapitalOne, "Big-Picture Thinking Leads to the Right Money Mindset," January 27, 2020, https://www.capitalone.com/about/newsroom/mind-over-money-survey/.

Chapter 1

1   John Amodeo, "Deconstructing the Fear of Rejection," *Psychology Today*, April 4, 2014, https://www.psychologytoday.com/us/blog/intimacy-path-toward-spirituality/201404/deconstructing-the-fear-rejection.

2   Susie Moore, "603: Creator of the Side Hustle Academy," July 24, 2017, in *So Money*, produced by Farnoosh Torabi, podcast, 39:40, https://podcast.farnoosh.tv/episode/susie-moore.

3   Janis Isaman, "When Rejection Trauma Triggers Our Childhood Wounds," *Elephant Journal*, April 2, 2021, https://www.elephantjournal.com/2021/04/the-trauma-of-rejection-can-suck-it.

4   Sarah Sorenson, "Understanding Rejection Trauma," *Dr. Kathleen and Team*, February 28, 2022, https://drkathleen.co.nz/understanding-rejection-trauma.

5   Katie Couric, "Commencement Address," May 21, 2014, Trinity College, Hartford, Connecticut, www.youtube.com/watch?v=AFzPYFmRE-Q.

6   Cory J. Clark et al., "Tribalism Is Human Nature," *Current Directions in Psychological Science* 28, no. 6 (2019): 587–592.

7   Yonat Zwebner et al., "We Look Like Our Names: The Manifestation of Name Stereotypes in Facial Appearance," *Journal of Personality and Social Psychology* 112, no. 4 (2017): 527–554, https://www.apa.org/pubs/journals/releases/psp-pspa0000076.pdf.

8   Luvvie Ajayi, "1505: Luvvie Ajayi Jones on How to Be a Good Trouble-maker," April 26, 2023, in *So Money*, produced by Farnoosh Torabi, podcast, 7:26, https://podcast.farnoosh.tv/episode/luvvie-ajayi-2/.

9   Deepa Purushothoman, *The First, the Few, the Only: How Women of Color Can Redefine Power in Corporate America* (New York: HarperCollins, 2022).

10   Deepa Purushothoman, "1316: Speaking to Power at Work and Defining Success on Your Terms," February 9, 2022, in *So Money*, produced by Farnoosh Torabi, podcast, 27:51, https://podcast.farnoosh.tv/episode/purushothaman/.

Chapter 2

1   Richard Weissbourd et al., "Loneliness in America: How the Pandemic Has Deepened an Epidemic of Loneliness and What We Can Do About It,"

Harvard Graduate School of Education, February 2021, https://mcc.gse
.harvard.edu/reports/loneliness-in-america.

2 Naomi I. Eisenberger, Matthew D. Lieberman, and Kipling D. Williams,
"Does Rejection Hurt? An fMRI Study of Social Exclusion," *Science* 302, no.
5643 (October 2003): 290–292, https://science.sciencemag.org/content
/302/5643/290.abstract.

3 José Ventura-León et al., "Fear of Loneliness: Development and Validation
of a Brief Scale," *Frontiers in Psychology* 11 (2020): 1–9.

4 Livia Tomova et al., "Acute Social Isolation Evokes Midbrain Craving
Responses Similar to Hunger," *Nature Neuroscience* 23 (2020): 1597–1605,
https://www.nature.com/articles/s41593-020-00742-z.

5 Julianne Holt-Lunstad, Timothy B. Smith, and J. Bradley Layton, "Social
Relationships and Mortality Risk: A Meta-analytic Review," *PLOS Medicine*
(July 27, 2010): https://journals.plos.org/plosmedicine/article?id=10.1371
/journal.pmed.1000316.

6 Louise C. Hawkley and John T. Cacioppo, "Loneliness Matters: A Theoret-
ical and Empirical Review of Consequences and Mechanisms," *Annals of
Behavioral Medicine* 40, no. 2 (October 2010): 218–227, https://academic
.oup.com/abm/article/40/2/218/4569527.

7 Jacob Sweet, "The Loneliness Pandemic," *Harvard Magazine*, January–
February 2021, https://www.harvardmagazine.com/2021/01/feature
-the-loneliness-pandemic.

8 Tara Schuster, "1475: Author of Glow in the F*cking Dark and Buy Yourself the F*cking Lilies," February 15, 2023, in *So Money*, produced by
Farnoosh Torabi, podcast, 35:42, https://podcast.farnoosh.tv/episode
/tara-schuster/.

9 Katie Sturino, "How I Stopped Saying Horrible Things to Myself," *The Cut*,
May 26, 2021, http://thecut.com/2021/05/excerpt-from-body-talk-by-katie
-sturino.html.

10 Katie Sturino, "1036: The Pandemic's Impact on the Influencer Market,"
April 29, 2020, in *So Money*, produced by Farnoosh Torabi, podcast, 39:12,
https://podcast.farnoosh.tv/episode/katie-sturino/.

11 Suzanne Somers, "1098: Suzanne Somers on Health, Wealth and
Reinvention," September 21, 2020, in *So Money*, produced by Farnoosh
Torabi, podcast, 33:44, https://podcast.farnoosh.tv/episode/
suzanne-somers/.

12 Bob Litwin, *Live the Best Story of Your Life: A World Champion's Guide to
Lasting Change* (Hobart, NY: Hatherleigh Press, 2016), 6–7.

13 Paris Stevens, "The 2021 Workplace Friendship and Happiness Survey,"
    July 19, 2021, https://wearewildgoose.com/usa/news/workplace-friendship
    -and-happiness-survey/.

14 John Cacioppo, "Researching the Effects of Social Isolation," Cengage
    Learning, October 19, 2012, educational YouTube video, 10:58, https:
    //www.youtube.com/watch?v=iyAlnObWfrE.

15 Maya Angelou, quoted in Helena Andrews-Dyer, "A Poetic Playlist in
    Honor of Maya Angelou," *Washington Post*, May 30, 2014, https://www
    .washingtonpost.com/news/reliable-source/wp/2014/05/30/a-poetic
    -playlist-in-honor-of-maya-angelou/.

16 Sheila Torabi, "415: Adam and Sheila Torabi," May 11, 2016, in *So Money*,
    produced by Farnoosh Torabi, podcast, 34:30, https://podcast.farnoosh.tv
    /episode/adam-and-sheila-torabi/.

17 Cacioppo, "Researching the Effects of Social Isolation."

Chapter 3

1 James A. Roberts and Meredith E. David, "The Social Media Party: Fear of
   Missing Out (FoMO), Social Media Intensity, Connection, and Well-Being,"
   International Journal of Human-Computer Interaction 36, no. 1 (July 2019):
   1–7, https://www.researchgate.net/publication/334717933_The_Social
   _Media_Party_Fear_of_Missing_Out_FoMO_Social_Media_Intensity
   _Connection_and_Well-Being.

2 Patrick McGinnis, "1327: The Financial Cost of FoMO," March 7, 2022, in
   So Money, produced by Farnoosh Torabi, podcast, 32:02, https://podcast
   .farnoosh.tv/episode/patrick-mcginnis-2/.

3 Chantel Chapman, "1415: Healing from the Trauma of Money," September 28, 2022, in *So Money*, produced by Farnoosh Torabi, podcast, 29:03,
   https://podcast.farnoosh.tv/episode/chantel-chapman/.

4 Julie C. Coultas, "When in Rome . . . An Evolutionary Perspective on
   Conformity," *Group Processes and Intergroup Relations* 7, no. 4
   (September 2004): 317–331, https://journals.sagepub.com
   /doi/10.1177/1368430204046141.

5 Chelsea Fagan, "1390: Stay Away from These Financial Moves," August 1,
   2022, in *So Money*, produced by Farnoosh Torabi, podcast, 31:37, https:
   //podcast.farnoosh.tv/episode/10626/.

6 Michelle Obama, "NPR News Interviews Michelle Obama, Reviews Her
   New Book," interview by Audie Cornish, NPR, November 9, 2018, https:

//www.npr.org/about-npr/666283346/npr-news-interviews-michelle-obama
-reviews-her-new-book.

7 Farnoosh Torabi, "FIRE Hype: Want to Retire Early? Not So Fast," CNET,
October 1, 2022, https://www.cnet.com/personal-finance/investing/fire
-hype-want-to-retire-early-not-so-fast/.

8 Adam Grant (@AdamMGrant), Twitter post, February 7, 2022, 9:08 a.m.,
https://twitter.com/AdamMGrant/status/1490688969096507400.

Chapter 4

1 Carlos Tilghman-Osborne et al., "Relation of Guilt, Shame, Behavioral
and Characterological Self-Blame to Depressive Symptoms in Ado-
lescents over Time," *Journal of Social and Clinical Psychology* 27, no. 8
(2007): 809, https://www.ncbi.nlm.nih.gov/pmc/articles/PMC4238306
/#R74.

2 June Price Tangney, "Constructive and Destructive Aspects of Shame and
Guilt," in *Constructive and Destructive Behavior: Implications for Family,
School, and Society*, ed. Arthur C. Bohart and Deborah J. Stipek (Washington, D.C.: American Psychological Association, 2001): 127–145, http://www.
rpforschools.net/articles/ASP/Tangney%201995%20Constructive%20
and%20Destructive%20Aspects%20of%20Shame%20and%20Guilt.pdf.

3 Levi Boxell, Matthew Gentzkow, and Jesse M. Shapiro, "Cross-Country
Trends in Affective Polarization," National Bureau of Economic Research
Working Paper Series (January 2020, revised November 2021), https:
//www.nber.org/papers/w26669.

4 Kaelyn Ford, "Why More Women Don't Report Sexual Assaults: A Survi-
vor Speaks Out," *ABC News*, September 27, 2018, https://abcnews
.go.com/US/women-report-sexual-assaults-survivor-speaks
/story?id=57985818.

5 Rakshitha Arni Ravishankar, "What's Wrong with Asking 'Where Are You
From?'" *Harvard Business Review*, October 22, 2020, https://hbr.org/2020
/10/whats-wrong-with-asking-where-are-you-from.

6 Emily Ladau, *Demystifying Disability: What to Know, What to Say, and How
to Be an Ally* (New York: Ten Speed Press, 2021).

7 Emily Ladau, "1333: Demystifying Disability and Closing Opportunity
Gaps," March 21, 2022, in *So Money*, produced by Farnoosh Torabi, podcast, 27:44, https://podcast.farnoosh.tv/episode/emily-ladau/.

8 Jasmine Vergauwe et al., "Fear of Being Exposed: The Trait-Relatedness

of the Impostor Phenomenon and Its Relevance in the Work Context," *Journal of Business and Psychology* 30 (2015): 565–581, https://link.springer.com/article/10.1007/s10869-014-9382-5.

9   Lee Bonvissuto, "1343: Overhauling Finances, Career, and Childcare in the Pandemic," April 13, 2022, in *So Money*, produced by Farnoosh Torabi, podcast, 31:52, https://podcast.farnoosh.tv/episode/lee-bonvissuto/.

10 Morgan Anderson, "1352: Afraid of Money? This Might Be Why," May 4, 2022, in *So Money*, produced by Farnoosh Torabi, podcast, 28:52, https://podcast.farnoosh.tv/episode/de-morgan-anderson/.

Chapter 5

1   Ursula K. Le Guin, *The Left Hand of Darkness* (New York: Berkley Publishing Group, 1969), 70.

2   Archy O. de Berker et al., "Computations of Uncertainty Mediate Acute Stress Responses in Humans," *Nature Communications* 7 (2016): 1–11, https://doi.org/10.1038/ncomms10996.

3   MasterClass, "Recency Bias Definition: How Recency Effect Impacts Decisions," April 7, 2022, https://www.masterclass.com/articles/recency-bias-definition.

4   Arabella L. Simpkin et al., "Stress from Uncertainty Predicts Resilience and Engagement Among Subspecialty Medicine Fellows," *International Archives of Internal Medicine* 4, no. 23 (2020), https://doi.org/10.23937/2643-4466/1710023.

5   Devin Tomb, "72% of Muse Survey Respondents Say They've Experienced 'Shift Shock,'" *The Muse*, updated August 30, 2022, https://www.themuse.com/advice/shift-shock-muse-survey-2022.

6   Cait Donovan, "1388: Suffering from Burnout? Why Your Job Might Not Be the Main Problem," July 27, 2022, in *So Money*, produced by Farnoosh Torabi, podcast, 33:47, https://podcast.farnoosh.tv/episode/cait-donovan.

7   Harvey Karp, "Why Breast Is Best," *NY Daily News*, August 5, 2012, https://www.nydailynews.com/opinion/breast-best-article-1.1128662.

8   Stef Ziev, "1161: How to Make Hard Decisions About Money and Life . . . Easy," February 16, 2021, in *So Money*, produced by Farnoosh Torabi, podcast, 36:55, https://podcast.farnoosh.tv/episode/stef-ziev.

9   Mercii Thomas, "Bonus: Understanding Financial Abuse," June 15, 2021, in *So Money*, produced by Farnoosh Torabi, podcast, 35:13, https://podcast.farnoosh.tv/episode/understanding-financial-abuse.

10 Rachel Wyman, "1177: How a Local Bakery (Barely) Survived the Pandemic," March 24, 2021, in *So Money*, produced by Farnoosh Torabi, podcast, 36:17, https://podcast.farnoosh.tv/episode/rachel-wyman/.

Chapter 6

1 Matthew A. Killingsworth, "Experienced Well-Being Rises with Income, Even Above $75,000 per Year," *Proceedings of the National Academy of Sciences* 118, no. 4 (January 18, 2021), https://www.pnas.org/doi/full/10.1073/pnas.2016976118.

2 Christina Blacken, "1363: Rewriting Your Money Story," May 30, 2022, in *So Money*, produced by Farnoosh Torabi, podcast, 31:18, https://podcast.farnoosh.tv/episode/christina-blacken/.

3 Ibid.

4 Barbara Huson (formerly Barbara Stanny), "33: Barbara Stanny and Building Sacred Success," February 13, 2015, in *So Money*, produced by Farnoosh Torabi, podcast, 31:11, https://podcast.farnoosh.tv/episode/barbara-stanny/.

5 Anonymous, "Confessions of an Overnight Millionaire: 'I Constantly Ask Myself, Do I Deserve This Money?'" *New York*, April 12, 2021, https://nymag.com/intelligencer/2021/04/confessions-overnight-tech-millionaire.html.

6 Wellcome Trust, "Why Losing Money May Be More Painful Than You Think," *Science Daily*, May 2, 2007, https://www.sciencedaily.com/releases/2007/05/070502072658.htm.

7 Katie Gatti, "1348: How Fear Can Drive Financial Excellence," April 25, 2022, in *So Money*, produced by Farnoosh Torabi, podcast, 32:51, https://podcast.farnoosh.tv/episode/katie-gatti.

8 Queen Latifah, "1054: Black Wealth Matters," June 10, 2020, in *So Money*, produced by Farnoosh Torabi, podcast, 27:29, https://podcast.farnoosh.tv/episode/queen-latifah.

9 Farnoosh Torabi, "Why I Caved and Altered My Retirement Portfolio," *Bloomberg News*, July 18, 2020, https://www.bnnbloomberg.ca/why-i-caved-and-altered-my-retirement-portfolio-1.1467316.

10 Geneen Roth, "What I Gained by Losing in Madoff," *Huffington Post*, February 7, 2009, https://www.huffpost.com/entry/what-i-gained-by-losing-i_b_156088.

11 Geneen Roth, "709: This Messy Magnificent Life Author," March 28, 2018,

in *So Money*, produced by Farnoosh Torabi, podcast, 39:50, https://podcast
.farnoosh.tv/episode/geneen-roth.

12 Geneen Roth, "I Was Fleeced by Madoff," *Salon*, January 7, 2009, https://www
.salon.com/2009/01/07/madoff.

13 Seth Godin, "25: The Meaning of Money and the Choice to Live a Happier
Life," February 5, 2015, in *So Money*, produced by Farnoosh Torabi, podcast,
37:28, https://podcast.farnoosh.tv/episode/seth-godin.

Chapter 7

1 Dan Ariely, Joel Huber, and Klaus Wertenbroch, "When Do Losses Loom
Larger Than Gains?" *Journal of Marketing Research* 42, no. 2 (May 2005):
134–138, https://journals.sagepub.com/doi/10.1509/jmkr.42.2.134.62283.

2 Arthur C. Brooks, "Go Ahead and Fail," *Atlantic*, February 25, 2021, https:
//www.theatlantic.com/family/archive/2021/02/how-overcome-fear-failure
/618130.

3 Candice Cook Simmons, "1165: Investing in Women, Disrupting the Legal
Industry, and Common Startup Mistakes," February 24, 2021, in *So Money*,
produced by Farnoosh Torabi, podcast, 33:51, https://podcast.farnoosh.tv
/episode/candice-cook-simmons.

4 Karen Rinaldi, "892: Author of (It's Great to) Suck at Something," May 29,
2019, in *So Money*, produced by Farnoosh Torabi, podcast, 40:07, https:
//podcast.farnoosh.tv/episode/karen-rinaldi-2.

Chapter 8

1 Ernest Becker, *The Denial of Death* (New York: The Free Press, 1973), xvii.

2 Martin D. Vestergaard and Wolfram Schultz, "Retrospective Valuation of
Experienced Outcome Encoded in Distinct Reward Representations in
the Anterior Insula and Amygdala," *Journal of Neuroscience* 40,
no. 46 (November 2020): 8938–8950, https://www.jneurosci.org
/content/40/46/8938.

3 Calvin Trillin, quoting his wife Alice Stewart Trillin, loosely quoting Ernest
Becker, "About Alice,'" *New York Times*, January 14, 2007, https://www
.nytimes.com/2007/01/14/books/chapters/0114-1st-tril.html.

4 Ian Sample, "Doubting Death: How Our Brains Shield Us from Mortal Truth,"
Guardian, October 19, 2019, https://www.theguardian.com/science/2019
/oct/19/doubting-death-how-our-brains-shield-us-from-mortal-truth.

5 C. Nathan DeWall and Roy F. Baumeister, "From Terror to Joy: Automatic

Tuning to Positive Affective Information Following Mortality Salience," *Psychological Science* 18, no. 11 (May 2016), https://doi.org/10.1111/j.1467 -9280.2007.02013.x.

6 Caroline Fer, Michel Guiavarch, and Pascal Edouard, "Epidemiology of Skydiving-Related Deaths and Injuries: A 10-years Prospective Study of 6.2 Million Jumps Between 2010 and 2019 in France," *Journal of Science and Medicine in Sport* 24, no. 5 (2021): 448–453, https://doi:10.1016/j .jsams.2020.11.002.

7 Cameron Huddleston (@cameronkhuddleston), "On this day a year ago, I learned that my mom had tested positive for COVID-19." Instagram, January 11, 2022, https://www.instagram.com/p/CYmrNQJbld/?igshid= MTA0ZTI1NzA%3D.

8 Elizabeth Gilbert, "Your Elusive Creative Genius," filmed February 2009, TED video, 19:15, https://www.ted.com/talks/elizabeth_gilbert_your _elusive_creative_genius?language=en.

9 Beth Richardson, "Your Grief Is Not About Your Child Being Transgender," *Just Plain Beth* (blog), February 8, 2022, https://www.justplainbeth.com /your-grief-is-not-about-your-child.

10 Mary-Frances O'Connor, "184: How Grieving Changes the Brain," April 2022, in *Speaking of Psychology*, produced by the American Psychological Association, podcast, 33:56, https://www.apa.org/news/podcasts/speaking -of-psychology/grieving-changes-brain.

11 Ellen Vora, "1321: Money and Your Mental Health," February 21, 2022, in *So Money*, produced by Farnoosh Torabi, podcast, 31:45, https://podcast .farnoosh.tv/episode/dr-ellen-vora.

12 Daniel Pink, *The Power of Regret* (New York: Riverhead Books, 2022).

Chapter 9

1 "Zahra Kazemi," *Committee to Protect Journalists*, accessed December 27, 2022, https://cpj.org/data/people/zahra-kazemi.

2 Emily Schmidt, Craig Helmstetter, and Benjamin Clary, "Poll: Most Americans Think Liberty Has Waned, Rights Will Further Diminish," *APM Research Lab*, June 30, 2022, https://www.apmresearchlab.org/motn/ what-americans-think-about-liberty-rights-freedom-may-2022.

3 Institute on Aging, "Aging in America," accessed February 2023, https://www .ioaging.org/aging-in-america/#caregivers.

4 Clarity, "Final Report: Aging in Place in America," commissioned by Prince

Market Research, August 20, 2007, https://www.slideshare.net /clarityproducts/clarity-2007-aginig-in-place-in-america-2836029.

5 Maggie McGrath, "Mahsa Amini: The Spark That Ignited a Women-Led Revolution," *Forbes*, December 6, 2022, https://www.forbes.com/sites /maggiemcgrath/2022/12/06/mahsa-amini-the-spark-that-ignited-a -women-led-revolution/?sh=89482fa5c3db.

6 Adam Grant (@AdamMGrant), Twitter post, February 18, 2022, 11:22 a.m., https://twitter.com/adammgrant/status/1494708914922 954759?lang=en.

7 Richard M. Ryan and Edward L. Deci, "Self-Regulation and the Problem of Human Autonomy: Does Psychology Need Choice, Self-Determination, and Will?" *Journal of Personality* 74, no. 6 (December 2006): 1557–1586, https://doi.org/10.1111/j.1467-6494.2006.00420.x.

8 Brit Marling, "Harvey Weinstein and the Economics of Consent," *Atlantic*, October 23, 2017, https://www.theatlantic.com/entertainment/ar chive/2017/10/harvey-weinstein-and-the-economics-of-consent/543618/.

9 Sunny Israni, "1228: On Financial Inclusivity and Feeling 'Safe' in the Financial World," July 19, 2021, in *So Money*, produced by Farnoosh Torabi, podcast, 32:01, https://podcast.farnoosh.tv/episode/sunny-israni.

10 Farnoosh Torabi, "Being a Mom Has Made Me Rich," *Money*, February 28, 2018, https://money.com/having-baby-mom-made-me-rich.

11 Melissa Banigan, "I'm Not Afraid of Commitment—I Just Love My Inde- pendence," *Washington Post*, March 24, 2016, https://www.washingtonpost .com/news/soloish/wp/2016/03/24/im-not-afraid-of-commitment-i-just -love-my-independence.

12 Elinor Cleghorn, *Unwell Women: Misdiagnosis and Myth in a Man-Made World* (New York: Dutton, 2022).

13 Kyung-Hwa Kwak, "Postdural Puncture Headache," *Korean Journal of Anes- thesiology* 70, no. 2 (April 2017): 136–143, https://www.ncbi.nlm.nih .gov/pmc/articles/PMC5370299/

14 Ellie Diop, "1426: Stimulus Check to 7 Figures, How One Single Mom Turned Her Financial Life Around," October 24, 2022, in *So Money*, pro- duced by Farnoosh Torabi, podcast, 31:21, https://podcast.farnoosh.tv /episode/ellie-diop.

INDEX

ABOUT THE AUTHOR

Farnoosh Torabi is an Iranian American journalist and one of the country's leading and most trusted personal finance experts. For more than twenty years, she's dedicated her career to helping people become financially empowered and lead richer lives. She's written multiple books, hosted a CNBC program, and worked alongside Oprah's editorial team. Today she hosts the long-running, Webby-honored podcast *So Money*, which has earned over 30 million downloads. Farnoosh holds a degree in finance from Penn State and a master's in journalism from Columbia University. She lives on the East Coast with her family.